And all that believed were together, and had all things common.   ACTS 2:44

ALL THINGS COMMON:

THE HUTTERIAN WAY OF LIFE

ALL THINGS COMMON

The Hutterian Way of Life

BY VICTOR PETERS

HARPER TORCHBOOKS

Harper & Row, Publishers

New York, Evanston, San Francisco, London

TO ELISABETH, BAMBI, AND KARL

The woodcut on the title page, showing Hutterians in contemporary
costume, is taken from *Historia von Münsterischen Widertauffern*
by Christoph Erhard (Munich, 1588)

This book was originally published by the University of Minnesota Press and
is here reprinted by arrangement.

FOREWORD

ALL THINGS COMMON is a sign and product of the capacity and persistence of Dr. Victor Peters, who wrote it, and of the scholarly interest of the University of Minnesota Press, which has published it. But it is also a mark and fruit of the foresight of those members of the Manitoba Historical Society who, in 1945, launched a series of "ethnic studies" and, some years later, invited Victor Peters to participate by undertaking a study of the Hutterians.

Ethnic studies are peculiarly appropriate in Manitoba because of the remarkable vigor and diversity of the ethnic groups to be found there. Few other areas of settlement have attracted groups that have been so large relative to the total population, and so frequently concentrated in particular geographic areas, as the Icelanders, Ukrainians, and Mennonites of Manitoba. With the support of their size and concentration, these and other ethnic communities have tended to preserve each a separate, lively culture. So apparent is this abundance of differentiated communities that it has been a fashion to refer to their total pattern as the Manitoba "mosaic," to contrast it with the conformity connoted by a "melting pot."

The "mosaic" metaphor, however picturesque, may easily convey an exaggerated conception of the pluralism of Manitoba's social structure, and a word of caution may not be out of place. Cultural diversity has been able to persist in Manitoba because a basic English-speaking population, predominantly from Ontario, and a French group, much smaller but self-conscious, gave the province a firm but flexible structure, maintained its cohesion, and have been generally successful in keeping the polity a reasonably harmonious one. With these essentials provided for, there was room to accept the view that cultural diversity did little harm and might do considerable good. Secondly, the diversity has not covered an unlimited spectrum, but consists in variations on a European outlook. Thirdly, while various ethnic communities have preserved colorful folkways and some use of their original language, nearly all were integrated long ago into the general economic and political environment for day-to-day purposes. Fourthly, assimilation in the direction of a homogeneous culture has been proceeding, in truth, at a pretty rapid rate; and exaltation of Manitoba's "mosaic" is probably already more of an exercise in nostalgia than a description of current reality. The one clear exception to this rule among ethnic communities is the Hutterian one: as Dr. Peters' present work makes clear, its eventual absorption into a general cultural pattern is problematic, and even unlikely. For the rest, groups will no doubt preserve a certain cultural separateness for a long time, but rather in the way that Scots recall their origins on Burns' Night, and have a special feeling for bagpipes. A program of ethnic studies in Manitoba was, therefore, not only appropriate; it was also timely in that distinctive communities (except for the Hutterians) may not be available much longer for study.

However suitable and timely a series of ethnic studies in Manitoba, its initiation was an act of great courage on the part of an Historical Society possessing only the most limited financial resources. Nor did success unfold smoothly: several of the studies commissioned have, for one reason or another, been long delayed in publication. But it can be said that the studies published have contributed substantially to our historical and social knowledge of Manitoba, and have justified the judgment and faith of the sponsors, as well as reflecting credit on their individual authors. These studies are: *The Ukrainians in Manitoba* by Dr. (now Senator) Paul Yuzyk (1953); *In Search of Utopia* (the Mennonites) by E. K. Francis (1955); *The Jews in Manitoba* by Rabbi Arthur Chiel (1961); and now the present volume on the Hutterians.

The Hutterians, by diverging much more than any other ethnic minority from the general cultural pattern of Manitoba, produce unusual social strains but also unusual insights into the processes of accommodation and assimilation. Their communities provide living demonstrations of European social life in the late Middle Ages (and of a primitive communism with still older roots). But they are a demonstration at the same time of how a medieval social structure can be adjusted in some (highly selective) ways to current technology and market organization, while remaining rigidly unchanging in other respects. With access to the capacities of an advanced civilization and level of medical care on one hand, but perfectly uninhibited in procreation on the other, the Hutterians appear to have the world's highest rate of population increase. Demonstrating a very low incidence of mental disorders, the Hutterians posit the important question, how far their record is attributable to the freedom of their members from the pressures of an individualistic society. Hutterian communities are also rare phenomena, surviving in only a few other (rather similar) jurisdictions outside Manitoba. These are the striking people about whom Dr. Peters writes.

Outstanding qualities of Dr. Peters' work are the sympathy which he displays toward his subjects, and the wealth of factual information he provides, covering both the history of the Hutterians since their origins and their present attitudes and circumstances. Probably not everyone will agree with all of the author's interpretations and judgments, tempered though he has sought to make them. Those who dispute him, however, will still rely gratefully on the facts which he provides.

H. C. PENTLAND, *President*
The Historical and Scientific Society of Manitoba

ACKNOWLEDGMENTS

THE RESEARCH for this study was made possible by a fellowship grant to me by the Manitoba Historical and Scientific Society, which I hereby gratefully acknowledge. I also owe a special debt of gratitude to the hospitality of the Hutterian communities. Though some of the Hutterians saw little merit in a study of this type, I was invariably made welcome at the colonies, even when my stay was prolonged over a period of weeks at a time. This courtesy, as far as I know, has been extended to all other students and scholars in diverse fields of work interested in Hutterian ways. Between 1956 and 1958 I visited all the Manitoba colonies, and some colonies outside the province, and have repeatedly returned up to the present time. I was with the Hutterian men at work on the fields, in the poultry houses, and in the shops; I observed the women at work in the kitchen and the gardens and the teachers in the schools; I joined the members for community meals and attended their religious services. I also interviewed colony ministers, colony stewards, heads of colony enterprises, helpers, converts, Hutterian teen-agers, and Hutterians who had left their colony. In all cases information was provided most willingly.

The field research also involved many non-Hutterians. In personal interviews or by correspondence I received information concerning the Hutterians and their colonies from municipal secretaries, government officials, staff members of the University of Manitoba, scholars at other institutions, farmers, businessmen, ministers, social workers, doctors, law enforcement officers, and others. The teachers of colony public schools cooperated willingly in suggested projects, filling out questionnaires and providing much pertinent data. Since much of this information, provided by Hutterians or outsiders, was often of a personal nature, I will abstain from listing any names except those of some people who were always available to spend some time with me whenever I was confronted with a special problem. These include Professor F. John C. Dallyn, formerly with the Department of Sociology, University of Manitoba; Senator Paul Yuzyk, Ottawa, then president of the Manitoba Historical Society; Mr. E. A. Fletcher, Q.C., solicitor for the Hutterian communities; Mr. Bernard Grafton, Supervisor of Special Schools for the Province of Manitoba; Rev. Peter Hofer, senior elder of the *Schmiedeleut'* congregations in Manitoba and South Dakota; Rev. Jacob Kleinsasser, Crystal Spring colony; the late Rev. Samuel Kleinsasser, Sturgeon Creek colony; Rev. Jacob Maendel and Mr. Peter Maendel, New Rosedale colony; Rev. Joseph Kleinsasser, Sunnyside colony; and Mr. Peter Entz, formerly of Elm Spring colony, Alberta, now Waldeck colony, Saskatchewan. I would like to thank especially Mr. Joseph Shechtman, of the University of Minnesota Press, who has been most helpful with his suggestions, and Professor H. C. Pentland, president of the Manitoba Historical Society, who contributed the foreword.

To this list I would like to add the names of those who helped me in my study by directing my attention to newspaper articles or other sources of informations on the Hutterians. They are Professors William Knill and John Bergen, University of Alberta; Professor Cornelius Krahn, Bethel College, Kansas; Professor W. C. Christen, Mankato State College, Minnesota; Mr. B. Bott, Winnipeg; and Mr. Alexander Rempel, Niagara-on-the-Lake, Ontario. To these, and to all those who must go unmentioned, I wish to express my most sincere gratitude.

Since making this study I have had an opportunity to continue my research in Hutterian history in Europe. While the bulk of the material in this book is based on the report which I submitted to the Manitoba Historical Society, some additional data of my study at Göttingen, in Germany, have been included. In this connection I would like to express my appreciation to Dr. and Mrs. Ernst Crous, of the *Mennonitische Forschungsstelle* at Krefeld, and to Professors Dr. P. E. Schramm, Dr. Will-Erich Peuckert and Dr. Helmuth Plessner, of the University of Göttingen. These scholars were most helpful in directing my attention to sources on early Hutterian history.

I also would like to express my appreciation to two friends and former teachers: Professor W. L. Morton, Provost of University College, Winnipeg, and Dr. E. K. Francis, Director of the Sociological Institute at the University of Munich. While they were not directly connected with my research on the Hutterians, their scholarship was a constant source of inspiration.

Finally I would like to thank my wife, whose interest and encouragement have accompanied the progress of this study at all times.

V. P.

Moorhead State College
Moorhead, Minnesota
August 1965

special thanks to Professor W. J. McCann, Provost of University College, xxx, and Dr. L. B. ... Director of the Sociology ... lectures on ... things survey. While my ... are not directly connected, I still owe ... research to little more than scholarship ... and ... inspiration.

Finally I extend ... to ... my wife, whose ... and ... throughout ... have accompanied the preparation of this ... at all times.

Richmond State College
... Minnesota
August 197

CONTENTS

Part Three. The Hutterians and the Outside World

Appendix

Illustrations between pages 96 and 97

ALL THINGS COMMON:

THE HUTTERIAN WAY OF LIFE

ABOUT THE HUTTERIANS

THE HUTTERIAN BRETHREN, also known as Hutterites or Hutterians, had their origin in Central Europe at the time of the Reformation. In their history of over four centuries they have experienced persecutions and migrations. Moravia, Slovakia, Transylvania, and Russia were the main stops on their long wanderings. It was not until the 1870's that the small group which had survived, numbering only a few hundred people, reached the United States and settled in what was then Dakota Territory. Today there are some 15,000 of these Hutterians in North America, two-thirds of them making their home in Canada and the rest in the United States. They live in cluster-type colonies known as *Bruderhöfe*, or communities of brethren. Over one hundred of these colonies are scattered across the Canadian prairie provinces of Manitoba, Saskatchewan, and Alberta, and about fifty of them are in the United States, largely in South Dakota and Montana.

The Hutterians have several unique characteristics which distinguish them from their Canadian and American neighbors. They are conscientious objectors to war. They practice common ownership of all property. They have retained the dress, the customs, and the simple manner of living of their early ancestors. While they speak English freely and use German in their church service, their everyday speech is an almost extinct Tirolean dialect. All these factors serve to set the Hutterians apart. At the same time they have a rich spiritual and cultural heritage and are unusually successful in transmitting it to every new generation of Hutterians. Their small colonies, averaging about one hundred people, are exemplary social and economic democracies. Their total egalitarianism assures the members of economic security from the cradle to the grave. Unlike monastic orders the colonies are not dependent on recruiting outsiders for membership in order to survive; they have one of the highest birth rates in the world.

My study of the Hutterians is concerned primarily with the colonies in Manitoba. But the Hutterians are a cohesive group, even though their colonies are scattered over the vast expanse of the Canadian-American prairies. Changes introduced in one place invariably affect the whole group. When an Alberta elder commissioned the publication of a songbook, the printed copies were distributed at all colonies; when an American colony experimented by sending its children to a large public school in a nearby town (they were later withdrawn), the development was closely observed by all the other colonies. Developments in agricultural technology introduced at one colony are adopted, when feasible, by others. It is thus impossible to isolate or confine a study of the Hutterians to any one province or state.

In the same way it has proved impossible to limit this study to either the history or the present-day life of the Hutterians. The events of the early sixteenth century are a living presence in Hutterian consciousness; they remember and revere the names and sufferings of the martyrs to the faith. A chronicle of the experiences of the Brotherhood is, like the Bible, to be found in every Hutterian home. My work is necessarily both a historical study (in the earlier chapters) and a sociological field report (in the later chapters); a more unified treatment could only have been achieved by a sacrifice of accuracy and explanatory force.

Held together by strong bonds of religion, culture, and economics, and by ties of blood and kinship, the Hutterians still face an uncertain future. Because they have resisted integration and assimilation to a greater degree than any other ethnic group of European origin, they pose a problem: will their members in time integrate into the larger society, sharing all its duties and privileges, or will they continue to perpetuate their introverted way of life? Sections of Canadian and American society feel that the Hutterian colonies form little culture islands which obstruct the conformative process of Canadianization and Americanization. There have been demands that provincial or state governments forcibly dissolve the Hutterian colonies.

Thus, whether regarded as a fragment of the Protestant Reformation that has survived unchanged in the modern world, as a *Gemeinschafts-*group that has proved uniquely resistant to the encroachments and segmental relationships of individualistic society, or, because of their nonconformist response to many widely held beliefs, as a test case of cultural pluralism, the Hutterians deserve closer attention than they have generally received.

Im übrigen ist es zuletzt die grösste Kunst, sich zu beschränken und zu isolieren. (For the rest of it, the last and greatest art is to limit and isolate oneself.) GOETHE

Part One

A HISTORY OF THE HUTTERIAN BRETHREN

I

THE ORIGIN AND BACKGROUND
OF THE HUTTERIAN BRETHREN

IT WAS in the eventful period when Sir Thomas More wrote his *Utopia*, when Erasmus of Rotterdam inveighed against war as "the sea of all calamities," when Luther took his stand and declared that he could not do otherwise, that the Hutterian Brotherhood was organized in Moravia. It was a branch of the Anabaptist movement,[1] with spiritual roots extending to the Swiss Brethren, who practiced adult baptism and opposed war. Adult baptism and nonviolence were, and have remained, two salient characteristics of Hutterian faith.

The Swiss Brethren

Barely had Luther and Zwingli broken away from the Catholic Church when some of their closest supporters pressed for still greater reforms. Among the foremost of these radical reformers were a group of Zwingli's followers in Zurich. They became known as the Swiss Brethren, but their membership was by no means confined to Switzerland. Their leaders included Conrad Grebel, Felix Mantz, and Georg Blaurock, among whom Grebel was outstanding. A son of one of the patrician families of Zurich, he had studied at Vienna and Paris. He broke with Zwingli when the latter found it expedient to compromise with the civilian authorities in the hope of support for his religious reforms.

As a reformer Zwingli went considerably beyond Luther, but, anticipating the support of the Zurich council, Zwingli, like Luther, was prepared to ally himself with civic authority. Thus at the public disputation of 1523 Zwingli declared, "My lords will decide whatever regulations are to be adopted in the future in regard to the Mass." Stumpf, a colleague of Conrad Grebel's, immediately challenged this declaration: "Master Ulrich, you do not have the right to place the decision on this matter in the hands of my lords, for the decision has already been made, the Spirit of God decides." [2]

Zwingli eventually persuaded the city council to abolish mass in the churches of Zurich, but the principle of waiting for worldly authority to intervene was unacceptable to the extreme wing of the reformers. For them the New Testament was the sole authority in spiritual matters. They maintained that once a man felt sure that the directive from Scripture was clear, it would be wrong for him not to comply with divine guidance. Since only a mature adult could be expected to assume this moral responsibility, the radical reformers rejected infant baptism.

Early in 1525 the radical reformers completed the break with the more moderate Zurich reformers by introducing adult baptism. Georg Blaurock asked Conrad Grebel to baptize him. Grebel, a layman, complied. Immediately after, Blaurock baptized about fifteen men and women who were present. It was in this manner that the *Täufer* (Anabaptist) movement had its beginning.

Meanwhile another event took place in the Germanys, including Switzerland, which was indirectly associated with the rise and spread of Anabaptism. This was the Peasants' War of 1524–1525. The insurgents, mostly peasants but including townsmen, artisans, teachers, recreant priests, and some nobles, wanted the Reformation to embody economic and political changes, as well as greater religious freedom. The rebellion failed, and Luther's endorsement of the old social order and his condemnation of the rebels disillusioned and alienated many of his supporters. As a result great numbers returned to the Catholic Church, and others joined the small clusters of Anabaptists. Subsequently Bullinger, friend and successor of Zwingli, was, mistakenly, to label the leader of the revolt, Thomas Münzer, "the initiator of Anabaptism."

Indeed, the spread of Anabaptism after 1525 was almost phenomenal. From the Rhine to Prussia, from the North Sea to the Tirol, no part of the Holy Roman Empire was free of it. Since the Anabaptists lacked a central authority to provide directives, the movement represented a wide spectrum of beliefs. Numerous conferences were held and attempts made to formulate Anabaptist doctrine. By 1527 a clearly defined confession of faith, known as the Schleitheim Confession, was adopted by the Swiss Anabaptists.[3] Its articles endorsed adult baptism, "given to all those who have learned repentance and amendment of life"; the use of the ban on those members who "fall into error and sin"; the observance of communion "in remembrance of the broken body of Christ"; and the authority of the elected minister of the church. The articles furthermore rejected the oath and the use of the sword. The strong stand the Anabaptists took against the sword, and violence in general, may in no small measure be attributed to the failure of the Peasants' War.

Even at the time there were not a few Anabaptists who favored adding an article on *Gütergemeinschaft* (common ownership of goods) to the list, in order to restore fully the ideals of the primitive church, where "all that believed were together, and had all things common" (Acts 2:44).

The early growth of Anabaptism may also be attributed to the extraordinary activity of its early missionaries. Men like Balthasar Hubmaier, Hans Denck, and Hans Hut, and many others, gave a tremendous impetus to the movement.[4] Hubmaier was born near Augsburg around 1480. He studied at Freiburg, where he was a student of Johann Eck, later famous for his disputations with Martin Luther. At an early age Hubmaier became the prorector of the university at Ingolstadt. Later he moved to Waldshut, a city close to the Swiss border, and pursued feverish missionary activity. He was one of the moving spirits behind the peasants' petitions, and one of the most zealous leaders of Anabaptism.[5]

From the outset Anabaptism was regarded as a danger to the very foundations of the state and the state church. The Anabaptists refused to accept office in, or to bear arms for, the state. Many of them endorsed some form of common ownership of goods. They claimed the right for the individual to worship as he pleased, accountable only to his own conscience. These were reasons enough for the state and the church, whether Roman Catholic, Lutheran, or Zwinglian, to regard all Anabaptists as either heretics or a seditious element. "The persecution of Anabaptism," says Holborn,[6] "by all political and ecclesiastical — Catholic, Lutheran, and Reformed — authorities was cruel, even beyond the usual measure of the century."

Zurich was the first to introduce the death penalty specifically for Anabaptists, on March 1, 1526. By the end of the year it was extended to those who attended Anabaptist meetings. Similar edicts were issued by numerous German cities and states. On January 4, 1528, Charles V decreed that Anabaptists were to be "exterminated by fire and sword," and the mandate was approved by the Reichstag at Speyer a few months later. Persecution became so intense in Switzerland and the Habsburg lands that many of the Anabaptists sought sanctuary in Moravia.

The Anabaptists in Moravia

At that time Bohemia and Moravia formed a kingdom within the Empire. At the death of King Louis II, on the field of Mohács in 1526, this kingdom, with Hungary, came under direct Habsburg control. However, because of the borderland nature of the country, the powerful nobility continued to enjoy considerable independence despite the Habsburg connection. These nobles were willing to grant asylum to the German and Swiss Anabaptists.

For centuries Germans had penetrated into Bohemia, introduced new industries, built cities, and increased the agricultural production of the land.[7] Moravia, lying east of Bohemia, had relatively few German settlers. Since many of the Anabaptists were skillful craftsmen and artisans, they were desirable immigrants. That they were religious dissenters, accused of sedition, did not unduly alarm the nobles. Bohemia and Moravia had experienced religious conflicts in their destructive fury a full century earlier, during the Hussite wars (1419–1436). The intermingling of Utraquists, Taborites, Moravian-Bohemian Brethren, Catholics, and more recently Lutherans, had brought about a religious tolerance still unknown in the Germanys.

Among the wealthiest families of Moravia were the Liechtensteins,[8] who owned vast estates and were lords over cities and towns, including one named Nikolsburg. After 1526 Nikolsburg and the surrounding area received a great influx of Anabaptists. Leonhard von Liechtenstein (1482–1534), the head of the family, was so taken with the Anabaptist teachings that he joined them, being baptized by Dr. Hubmaier.[9]

Soon Nikolsburg came to occupy a pre-eminent position for the Anabaptists. The overt sympathies of the Liechtensteins drew to the town such Anabaptist leaders as Hubmaier and Hans Hut, who arrived in 1526, and the Zurich printer and publisher Sorg, commonly known as Froschauer, who fled to Moravia and was invited by Liechtenstein to make his home in Nikolsburg. These men formed but the spearhead of the movement, for soon Anabaptist refugees arrived from every German and Swiss state, canton, and city.

The Anabaptists were united in their opposition to the authority of the state in matters of conscience and to the state church. At the same time their very individualistic approach to doctrine fragmented their own ranks. Moreover, they had come to Moravia from diverse parts of the Empire and the natural differences contributed to disharmony. It was for these reasons that almost from the beginning two main factions of Anabaptism emerged. One group was led by Hubmaier, who counseled moderation in the doctrine of "avoidance of the world" and insisted that the government had a right to levy war taxes in order to protect its citizens.[10] His followers were thereupon labeled by their opponents the *Schwertler* (swordbearers). The other group, led by Hans Hut and Jacob Wiedemann, held strictly to nonviolence and refused to pay war taxes. This radical party was dubbed the *Stäbler* (staffbearers).

However, neither Hubmaier nor Hut was destined to continue his activities for very long. The former's prodigious literary output drew the Viennese government's attention to him, as it had before. He was captured and charged with sedition for his share in the Peasants' War. Even Liechtenstein, his powerful patron, could not protect him against this charge, and Hubmaier was burned at the stake in Vienna on March 10, 1528. Hut had died under mysterious circumstances in an Augsburg prison the year before.

Though the two leaders had died, the intra-Anabaptist differences remained divisive, the more so since special war taxes continued to be levied. At this time the Turks had penetrated deep into the Habsburg empire. Under Suleiman I they captured Belgrade in 1521, defeated the Hungarians in 1526, and stood before the gates of Vienna in 1529. In 1528 the imperial government used all its power to press the nobles into service in order to buttress the empire's defenses. When Liechtenstein hesitated to lend his support, an imperial emissary threatened him with force. Liechtenstein retorted that if the royal troops should invade his estates they would be met with bullets.[11] This was too much for the *Stäbler,* the nonresistance group, whose opposition to violence went so far that they refused protection by arms. Addressing himself to Liechtenstein, Wiedemann, the leader of the group, said, "Since you threaten to protect us, we cannot stay."

It was under these circumstances that Wiedemann and about two hundred followers left Nikolsburg. Friends bade them farewell, and Leonhard von Liechtenstein and his retinue of mounted escorts accompanied them to the limits of the principality. Liechtenstein was so well disposed toward them that he even refused to extract the customary tax from his departing tenants. Once outside the boundaries of Nikolsburg, with no shelter under the open sky, the group decided to pool all its resources. Two stewards were elected, and, according to the Old Hutterian Chronicle, these men spread a cloak on the ground on which everyone "freely and without compulsion laid his possessions." [12] This memorable incident occurred in 1528. It marked the first step in total communal ownership of property. In time this feature became the chief doctrinal characteristic of this branch of Anabaptism.

The leaders of the group next appealed to the von Kaunitz brothers for permission to settle on their estates.[13] The four Kaunitz brothers declared that the group was welcome even if "there were a thousand of them." In this way Austerlitz, the part of the von Kaunitz estates where the voluntary refugees settled, became a haven for the German Anabaptists as remarkable as Nikolsburg had been.

Jacob Huter

The people of Austerlitz helped the newcomers, and the Kaunitz brothers provided them with lumber for the building of homes. They also exempted their new tenants from taxes and statute labor for a period of six years. The new settlers were determined to live communal lives, and this purpose was strengthened by a new leader who appeared, Jacob Huter.

Little is known about Huter's early life.[14] The date of his birth is unknown, but the Old Hutterian Chronicle reports his presence in Austerlitz in 1529. The entry records: "There came a man by the name of Jacob, by trade a hatter [German *Huter*], born in the hamlet of Moos, half a mile away from Bruneck, in the Pustertal [South Tirol]." [15]

Anabaptism had received widespread support in Tirol. Jacob Huter had been one of its earliest adherents, and was an elected minister of a congregation. When the Tirol Anabaptists heard of the large congregations in Moravia, they delegated Huter to establish contact with them. From this mission Huter returned in 1529, satisfied that his people's beliefs and those of the Brethren in Moravia were the same. Meanwhile a wave of terror was released on the Anabaptists in Tirol. The spread of the faith had weakened Tirol's military position. So intense was the persecution, and so many men and women were burned at the stake or drowned, that communities began to complain of the number of orphans the Anabaptists left behind. In 1529 the small city of Kitzbühel alone had from forty to fifty Anabaptist children in its orphanages.[16] Huter's task was to guide to Moravia the refugees who escaped the executioner and whose homes had been burned to the ground.

But Austerlitz and the neighboring Anabaptist congregations were little prepared to receive the destitute new arrivals. The existing homes became too small, and additional dwellings had to be erected. This was a great strain on the community people, who had established themselves only the year before. Many of the members were not prepared for the selfless sacrifices which communal life demanded. Soon some members charged that the leaders selected the better homes for their own families, and that the kitchen served them better food. In addition there was rivalry among the leaders, who, when they became Anabaptists, were of entirely different social strata. There were men like Marpeck, a former civil engineer, Wiedemann, a plain laborer, and Reublin, a graduate of Freiburg university. Reublin, who had been the first Swiss priest to enter into marriage (in 1523) and had rebaptized Hubmaier, repeatedly challenged Wiedemann's position in the congregation.

Huter saw that the congregations lacked firm leadership and spent too much time on internal disputes. He also perceived that the practice of common ownership was not always followed. A strong organizer, Huter proceeded to weld the amorphous Moravian groups into tightly knit community-congregations. In 1533 he was elected leader and occupied the position for three years. Early in 1536 he was captured on his way to Tirol and was condemned to death by fire. He died at the stake at Innsbruck on February 25 of that year. It is from him that the community-minded Anabaptists took their name, and thenceforth called themselves the Hutterian Brethren.[17]

Peter Riedemann

Huter's successor as leader, or *Vorsteher*, as he was known by the Hutterians, was his former assistant, Amon. Amon bridged the short period between Jacob Huter and another leader who, like Huter, was a key figure in the history of the Hutterian Church. This was Peter Riedemann. Riedemann was in Hesse when his home congregations wrote him that if he could be spared from the mission field he was to return to Moravia. Riedemann, who was now thirty-six years of age, had already made his most lasting contribution to the Brotherhood. Two years earlier, in a Marburg jail, he had written his *Confession of Faith*,[18] the standard Hutterian doctrinal interpretation accepted to this day.

Huter's ideal had been total communal life. To him, says the historian Heimann, "the economic security of the brotherhood [was] the condition for the full development of a sacred community."[19] Riedemann's contribution was to translate this ideal into a practical pattern for life and to provide for it a sound doctrinal basis. To Riedemann "All God's gifts — not only spiritual, but also material things — are given to man, not that he should have them for himself, or alone, but with all his fellows."[20] To the German socialists of the nineteenth century this stand appeared sufficiently revolutionary to qualify the early Hutterians as "forerunners of modern socialism."[21] But this is a retrospective interpretation of Riedemann and Hutterian doctrine. The whole tenor of Riedemann's *Confession* and of the Hutterian pattern of life molded by it emphasizes *Gütergemeinschaft* not as a new economic system but as a realization of primitive Christianity.

The Hutterian Communities in Moravia

Riedemann's tenure saw a great expansion of Hutterian communities. Partly this expansion was due to natural increase, and partly to the work of missionaries. One German source lists a total of eighty-five communal "households" for the period from 1529 to 1622, and there may have been as many as sixty-five of them at any one time.[22] The Czech historian Frantisek Hrubý, who classified the Hutterian households according to the number of estates on which they could be found, lists twenty-six lordly manors.[23]

The communities were Germanic islands set in predominantly Slavic areas. Their contribution to the economic development of southern Moravia has been amply documented by Hrubý. A large number of the Brethren were employed at home; others were administrators of estates or supervised the manorial enterprises. Many were millers. Then there were masons, farriers, scythemakers, sicklesmiths, coppersmiths, locksmiths, plumbers, tanners, furriers, shoemakers, harnessmakers, saddlers, cartwrights, bookbinders, toolmakers, hatters, tailors, thatchers, weavers, ropemakers, sievemakers, glaziers, potters, brewers, surgeons, cutlers, and many others.

"Each shop," reports one Hutterian chronicle, "was looked after by the man in charge, who accepted the job to be done, performed it, returned the finished article or sold the products of the shop according to their value, and turned the honest profit over to the community." [24] Hrubý reprints a letter sent by a leading Moravian to a Hutterian community. The writer asks whether the carriage he has ordered is ready, requests the services of some of the Brethren for the installation of water pipes in his palace, and concludes with an order for a new glass inkwell. [25] Another Czech scholar, Cernohorský, has pointed out the excellence of early Hutterian ceramics, evidence of which has been preserved in the museums of Vienna and Brünn. [26]

There were, however, some occupations and assignments which the Brethren refused to accept. When the Count of Thurn and Taxis planned an ostentatious wedding for his daughter, the Hutterians refused to assist in the preparations because the occasion was to be marked, in their opinion, by "pride and immoderate drinking." The count summarily dismissed his uncooperative servants. Again when the powerful Moravian noble Zierotin, engaged in maneuvers against the Turks, asked some Brethren to move his war tent and its contents, consisting largely of arms, they resisted with the objection that to do this was contrary to their faith. [27]

Every Hutterian enterprise abided strictly by the hard and fast rules laid down by Riedemann. The tailor, for instance, knew that whatever "serveth but pride, magnificence, and vanity" he was forbidden to make. The artisan was prepared to make bread knives and axes, but refused to make swords and spears. Moreover, the rigid code of craftsmanship observed by the Hutterians, and the supervision of their shops by their own men, combined to warrant the quality of their products. In a way these workshop enterprises anticipated the industrial age. The communal enterprises were more economical and efficient than the small workshops of individual craftsmen.

Persecution and Expulsion

The Anabaptists had originally fled to Moravia in order to escape persecution. But through the following years the power of their protectors, the Moravian nobility, waned as the power of the imperial government in

Vienna increased. From time to time government troops, assisted by local informers, would comb the country for Anabaptists. In such times the protection extended to them by the nobility, in direct opposition to royal mandates, would avail little. The Hutterian chronicles report that the Brethren would flee on such occasions to the mountains and the caves. In modern times these caves (Czech *lochy*, from the German *Löcher*) have been explored. They are not caves in the accepted sense of the word, but elaborate excavations more like air raid shelters, with winding passages, containing trapholes, living quarters, and hidden exits. Cernohorský maintains that only the highly organized Hutterians, having many skillful workers available, could have engineered these cave shelters, which are found in areas at one time inhabited by the Brethren.[28]

Another threat was the Turkish wars. The whole population suffered from them, but the Hutterian communities were especially vulnerable because they contained central food stores and community kitchens, and were thus ideally suited for quartering troops. In 1593 the Turks once again thrust deep into the Empire, and, on retreating, took with them many captives, especially women. In this connection the experiences of one Hutterian, Solomon Boeger, are of special interest. Boeger had lost his wife and child to the Turks and set out to find them. In his search, which extended over many years and took him to the heart of the Ottoman Empire, Boeger found and helped many Hutterians. His tireless quest for his own family, however, went unrewarded, and it is assumed that Boeger himself was finally murdered.[29]

In 1618 a war that was to convulse Central Europe for thirty years began in Bohemia. When the emperor's army routed the forces of the elector of the Palatinate outside of Prague in the fall of 1620, the entire Protestant nobility of Bohemia and Moravia fled the country. Twenty-seven nobles who were captured by the imperial forces were publicly executed in Prague and their estates were confiscated. With the nobility the Hutterians lost their staunchest friends. Many of the Catholic nobles also had Hutterian tenants on their estates, but it was no longer safe to keep them. On September 17, 1622, Cardinal Dietrichstein received instructions from Vienna that the "Anabaptists be driven unconditionally out of Moravia."[30] This order was carried out to the letter, though the cardinal made a personal attempt to lessen the blow by trying to persuade the Hutterians to remain and relinquish their faith.

As the first century of Hutterian history drew to a close, the Brethren once more became homeless wanderers. They left behind in Moravia their communal holdings to cross the March River into Slovakia, where the emperor, as king of Hungary, wielded considerably less power at this time.

During the Moravian period the Hutterian Church received its mold. The communal organization of its enterprises expressed their ideal of a Christian spiritual community. Moreover, this community also provided for the economic security of its members. That the Brotherhood members were almost all Germans and formed culture islands in a largely Czech-peopled country strengthened their sense of *Gemeinschaft,* their in-group feelings, and reinforced their deliberate attempt to avoid contact with the outside world. The community-congregation as an expression of the Hutterian concept of the primitive church thus took shape in Moravia. This religious, cultural, and economic entity, in and by itself in every way almost entirely self-sufficient, may be regarded as the most lasting Hutterian heritage of the Moravian period.

II

HUTTERIAN MIGRATIONS

THE FIRST Hutterian community in Hungary was established as early as 1546, when the Brethren purchased a mill at Sabatisch.[1] This place was immediately across the border from Moravia, in what is today Slovakia. Soon more Hutterian colonies were established in this region, and after the Moravian exodus a Hutterian community was established at Alwintz, in Transylvania, a territory now part of Rumania. It becomes evident that in a discussion of the Hutterian sojourn in Hungary we are dealing with a geographical region of the seventeenth and eighteenth centuries rather than with the modern political entity.

Since 1526, after the Mohács disaster, Hungary had been in a most unhappy condition. The Turks shortly gained control of four-fifths of the country, and they remained in Buda until 1686. In the west the Habsburgs retained nominal possession of a slice of territory, and in Transylvania the Zápolya family, and later the Bethlen family, protégés of the Turks, ruled the country. Until the defeat of the Ottoman Turks in the Battle of Vienna in 1683, the history of Hungary was marked by incessant wars and internal disunity.

Yet it was to this country that the Hutterians looked for shelter and safety when they left Moravia during the first phase of the Thirty Years' War. Despite Turkish occupation, the Magyars were not entirely outside the European community. They too were strongly affected by the Reformation, and many of the best known families became Calvinist or Lutheran. Later Cardinal Peter Pázmány (1570–1637), a born Calvinist turned Catholic, directed the Hungarian Counter-Reformation, and succeeded in regaining the bulk of the population for the Roman Church. Transylvania, which had received German immigrants from the Rhineland and the Palatinate as early as the twelfth century, became strongly Protestant. Here Catholics, Lutherans, Calvinists, and Unitarians had equal rights and complete freedom of religion, and here the Hutterians sought a new home.

The Communities in Hungary

Within a year after Sabatisch was established in Slovakia, twelve small Brotherhood communities mushroomed in its immediate neighborhood. The Hutterians did not displace a native population, but rather took up land that had been left by people who had migrated to safer regions after great numbers of their neighbors had been destroyed by pestilence and war. The nobility, who owned the land, used every inducement to attract new settlers.[2]

In 1588 a community was established at Lewär,[3] about thirty miles north of Pressburg (Bratislava), and it soon became a springboard for further expansion in this area.

The third Hutterian settlement was established at Alwintz, near Hermannstadt,[4] in 1621 when Gabor Bethlen (1580–1629) invited 183 Hutterian refugees to move to Transylvania, and a little later this group was strengthened by more migrants from Moravia. Proclaimed Prince of Transylvania in 1613, Bethlen, an ardent Protestant, declared in 1622, "Since I have heard that the Moravian Brethren have been dispossessed and driven from their homes, and I have known them as excellent tradesmen and artisans, I have invited them to Alwintz and turned over to them land and vineyards."[5]

The communities in western Hungary suffered severely during the Thirty Years' War. A Hutterian chronicle records that in 1626 the imperial general Wallenstein invaded Hungary with "a very large armada, 50,000 strong, on horse and foot," to meet "Prince Bethlen and his array of Hungarians, Turks, and Germans," and their "armies remained in their camps for four months."[6] An outright clash was avoided because Bethlen had already made peace with Emperor Ferdinand II when Wallenstein turned his forces from Silesia to Hungary. Both military camps remained inactive but refused to depart because neither side trusted the other. Since both armies lived off the land, the result was disastrous to the country.

The Hutterian chronicler laments that the soldiers pillaged and robbed what had been acquired "by the sour sweat of labor."

The excesses of the prolonged wars excited the minds of many people. Some thought that they were witnessing the gathering for Armageddon, the great final conflict. Among the Hutterians at Lewär this belief gained converts, and many of them held that the Last Judgment had arrived.[7] A turner would leave his lathe, a miller his mill, or a cook her kitchen, to wander away and spend the rest of the day in prayer. Many refused to attend church services, where they would be found by the Lord associating with less saintly believers. This behavior not only threatened the spiritual community but also affected the economic life of the colony. Order was not restored until the dissidents were read out of the church by the assembled Brotherhood.

As the Thirty Years' War proceeded, spreading havoc and destruction, it brutalized the peaceful citizenry. Peasants and laborers who had formerly quietly followed their pursuits had their homes and villages pillaged until they saw no redress but to join the plunderers and bandits. Since one of the major tenets of the Hutterians was the rejection of all violence, they had to stand idly by and see small bands of roving brigands raid their homes, farmyards, and storage rooms. This was hard, especially for the younger members; sometimes they would resort to flail, pitchfork, or stick and protect what was their own. As a result the church elders drew up strict regulations which prohibited the use of force and violence whatever the provocation might be.[8]

Despite the incessant wars, the Hutterian communities in Hungary appeared prosperous when compared with their neighbors. A German writer of the time, Johann von Grimmelshausen (*ca.* 1621–1676), a Catholic, visited them and has left an almost idyllic picture of Hutterian colony life:

They had treasures laid up and more than enough to eat; yet they wasted nothing. One heard no grumbling or cursing among them, not even unnecessary words. I saw craftsmen working in their shops as if they were doing piecework. Their schoolmaster taught the children as if they were all his own. Nowhere did one see men and women mixed; each sex was doing its assigned work in its assigned place. I saw lying-in rooms where there were only young mothers, who were well taken care of — as were the babies — by other young mothers, without the interference of husbands. Other special rooms contained nothing but babies in cradles; women fed the babies and kept them clean and cared for them. The mothers came in only three times a day in order to breast-feed the infants. Only widows were used as children's nurses. In another hall women were working at more than a hundred spinning and carding wheels. Some women were exclusively laundresses, some bedmakers, cattle-feeders, waitresses, in charge of china or linen, and so on; each had her job and knew how to do it. Similarly, the men had their assigned activities. If a person got sick, he or she had a special nurse; and there was a doctor and pharmacist for the group, though because of good food and healthy living hardly anyone was ill. I saw many an old person living quietly to an extreme age among them, and that is seldom found elsewhere. They had their appointed hours for eating, for sleeping, for working, but not a single minute for play or for promenading, except for the youngsters. After each meal, for the sake of health, the youngsters went walking for an hour with their teacher. During this time they also had to pray and sing hymns. There was no anger, no zealotry, no vengefulness, no envy, no enmity, no worry about worldly goods, no pride, no regret. In short, there prevailed such lovely harmony as seemed to purport nothing but the honorable increase of the human race and of God's kingdom. No man saw his wife except when he met with her at the appointed hour in their bedroom, which contained nothing but their well-made bed plus a chamber pot, a washbasin, a pitcher filled with water, and a white towel, so that he could fall asleep and go to work next morning with clean hands. They all called each other "brother" and "sister," and yet such familiarity never caused lewdness.[9] *

Andreas Ehrenpreis

The Hungarian interlude also produced the first great leader who was born into the community,[10] Andreas Ehrenpreis (1589–1662). He instilled human warmth into the institutionalized, rigid Huter-Riedemann community, making the austere Hutterian life practicable and viable. Though Ehrenpreis lived to see the Brotherhood decline, nevertheless his influence transcended the generations, and the atmosphere of the communities today in large measure reflects his ideal.

Ehrenpreis was born to Hutterian parents in Moravia. A miller by occupation, he was elected minister at the age of twenty-two, and after the customary Hutterian period of trial, a period that varies in length, he was ordained in the ministry two years later, at Sabatisch. He spent the rest of his life there. In 1639 he was elected *Vorsteher*, and was in charge of all Hutterian communities in Hungary. Ehrenpreis's work consisted in providing sound, practical leadership in the administration of the com-

* From Johann Jakob Christoffel von Grimmelshausen: *Simplicius Simplicissimus*, translated by George Schulz-Behrend, © copyright 1965 by the Bobbs-Merrill Company, Inc., reprinted by permission of the Liberal Arts Press Division of the Bobbs-Merrill Company, Inc.

munities, in collecting old and drawing up new ordinances which regulated communal behavior and work, and in carrying on an extensive literary activity which took the form of letters, addresses, and hymns. He was also the author of a small book, *Ein Sendbrief* (epistle).[11]

This work, which remains one of the most influential expressions of Hutterian doctrine, has a lengthy introduction, but in the second chapter the author arrives at his favorite theme that "true community" is not the result of "force and pressure," but is the voluntary surrender and integration of the individual, his total submergence in the *Gemeinschaft* (community). He develops his point in a simile in which the brethren and sisters are compared to the bread and wine at the Lord's Table.

"As bread cannot come of corn unless it be broken and finely ground," wrote Ehrenpreis, "so also shall those who would take communion be broken and crushed by the millstone of the word of God, break their own mind and will and be no more vain in themselves, but rather restrain and compel body, mind and will into Christian service. Just as the grains of corn must be completely mixed and blended and each must render its share to produce flour and bread, while any single grain which remains whole and retains its own properties is unworthy, and cast out for it belongs not therein. The same is the wine, where the press crushes each tender berry, each in turn yields all its juice and strength towards the cider or wine, so that the qualities of each single berry are no longer evident, but are part of the whole wine. . . . If any single berry escape the press and is not crushed, but retains its own strength and form, it belongs not in the wine, for it is unworthy, useless, and is cast out. . . ."[12]

This is the message of Ehrenpreis, and the rest of the book serves to instruct how the personality is to be submerged in the community. Ehrenpreis warns against too much learning, and against intermarriage with worldly outsiders; he insists on the retention of the ban for repeated transgressors, and pleads for stricter discipline in the rearing of children. He warns against avarice, a "vice equal to the worst sins."

It is significant that Ehrenpreis was born in a Hutterian community: these communities no longer needed revivifying influences from without, but had by now established their own traditions, evolved an informal behavior pattern, and could extend and codify this pattern for themselves. The organization of communities where "three, four or even six hundred people" used "one kitchen, one bakery, one communal dining room,"[13] where young mothers jointly used one nursery, and where the men divided the work among themselves, required, according to Ehrenpreis, a distinct code that would be a guide to the Brotherhood. It was out of this need that the *Gemeindeordnungen*[14] (community ordinances and regulations) were born.

Only a few of the regulations can be mentioned here, and these but briefly. They indirectly point to the human frailties and shortcomings that confronted the Hutterian communities. One of the first ordinances is a reminder to the members to see that the younger people devote more time to reading the Hutterian hymns, letters, and accounts in order to acquaint themselves more fully with their own heritage. Members are admonished to spend a minimum of money on clothes and appearance; they are warned that the Church does not recognize bequests to or by individual members. Young and old, reads another injunction, are to spend their time at work, and are not to absent themselves for trivial reasons. Nor are the wives to spend too much time visiting their husbands in the workshops, as this contributes to annoyance and disharmony. Beggars and paupers should be directed to one source of distribution in the colony, as they could very easily exploit unwarranted liberality if everyone felt free to hand out what he pleased. Brethren and sisters are warned to avoid places of entertainment unseemly for Christians, like public executions. The community ministers and teachers are charged to see that these regulations are observed, "for if a sheep is lost or goes astray, one inquires of the shepherd for its whereabouts." [15]

The Dissolution of the Communities

Ehrenpreis had striven hard to infuse a new spirit into his Brotherhood, which was showing increasing signs of disintegration. The communities had lost the missionary zeal of the previous century. Moreover, the Brotherhood had grown tired of persecution. During the formative years of Hutterianism persecution had been violent and punishment swift and severe. The conditions the Brethren faced now were different but equally oppressive. The Treaty of Westphalia (1648) terminated the Thirty Years' War. States began to consolidate their holdings. Hungary was a Habsburg domain, and the Habsburgs, with the assistance of the Jesuits, set about to Catholicize their subjects, and to harass those that clung to their faith.

The Hutterian communities were taxed mercilessly. The nobility, anticipating government confiscation of the communal households, determined to get their share of the spoils. One Hutterian writer laments that "Count Uhrich removed from Lewär 10 pails of wine from the cellars, 2 wagons, 3 harrows, 3 ploughs and a yoke, and 15 loads of hay" while the Brethren stood helplessly by. The action of the nobility was the signal for the neighborhood, itself impoverished by pillage. All restraints were dropped, and the mob took over. Now the government moved in, and removed oxen, cows, and sheep. The officials barely waited for the Hutterian custodians to assist them. When they found, at one colony, that the shoemaker's and tailor's shops were locked, they smashed the doors and windows to get at the contents more quickly. Left completely destitute, the Hutterians dissolved their community of goods in 1685, and appealed to the government to consider them henceforth as individual householders.[16]

Though the Hutterians discarded the practice of community of goods, they still continued as congregations. Then in 1688 the Lewär congregation was visited by Cardinal Kollonitsch, a genial man but noted for his religious zeal. The cardinal intimated to the Brethren that their children should receive the sacrament of baptism. A little later the same year, a government mandate decreed that "no child should die without having been first baptized."[17] Failure to have a child baptized was punishable by exile. Exiled families were forced to relinquish their children, who became wards of the Catholic Church.

The Hutterians circumvented this law by permitting their infants to be baptized by priests ("getting a bath," they called it) only to have these same children later, when they came of age, baptized by their own ministers. There were, however, other difficulties. Hutterian leaders were subjected to severe inquisitions, and Hutterian homes were continually raided by the police, accompanied by representatives of the Jesuit order. At these domiciliary visits all non-Catholic religious books were ferreted out and confiscated.[18]

Finally the last glimmer of Hutterianism was extinguished during the reign of Empress Maria Theresa, who inherited the crown in 1740.[19] The Hutterians by now had become for the most part nominal Catholics, but they continued to assemble in private homes for church services. Their children were instructed in their own faith at home, and the dead were buried in their own cemeteries. Though baptized in childhood by priests, the Brethren refused to attend mass or observe the customary Catholic holidays. Under the young empress this changed. The ministers were placed in confinement; the last Hutterian *Vorsteher* in Slovakia, Zacharias Walter, spent most of his life imprisoned at a Jesuit monastery at Ofen.[20] Other obstinate members were either pressed into army service or placed in "correction homes."[21] The rest of the Brotherhood finally conformed. Members who refused to attend mass would be whipped into obedience by Jesuit mercenaries. An official entry for March 31, 1763,[22] states that "Abraham Roth received three, Jacob Albrecht eight, and Johannes Schmidt eighteen lashes" before they promised to attend mass.

The final official Jesuit report for Sabatisch, dated May 27, 1763, states that the conversion by that time was complete: *omnes*. But this was a slight exaggeration. Twenty years later fifty-six Hutterians escaped from Slovakia and reached Russia, where their Transylvanian brethren had established a colony on the Desna River. Among them were Jacob Walter and his family; Walter was the son of that Zacharias Walter who was the last *Vorsteher*. The plan for the escape was organized in part by two Brethren from Russia, Glanzer and Müller, who visited Slovakia "as subjects of the Prince Romanov."[23]

There remains but a postscript to be added for the Slovakian period. Because the Hutterians lived in large communal homes they were sometimes known in Slovakia as the *Haushaber* (homeowners), which was corrupted to *Habaner*. Though they were converted to Catholicism and in time lost all knowledge of their Hutterian past, these *Habaner* persisted in remaining aloof from their Slovakian neighbors. When an Austrian historian visited them in the 1920's, the old homes, dating back to the early eighteenth century, were still occupied by people known in the neighborhood as *Habaner*. They still bore the old Hutterian patronyms, and had even retained some of the Hutterian customs and practices.[24]

Later several attempts were made by the Canadian and American Hutterians to establish contact with these *Habaner*. In 1938 David Hofer, of Manitoba, and Michael Waldner, of South Dakota, visited Slovakia.[25] But there was no response to their invitation that the *Habaner* establish a community of goods. That old ideal had been extinguished and could not be revived.

In the seventeenth century the Hutterians repeatedly attempted to establish their communities in the Protestant states of Germany. In 1603 and in the years immediately following an attempt was made to establish a colony at Elbing, in East Prussia, where there were already a considerable number of Mennonites. But the attempt failed. In 1654 the congregation at Sabatisch sent emissaries to the Calvinistic elector of the Palatinate, at Heidelberg, and permission was secured to establish a communal holding near the newly founded city of Mannheim. At first this community thrived, but then it too failed. It would appear from these ventures that the tightly knit Hutterian community could continue successfully only on foreign soil, where natural differences between the community people and the surrounding populations reinforced the isolation of the *Bruderhof*. In their native German soil social and economic integration developed and accelerated at a pace which invariably ended in a dissolution of the community.

Throughout the years of sojourn in southeastern Europe, the Hutterians remained in touch with the Mennonites of Germany and Holland, and through them, no doubt, established contact with the English Quakers. In 1662 two Quakers, John Philly and William Moore, visited the Hutterian colonies in Hungary. They called these communities "families," which they indeed resembled, and sent a report home to London in which they described their impressions. One Quaker historian intimates that their report may have influenced George Fox (1624–1691) to make his recommendations that compact working communities with approximately one hundred members be established, and that these accept the responsibility for the care of widows, orphans, and old people. Moore wrote that they had visited the "Hottersche Brethren, about a Day's Journey from Presburgh in Hungaria, where we were pretty kindly entertained." His letter recounts in some detail the chaotic conditions existing in Hungary, where the Quakers spent some time in prison. He describes the Hutterian tribulations, as in one area where there had been "nine Families [communities] there is but one remaining, and the rest were burned, with the Value of many Thousands in them, and about two Hundred of the Men were slain and taken captive." [26]

Transylvania and Wallachia

The subsequent history of the Hutterians was greatly affected by a development which initially had little to do with Hutterianism. In the sixteenth century the cause of the Reformation had gained a considerable following in Austria, but these Habsburg domains were reclaimed for the older faith by the Counter-Reformation. However, in the eighteenth century a renascent movement quite spontaneously developed in the provinces of Carinthia, Salzburg, Styria, and Tirol. Lutheran Bibles and writings found their way into peasant homes, and the country stirred with religious unrest. This revival of Lutheranism disturbed not only the Catholic clergy but also Empress Maria Theresa, who decided on a large-scale resettlement policy that was to transfer thousands of her Protestant subjects to Transylvania.[27]

One contingent of these transmigrants attached itself to the small Hutterian group which had come to Transylvania at the invitation of Gabor Bethlen. There is little doubt that this *Anschluss* made the survival of the enfeebled Brotherhood possible. The Carinthian patronyms — Kleinsasser, Hofer, Waldner, Wurz, Glanzer — to this day form the core of the Hutterian family names in the North American communities.

But Transylvania was still part of the empire, and before long the same persecution pattern that had been so effective in Slovakia repeated itself in Transylvania, this time directed exclusively against the Anabaptists. The Hutterians thereupon planned a mass flight across the Transylvanian Alps to Wallachia, a principality then under Turkish suzerainty. Since emigration was forbidden by the authorities, the Hutterians planned this flight in great secrecy. Women and children were organized, the blacksmiths made keys for the community members in prisons, and illegal border guides were hired to assist them in the escape across the guarded border. Three times the date set had to be postponed on account of reneging by the guides, who faced death by impaling or hanging if captured. In the end they must have considered the risk of shepherding the entire community across the border as too great, and they abandoned the project.

The Brethren now proceeded on their own. The move took the local authorities by surprise, and before it could be stopped the caravan of sixty-seven "souls" and their horses and wagons had crossed the mountains and forded the river into Wallachia. Although the travelers were completely exhausted before they reached their destination, they pushed relentlessly on in order to escape pursuers. "Many discovered," records a Hutterian chronicler, "what before had seemed incredible, that you can sleep while walking, or walk while sleeping."

The flight into Wallachia took place in the fall of 1767. Once safe the community dispatched two men to return to Transylvania to inform the remaining members, some of them still in prison, where the main body of the congregation could be reached. Two other men sent to Bucharest to find suitable land for settlement met there a well-to-do German by the name of Wölfl, who assisted them in locating land where they could erect temporary quarters. It lay about one mile out of Bucharest.

Johannes Waldner, the Hutterian chronicler who later recorded the events, was an impressionable young man of eighteen at this time. He describes their first homes, which served as a pattern for the Hutterians more than a hundred years later, in Dakota Territory.

"Winter was at the door," writes Waldner, "and we had no shelter. In our need we therefore built homes for ourselves out of sod, as do the poor natives of this land. We dug a hole about three feet deep, and as wide and as long as required. At both ends we erected posts as supports and placed a beam across, resting on the posts. . . . We covered the top with boards by placing one end of the board on the ground, and the other resting on the beam. These boards we covered with straw and earth. In the gable at the end we placed one or two windows; while the entrance was at the opposite end. The stove was placed wherever it was most convenient. We completed five or six of these homes. . . . They appeared strange at first, but we were satisfied, for we had peace and religious freedom." [28]

That winter their friend Wölfl died. The Hutterians bought "his home, orchard, and land, ten head of cattle, and twenty-four hives of bees." In spring their carpenters began an extensive building program, while others tilled the land and planted vineyards. Still others opened shops as weavers and potters. There was so much activity at the new community, and this in turn elicited such interest in drowsy Bucharest, that often there were "seven or eight carriages" of boyars who watched the Hutterians at work. It appeared that the Brethren at last had found a place where they were not only tolerated, but valued for their industry and peaceful ways.

The year after the Hutterians arrived in Wallachia, 1768, when Russia was occupied by one of the periodic Polish disorders, Turkey declared war on Russia, which was suspected of having designs on the principalities of Moldavia and Wallachia. The Russians retaliated by launching a simultaneous attack by sea and land, and defeated the Turks. By the peace signed at Kuchuk Kainarji, in 1774, Russia gained control of the entire Dnieper basin. Only internal conditions of unrest, especially the outbreak of the Pugachev rebellion, prevented Russia from fully exploiting her military successes by annexing the two principalities.

The unexpected outbreak of the war placed the Hutterians in Wallachia in a most precarious position. Finding themselves in the vortex of retreating and advancing armies and plundering Albanian freebooters, they had to recognize that what they had accepted as a remote and peaceful principality was actually an apple of discord between two powerful empires, Turkey and Russia. When the opportunity offered itself, the Hutterians decided to leave their war-scarred home and seek a safer domicile.

The Russian Sojourn, 1770–1874

For over a century Russia, or rather Ukraine, provided a home for the Hutterians. Russia, under its young empress, Catherine the Great (1762–1796), had just organized the area north of the Black Sea into the New Russian Territory. The next task of the imperial government was to attract settlers to these new domains, as well as to the Volga region, which had been devastated by the Pugachev uprising. Already, in response to Catherine's Manifesto of 1763, 23,000 Germans from the Palatinate and a small party of Moravian Herrnhuter[29] had settled in the Volga area. The Manifesto offered foreign settlers virgin lands, tax concessions, and privileges, including complete religious freedom, but excluding the right to proselytize among members of the Orthodox faith.[30]

The Russians expected the foreign settlers to fill two roles. They were to colonize the steppes, and to serve as models for the native population in farming techniques. To supervise the immigrant settlers a special government agency was set up at St. Petersburg.[31]

News of the inducements offered by the Russian government apparently did not reach the Hutterians. But during the Russo-Turkish war they had approached the Russian commander-in-chief, Count Rumiantsev, for help.[32] Rumiantsev invited the Hutterians to settle on his estate north of the city of Kiev. His written pledge offered them complete religious liberty and freedom to live in community, exemption from military service and from swearing of oaths, a three-year period of tax exemption, an advance payment in flour and lumber, and permission to retain the income from the sale of their home industries.[33] The Hutterians accepted this generous offer, and after an arduous trek of over a month arrived at Rumiantsev's estate in the early autumn of 1770. The estate was located on the Desna River, a tributary of the Dnieper.

The small community, known by the Russian name of Vishenky, soon had a water mill, a windmill, a school, and an ice-cellar. Farming, the raising of rye and winter wheat, was the main industry, but the Hutterians also planted a large orchard, and began several thriving enterprises: a weaving mill, a pottery, a blacksmith shop, and a distillery.

Vishenky flourished and became Rumiantsev's showplace, to which he sometimes took foreign diplomats. But in 1796 the old count died, leaving his estate to two sons. Though the two young Rumiantsevs, who spent most of their time in Moscow and St. Petersburg, were aware of the special status of their Hutterian tenants, they attempted to reduce them to the position of their regular serfs. The Hutterians were fully alert to the dangers that confronted them and sent a delegation to Emperor Paul I, who had just succeeded Catherine on the throne.

The tsar assured the delegates that their agreement with the senior Rumiantsev was valid, and that henceforth they would officially have the rights and privileges granted to the Mennonite colonists.[34] Although Paul was assassinated a little later, the Hutterian status was confirmed in a ukase by his successor, Alexander I.[35] The government's decision may well have been prompted in part by another development. At this time the Mennonite emigration from Prussia, begun in 1789, was about to resume and bring thousands of new settlers to the Russian steppes. A decision adverse to the Hutterians, who were in touch with the Prussian Mennonites, unquestionably would have deterred Mennonites from migrating to Russia.

The Hutterians now left Vishenky and moved to crown lands at Radichev, only twelve versts (about eight miles) away from their old home. For administrative purposes the government classed them as Mennonites, extending to them and their descendants complete religious freedom, including exemption from military service. Each family was granted sixty-five dessiatines (1 dessiatine = 2.7 acres) of crown land, for which 14 kopeks per dessiatine were to be remitted to the crown annually as a tax. The pioneer years had not been easy, and their chronicle carries this entry: "Vishenky was our home for 32 years less 36 days. During this time many brethren, sisters, and children fell asleep in the Lord, and 172 of them are buried there." [36]

There were now 44 families at Radichev, and the population numbered 99 males and 103 females.[37] The Brethren immediately set up their enterprises again, and a little later a government official, Kontenius, could report that "their fine linen matched the Dutch product in quality." Presumably the Hutterians also introduced the silk industry, for the same writer mentions that "the first 1000 mulberry trees" of an orchard of 5000 trees had been planted.

The community at Radichev was established on the northern bank of the Desna, where most of the arable land lay, while the hayland, the meadows, and some wooded areas were across the river. The settlement was laid out in a 490-foot square enclosed by a brush fence. Within this square were the buildings. The workshops occupied the ground floor of each building and the second floor held the parents' sleeping quarters, known as *Örtel*. The older children, segregated according to sex, had their own *Örtel*, each accommodating from twelve to sixteen persons.

In 1818 Radichev was visited by a government official named Bunin. His report, submitted to the ministry of the interior at St. Petersburg, contains his impressions of communal life as he found it. Bunin wrote that religious services were held "in a special room bare of all sacred images." The Brethren gathered "on Sundays, on holidays, and on every evening of the week for prayer." The service consisted of a sermon and some congregational singing. Bunin thought the members rather poorly dressed, but found them "well-mannered, friendly, obliging, hospitable, and willing to extend every courtesy."

Bunin was impressed with the social organization of the community. "Before confinement," he writes, "the woman is placed in a special warm room, where delivery takes place." The young mother occupied these quarters, together with other women who had given birth to babies, until the child reached the age of one and a half years. During this entire period she spent the nights away from her spouse. Then the mother joined her husband, while the child was placed in a separate room under the supervision of an older woman, "usually a widow who was elected to her position." This room was equipped with special beds and cradles, and had its own kitchen. At the age of four the children were placed in still another room where they lived, under similar supervision, until they were seven. Then the children were separated according to sex, and the boys were placed under male, the girls under female teachers. Both groups received instruction in reading, writing, arithmetic, and religion. Parents were permitted to visit their children, or have them visit the parents' quarters.

"Meals are taken in the community dining room," writes Bunin, but he observes that the male and female members sat at separate tables. Grace was said before every meal. Dinner was served at 11:30, supper at dusk. The members of the community rose at five in the morning, and went to bed at nine. "In this manner," concludes Bunin, "the community flourished, praising God and the emperor, and eliciting the admiration of the neighborhood."

Despite this auspicious beginning Radichev, after a few years, began to decline. There was too little land for the growing community, but the leaders refused to establish a daughter colony that would absorb the surplus population. Since there was no land nearby, it was feared that the two colonies, separated by too great a distance, would be submerged in the surrounding native population. They saw this happen to the Herrnhuter Sarepta Brethren, with whom they were in contact. These people were active missionaries, whose very industries — the manufacture of fineries, the operation of spas and rest homes — had been introduced with an eye to attracting people to their colony. The result was that they gained converts, but were too small a group to assimilate them. In the end the influence of the outsiders prevailed, and Sarepta disintegrated.[38] When, however, the general impoverishment of Radichev and the decline of the enterprises reached the stage of bankruptcy, it was too late to branch out to form a second colony.

After considerable internal friction, the Hutterians appealed to the government for assistance. The government, in turn, directed them to Johann Cornies, a leading Mennonite landowner who had done much to help the development of the Mennonite settlements in Russia. Cornies's plan was to relocate the Hutterians on one of the Mennonite settlements in the province of Tauridia, in southern Russia, where there was land available. This plan was carried out in 1842.

Though the Mennonites were Anabaptists, like the Hutterians, they did not practice community of goods. Nor did they insist on the conformity in dress and behavior so strictly enforced by the Hutterians. Cornies required that the Hutterians settle in Mennonite-type villages and as individual farmers. Since the Brethren had lived for over seventy years in great isolation, their industrial skill and methods of farming had stagnated. To acquaint them with modern farm operations Cornies apprenticed young Hutterian men and women on Mennonite farms. Within two years the Hutterians were economically solvent, and appeared to face a prosperous future. However, the old ideal of total communal life was too strongly ingrained to be discarded for economic prosperity. Within a few years about half of the Brotherhood reverted to the practice of *Gütergemeinschaft*.

At this stage events over which the Hutterians had no control determined their future. In the nineteenth century Russia had become increasingly nationalistic, and in 1864 a law was passed making Russian the language of instruction in all schools, and at the same time placing all schools under the supervision of the state. The object of this law was the gradual russification of subject races and of foreign colonists. A little later St. Petersburg announced that universal and compulsory military service would be introduced in Russia within ten years.[39]

These developments caused great consternation among the foreign settlers, from the Baltic to the Black Sea, but especially among the Mennonites and Hutterians, who were by their religion conscientious objectors to military service, and who regarded their schools as one of the chief bastions of their faith.

Both groups decided that their survival demanded emigration, and in 1873 a group of delegates left Russia to explore the possibilities of settlement in the United States and Canada. The Russian government at this point showed some concern at losing them as settlers, and the tsar gave assurance that the Mennonites and Hutterians would receive concessions, but it was too late to halt the emigration of the initial group. About 18,000 of them left Russia. This represented about one-third of the Mennonite group, but it included the entire, numerically small, Hutterian congregation.

The Hutterian emigration proceeded in several stages. The communal and individual holdings were disposed of to Mennonite and German settlers. The first Brethren to leave Russia were under the leadership of Michael Waldner. This group of 109 people, both adults and children, entrained at Alexandrovsk (now Zaporozhe) on June 7, 1874, and continued by railway through Kharkov, Smolensk, and Berlin, as far as Hamburg. Here the party boarded the ship *Harmonia* and reached New York on July 5, after a stormy Atlantic crossing of sixteen days. The second community group left in the fall of 1874, and the third and last group left in 1877. Between the years of 1874 and 1879 all the other Hutterians, who no longer lived in community but had joined the Mennonites, also left Russia.

In 1922, half a century after the Hutterians had left Russia, one of them returned to visit his native village. Russia had just gone through war, revolution, and famine, and a group of Mennonites from North America came to help their coreligionists who had remained in Russia. Among the men sent out to Russia to administer the distribution of food and clothing was one David M. Hofer. Hofer, who was no longer a Hutterian and lived in Chicago, was impressed with the appearance of his native Johannesruh, which he called a "magnificent model village." [40] Hofer relates how he went through his ancestral home, saw the cupboard, carved out of walnut by his father, visited his grandfather's blacksmith shop, and in another place found some century-old manuscripts left behind by the Brethren. The fine homes and barns, shut off from the street by brick walls, remained as the only testimonials of Hutterian industry and prosperity.

The stay in Russia left its stamp on the Brotherhood, particularly because of the association with the Mennonites. From 1770 to 1842, when they lived in Vishenky and Radichev, the Brethren were completely isolated. During this time, and indeed for the whole century which they spent in Russia, there is no record of intermarriage with Russians or Ukrainians. But after 1842 the proximity of the Mennonite settlements influenced the Hutterian way of life and blurred its sharp contours. Some marriages with Mennonites also took place.

Although the Mennonites spoke their *Plattdeutsch* and the Hutterians their Tirolean dialect, both groups used standard German in school and in church. Both groups had a common religious heritage, and both stressed *Gemeinsinn* (devotion to the common good) and the interdependence of the members of the community. Though the Mennonites did not practice community of goods, their creed maintained that the congregation had the responsibility of looking after the spiritual and economic needs of every member. Under these circumstances it is not surprising that about half of the Hutterians were prepared to forsake total communal life for the more elastic and more individualistic Mennonite form of community life.

On the other hand, it is significant that even the close association with the spiritually kindred and numerically many times stronger Mennonites could not permanently cloud the Hutterian ideal of total community. And while the differences between its supporters and those who were prepared to compromise on this point were not very clear in Russia, the break was made in the United States. The Hutterian transfer to the Mennonite settlement proved a benefit in that it removed those members from the Brotherhood who were only lukewarm toward communal life. That these were absorbed by the Mennonite congregations was fortunate in that the gradual estrangement and final parting of ways avoided an intragroup conflict. Moreover, the thirty years that the Hutterians spent with the Mennonites, "the very best farmers of Russia," [41] provided them with the necessary training and skill in agricultural enterprises that enabled them to face the pioneering years on the American prairies.

III

FROM THE STEPPES TO THE PRAIRIES

THE HUTTERIAN ARRIVAL in North America coincided with the opening of the American West to large-scale settlement. Even as the War of Secession was in progress, President Lincoln signed the Homestead Act, and Congress granted charters to the railway companies that were to contribute so much toward building the West. The railway companies not only received financial concessions but were also granted enormous tracts of land. Easterners and European immigrants were encouraged to move west, where land was free and plentiful. The railways in turn were stimulated to extend their lines, for as the new settlers poured in the land rose in value. Similar conditions prevailed in Canada, where the government took over the Northwest, which had until then been held by the Hudson's Bay Company. In 1872 the Canadian government passed the Dominion Lands Act, and also promoted the building of an all-Canadian railway to the Pacific coast.

The stage was thus set for mass immigration. But the 1870's saw a steady decline in the number of people coming from the countries that had previously furnished the bulk of new settlers. England discouraged emigration; resurgent Germany provided employment for its population at home. Similarly many of the other Western European countries succeeded in keeping their people at home.[1] The heavy influx of Slavic immigrants into Canada was still almost twenty years off. The immigration recruiting agents of the United States and Canada in the 1870's concentrated their activity on the German population pockets in Austria-Hungary and Russia.

The Mennonites in Russia, and the Hutterians were considered by now a component part of the Mennonites, were regarded as good prospective immigrants. Even before their delegation left Russia they received assurances from the Canadian government, through its agent William Hespeler, that the Mennonites would enjoy exemption from military service if they settled in Manitoba. The delegation, consisting of ten Mennonites and two Hutterians, did not make the ocean voyage together, nor did they inspect the available land, stretching from Manitoba to Texas, together. But they met periodically at convenient points to discuss and compare their findings. The Hutterian delegates, Paul Tschetter and his nephew Lorenz Tschetter, left Russia on April 14, 1873, and returned on July 27 of the same year.

Parenthetically it should be stated that Russia did not permit immigration agents to canvass for emigration. Canadian and American shipping companies employed diverse ruses to bypass the Russian regulations. They generally offered free maps or travel tips. One Canadian agency placed the following German advertisement in a book printed in Russia: "The undersigned do not want to persuade anyone to turn his back on his beloved homeland to face an uncertain future in a strange country. To those, however, who have already decided to leave for Manitoba, or the Canadian North West, it should be said that the shortest, cheapest, and fastest route there is not by way of New York, but via Quebec." [2]

The Delegation

The two Hutterian delegates to America made the entire exploratory journey together. Paul Tschetter, the senior deputy, kept a diary in which he recorded his impressions.[3] The two Tschetters left Odessa by train, traveling third class "with a mixture of people consisting of Jews, women, and children," and reached Berlin, where they were astonished to see buildings, some "five stories high." "In such a large city there are enough bad people," wrote Tschetter, and the two men, before they retired, prayed for divine protection, and carefully tied the door of their room.

In Hamburg they booked passage on a German boat. The sea voyage itself passed uneventfully, except that the passengers appeared too gay, and were dressed in frivolous clothes, "as if they did not realize the seriousness of their position." When the two delegates attended a Sunday service, they found the sermon good, "but too soft, especially for this godless rabble."

Debarkation took place in New York, and the delegates immediately proceeded to Elkhart, in Indiana, where they were the guests of the Mennonite congregation. Tschetter recorded his impressions of the condition and price of land, the size of farms, and the crops raised. Beyond that he noted down the Mennonite experiences during the Civil War, and inquired about the use of German in school and in church. The delegates also attended an American revival meeting. Since the Hutterian service was marked by an austere dignity, the antics of the minister took Tschetter by complete surprise. This experience may have indirectly encouraged him to recommend emigration to America, with the thought that if the country tolerated this, it would tolerate anything. At first Tschetter thought the minister had gone mad, for "he shouted," "ran from one side of the platform to the other," "hit his chest with his fist," "pointed up to heaven and down to hell," "in short, a madman could not have behaved in a worse manner." "The man preached the gospel truth," sums up Tschetter, "but with great human folly."

From Indiana the delegates traveled by way of Chicago to St. Paul, where they were joined by some members of the Mennonite delegation. The route they now took covered central Minnesota, from Duluth to Moorhead. Here they crossed into the Dakota Territory, and went west as far as the James River. Tschetter was impressed by the flatness of the prairie, but not by the soil, for the grass was sparse, and was getting thinner as they proceeded westward.

The delegates returned, and from Fargo they went by boat, on the *International*, down the Red River. At Pembina, near the Canadian border, they saw the first American soldiers and some cannons. They reached the "very small city" of Winnipeg, which they found heavily garrisoned. The Manitoba government, headed by Premier Clarke, tendered them a reception. The Hutterian delegates were in Manitoba ten days in all, spending many nights camping in tents. "There were so many mosquitoes," wrote Tschetter, "that one was hardly able to defend oneself." The settlers, he reports, were very friendly, and the people everywhere encouraged the delegation to recommend the move to Manitoba. Several of the Mennonite delegates spent more time in the province; the Hutterians did not go beyond about fifty miles of Winnipeg. They were directed to the Morris area, and to the land east of the Red River. Tschetter reported on the soil as between good and marginal (sandy), but very swampy in places.

The Canadian government assured the delegation that it was prepared to extend "entire exemption from Military Service" and complete freedom in the education of their children in schools.[4] Washington too displayed a most encouraging attitude. The Hutterian delegates were cordially received by President Grant. They presented Grant with a petition in which they asked for exemption from military service and the right to operate their own schools. The president could make no promises since these were "matters that fall under the jurisdiction of the various states in which they wish to settle." "It is true, however," stated a note from Secretary of State Hamilton Fish to the delegation, "that for the next fifty years we will not be entangled in another war in which military service will be necessary." [5]

After the Mennonite and Hutterian delegates had returned to Russia and made their recommendations to their respective congregations, about 8000 of the more conservative Mennonites moved to Manitoba. The more liberal Mennonite congregations, numbering about 10,000 members and children, decided to move to the United States, where most of them settled in Kansas, while others established themselves in Nebraska, Minnesota, and Dakota Territory, or remained in the East. The Mennonite split did not affect the Hutterians. The community people as well as those favoring individual ownership, the two groups numbering roughly 700 adults and children, migrated to the United States and settled in what is now South Dakota.

New Homes in Dakota

The first Hutterians, a party of a little over one hundred, reached New York on July 5, 1874, and proceeded to Lincoln, Nebraska, where they were housed in temporary shelters. The land in the Dakotas where they would settle had not yet been definitely selected, and some men were delegated to go north to purchase suitable land for settlement. In the meantime the adult males of the group went to work as day laborers for the farmers in the Lincoln area. An epidemic of dysentery which struck Lincoln at this time took a very heavy toll, especially among the immigrant children. Thirty-six of them died.[6] To escape the epidemic the Hutterians decided to take up transient quarters at Yankton, the territorial capital, in the southeastern corner of the Dakota Territory. They arrived on August 8, 1874.

The Territory, which included the present states of North and South Dakota, was largely unsettled.[7] As a destination it had the reputation that "the coward never started, and the weak died on the way."

The Hutterians did not choose to take up homestead land, partly because they thought it would place them under an obligation to the government, and partly because the conditions under which it was granted did not favor concentrated bloc settlement. Instead the first group bought 2500 acres of land from a private owner, Walter A. Burleigh, a former Indian agent. They paid $17,000 in cash, and arranged to pay the balance later. This settlement, which became known as the Bon Homme colony, was located near the Missouri River. The senior elder of this congregation was a blacksmith by trade, Michael Waldner. In time his congregation became known as the *Schmiedeleut'*, or "the blacksmith people."

The second group moved to Silver Lake, and like the Bon Homme people spent the very severe first Dakota winter in sod huts. In the spring they bought 5400 acres on the James River, a tributary of the Missouri. Located north of the Bon Homme colony, this second settlement became known as the Wolf Creek colony. The senior elder of this congregation was Darius Walther, hence the congregation was known as the *Dariusleut'*. Both groups began building permanent homes early the following spring. For building material they used the cream-colored chalk rock which is found on the banks of the Missouri.

These Hutterians who had relinquished communal life spent the first winter with the American Mennonites at Elkhart, in Indiana. Early in 1875 they too moved to Dakota, settling largely along the James River. They took up land as individual homesteaders. However, in 1877, the third and last party of community Hutterians arrived from Russia and bought 5440 acres of land north of the Wolf Creek colony. This settlement was known as the (Old) Elmspring colony. The senior elder of this group was Jacob Wipf, a teacher. His congregation became known as the *Lehrerleut'* (the teacher's people).

There were over one hundred Hutterian families in all, numbering about seven hundred adults and children. All of them settled in the Dakota Territory. About half of them settled in communal colonies known as *Bruderhöfe,* the other half lived *im Eigentum* (as individual farmers). The latter were known by the communal people as the *Prairieleut'*. These in time became completely integrated with the German-Swiss Mennonite congregations, and all social and familial relationships between them and the communal Hutterians ceased.

For over forty years, from 1874 to 1917, the Hutterian communities showed remarkable progress and stability. By 1915 there were about 1700 Hutterians, adults and children, living on seventeen colonies. Fifteen of these communities were in the southeastern part of South Dakota and two of them in Montana. Perhaps the most characteristic feature of these colonies was their complete seclusion. They took only a passive interest in the world about them, and the world in turn took no notice of them.

This isolation was to change dramatically with the entry of the United States into war in 1917. For centuries the Hutterians had been exposed to persecution because of the prevailing religious intolerance. In America, however, the roots of intolerance lay in nationalism. "Henceforth," wrote a minister of the gospel, "there is to be but one national ideal — the American ideal. There is to be but one language — the American language. There is to be but one school — the American school." [8] This was the mood of America, and the German-speaking, outlandishly dressed Hutterians, who objected to military service as well, had no place in this America. They were treated as enemy aliens.

The Hutterians were not the only ones who suffered because of the war hysteria. Many German-Americans experienced indignities and public censure. Nor were the Hutterians the only group to claim exemption from military service. There were the Friends (Quakers), the Mennonites, and the political pacifists.[9] But the Hutterians were more vulnerable because their compact colonies were readily recognized and known by their neighborhood. Moreover, their young men were not as educated as, for example, the intellectual pacifists. As a result, when they appeared before the military board of inquiry which was to judge their service status, the officials in charge often simply classified them as stubborn and obstinate peasant-farmers, and sent them to military training camps.[10]

Meanwhile the Hutterian communities sustained economic losses. Their Brethren refused to buy war bonds, the so-called Liberty Bonds, as they felt they would thereby support the war effort. Instead they donated to relief work and to the Red Cross.[11] Their failure to buy war bonds infuriated many local patriots, and often these resorted to overt lawlessness. The Bon Homme colony had a mill which ground flour for the colony and also for many of the neighboring farmers. A rumor was spread that the colony minister, who was also the miller, performed acts of sabotage by grinding glass into the flour. A government investigation cleared the colony of the charge. At another community, the Jamesville colony, a mob drove off a herd of 200 steers and 1000 sheep, and the action was applauded by a county newspaper.

The Hutterian colonies would possibly have been prepared to sustain considerable economic loss before emigrating, but there was the question of military service. The government at Washington offered no clear alternative for those claiming exemption. Secretary of War Newton D. Baker simply advised conscientious objectors to respond to the draft and request noncombatant duty at the camps. Thus the treatment the objectors were exposed to depended upon the officers in charge of the particular camp board of inquiry. There were instances where mock courts-martial were held. The objector was "sentenced" to be shot and led out to face a firing squad, the minutes were counted off, and the command to fire was issued. But no shots were fired; the victim was told he had been reprieved.[12]

An extreme case was the treatment accorded to the three Hofer brothers, John, David, and Michael, and to John Wipf, who, like many of the other Hutterians, were not granted the status of conscientious objectors. They spent their confinement mostly at Alcatraz and Fort Leavenworth, where they were ill-treated, had to spend hours outside in the cold, were refused clothes and blankets, and were manacled to bars so that they had to stand on their toes. Two were later discharged, completely broken, while the other two died in the camp.

It should be added that there were also voices and advocates of reason. Many of the Hutterians' neighbors refused to engage in anti-colony activities. At the beginning of the war Senator Thielman introduced a bill in the South Dakota legislature providing alternative service for conscientious objectors. The bill passed the Senate by a vote of 24 to 12, but it failed to pass the House of Representatives.

The Hutterians now sent a petition to President Woodrow Wilson, which was followed, early in 1918, by a delegation of Hutterian leaders. The delegates, David Hofer, Elias Walter, and Joseph Kleinsasser, attempted to persuade government leaders in Washington that since not a single Hutterian sentenced to prison or military camps had changed his position, the government should provide some alternative for military service for young Hutterians. The leaders also explained to government officials that if the government remained adamant, the Hutterians would consider emigration. But Washington was unwilling or unable to do much for the Hutterians, though Secretary of War Baker's secretary advised them not to take any hasty steps.

However, the treatment accorded to the drafted young men made it necessary, in the opinion of the colony people, to explore the possibility of emigration. While the original plans envisioned the establishment of a few colonies in Canada and the transfer of all men of military age from the United States to them, an increased number of call-ups of young men and the increased hostility of some excessively patriotic neighbors persuaded the colony leaders to undertake total emigration. The agitation against the Brethren had produced a political climate in the state which threatened the very existence of the colonies. The climax was reached in 1919 when suit was brought by the State of South Dakota in the Circuit Court of Beadle County against the Hutterians, asking for their dissolution as a corporation. The charges were that the incorporation was false because the Hutterians transacted business, that the leaders had a bad influence on their members, that the colony regulations and practices were contrary to the laws of the state, and that the Hutterians refused to support the nation in time of war. Judge A. E. Taylor ruled that the Hutterian "corporation should dispose of all its property exceeding fifty thousand dollars; amend its by-laws so as to exclude therefrom all provisions with reference to the transaction of secular business and submit such amended by-laws to the court for approval; and should no longer engage in farming, stock raising and other secular pursuits and businesses not authorized by the charter." [13] The overt object of this decision was to "absolutely exterminate" the Hutterians in South Dakota.[14]

The Hutterians had acted before the ruling was handed down. In 1918 advance parties had already prepared temporary homes in Canada, and almost immediately a general exodus had taken place. However, the court's decision made it necessary for the Hutterians to dispose of their property in great haste, and at a substantial financial loss. The first chapter of Hutterian history in South Dakota closed with all but one of their seventeen communities leaving for Manitoba and Alberta. Only Bon Homme, the oldest colony of all, remained behind.

The Hutterians in Canada

The Canadian authorities had had considerable experience with diverse ethnic and religious groups when they encouraged the migration of Hutterians to Canada in 1918. In the 1870's the Mennonites had arrived on the prairie and had founded villages of a type until then unknown in the New World. A little later the Icelanders came and for a short time established a tiny republic on the shores of Lake Winnipeg with its own four-member *thingrad,* or council. When the American antipolygamy laws went into effect the Canadian authorities permitted many Mormons to come to Canada. Already Canada had accepted as immigrants tens of thousands of Ukrainians, and to these were added the Doukhobors, a Russian religious sect with peculiarities of their own, who had come to Canada in 1899.

The Canadian government was of course fully aware that the Hutterians left the United States because the safeguards of their faith had been violated there and it might well have feared that the political climate and public opinion in Canada would move in the same direction, accelerated and accentuated by the war. In the opinion of the immigration officials, however, this factor was no doubt offset by another, the acute manpower shortage on the prairies. The war had drained off Canadian manhood and the government was already considering sending boys from Ontario and Quebec, dressed in khaki uniform and described by the press as "soldiers of the soil," to help western farmers. Western agriculture was one of the most important elements of the Canadian war effort, and a weakness here could seriously cripple Canada's contribution to the Allied cause. To the government and to the immigration authorities the incoming Hutterians with their excellent reputation as farmers were most valuable immigrants at a time of the nation's need.

The Hutterians were not unknown to the Canadian immigration officials. In 1873 the Hutterian representatives had visited Manitoba, together with the Mennonite delegation. Again, in 1898, at the beginning of the Spanish-American War, when the Hutterians considered emigrating to Canada, they had sent a delegation of three men to Winnipeg. At that time the immigration office in Winnipeg immediately sent an agent to the colonies in South Dakota to report on these prospective immigrants. The agent was impressed with what he saw and wrote to Ottawa that "any inducement possible should be made to secure them." [15]

The Hutterians in turn outlined their demands in a petition to the commissioner of immigration at Winnipeg, who forwarded it to Ottawa. Ottawa responded favorably to these demands, as is indicated by the following letter: [16]

Department of the Interior,
Ottawa,
27th October, 1899.

To W. F. McCreary, Esquire,
Commissioner of Immigration,
Winnipeg, Manitoba.

DEAR SIR,

I have your letter of the 12th instant, No. 21,759, enclosing a petition from certain members of the Hutterite community in which they ask that in coming to Canada they be assured of certain privileges.

(1) As to their request for exemption from military service, this question has already been dealt with, and I enclose you a copy of the Order-in-Council authorizing their exemption.

(2) These people will not be molested in any way in the practise of their religious services and principles, as full freedom of religious belief prevails throughout the country. They will also be allowed to establish independent schools for teaching their children if they desire to do so, but they will have to be responsible for their maintenance themselves. The children will not be compelled to attend other schools if their education is properly provided for.

(3) The law does not compel the taking of an oath in court by persons who have conscientious objections to doing so, and there is no compulsion as to voting for or holding offices, but the privilege of doing so is generally most highly prized.

(4) There will be no interference with their living as a commonwealth, if they desire to do so.

(5) The Dominion Lands Act makes provision for the locating of people as communities and their being allowed to live in villages instead of being required each to live separately on his own land.

(6) The privileges asked for in the last four sections cannot be more firmly established by any further official document than they are by the established laws of the country, and the members of the Society in question may rest assured that the statements made above are of as full value to them as they could be made by an order of the Governor-in-Council or any document of that nature.

Yours truly,

(*Signed*) Jas. A. Smart,
Deputy Minister.

The Deputy Minister's letter thus made it quite clear that most of the "privileges" asked for by the Hutterians were the accepted rights and privileges of Canadians in general.

While these negotiations were carried on a small group of Hutterians were already in Canada. In 1899 they had established a colony on the Roseau River east of Dominion City, in Manitoba. The land was unsatisfactory; floods repeatedly inundated the crops. Since, in addition, the war between the United States and Spain was of short duration, the result was that the Hutterians, after a five-year stay in Manitoba, returned to South Dakota.

In 1917 the Hutterian leaders resumed negotiations with the Canadian immigration officials. The commissioner of immigration in Winnipeg in a report sent to Ottawa and dated January 30, 1918, wrote: "It would appear to me that these people are very desirable; that they are clean, honourable, industrious and law-abiding, and that if they could be assured . . . that the conditions . . . provided for in Privy Council No. 1676 of August 12th, 1899, would apply to them, they would be satisfied." [17] The response from the deputy minister of the interior was favorable.[18] Consequently the immigration officials in Winnipeg, according to the *Winnipeg Free Press* of October 16, 1919, did "what they could to encourage Hutterite migration." They were, the paper continued, "activated by the view which until this time has had universal sanction and which regards as desirable all new settlers who are of thrifty and law-abiding habit."

The immigration of a German-speaking group of conscientious objectors to war was, as might have been expected, not met by the general public without some protest. The Hutterians arrived in the fall of 1918 and reports of their coming were sandwiched in between long newspaper columns announcing the extermination of German armies and demanding the hanging of the kaiser. There were some demonstrations against the admission of the new immigrants, and there was even talk of deporting those Hutterians already in Canada.

The war soon ended, and with this the initial opposition to Hutterian settlement, especially in the rural areas affected, gave way to a friendlier feeling. One of the Elie farmers, George Roy, wrote to the *Winnipeg Free Press*: "At the present time I farm about 1,800 acres of land, and my farm is not for sale, and I have a colony of Hutterians on each side of me. They settled there last fall and I wish to say from my personal experience in operating with these people as neighbors I find them quiet, peaceable, law-abiding citizens and good neighbors." [19]

Even the war veterans, who had spearheaded the opposition to Hutterian immigration,[20] modified their stand. When W. C. Angus, secretary of the Manitoba command of the Great War Veterans' Association, visited the colony early in 1919 he was relieved to find that the Hutterians had no political connections with Germany, and he was impressed with the organization of colony life.[21]

Moreover, in South Dakota the Hutterians had reached a compromise with the public school system. As long as the public school was located on the colony under the watchful eyes of the community people, they did not object to it, or to the learning of English in school. Since Manitoba had had considerable trouble introducing the public school in different ethnic areas, the press noted with satisfaction that the Hutterians were prepared to accept the public school without a murmur of protest: "The Hutterites, although a German sect, differ from the Mennonites in one important regard. They are not opposed to the school laws of the country in which they live, and while in the United States have never caused trouble such as the Mennonites have occasioned in Manitoba." [22]

Thus in a few years the public, which had opposed Hutterian immigration, completely reversed its position and now regarded them as very desirable settlers.

A parting of ways took place among the Hutterians in their migration from the United States to Canada. The *Schmiedeleut'* congregation, descendants of the first colony established in South Dakota, without exception moved to Manitoba. The *Dariusleut'* and *Lehrerleut'* congregations all moved to Alberta. The *Schmiedeleut'* had bought 9000 acres of land from Senator Aime Benard, who had extensive landholdings near Elie, in the rural municipality of Cartier. By the end of 1918 they had set up five colonies: Rosedale, Milltown, Huron, Bon Homme, and James Valley, all located in Cartier. The town of Elie and the municipality of Cartier are predominantly settled by French-Canadians. The initially ready acceptance of the Hutterians in Manitoba may be partly explained by their settlement in the Elie district. The French-Canadians had their own reasons for objecting to military service overseas, and showed greater tolerance to the new immigrants than Anglo-Saxon neighbors might have been prepared to extend to them.

The other two Hutterian groups bought land in the southwestern corner of Alberta. By the end of 1918 the *Dariusleut'* had established six colonies: Stand-Off, East Cardston, Rosebud, Springvale, West Raley, and Wilson Siding. The *Lehrerleut'* had established four: New Elmspring, Old Elm, Milford, and Rockport.

Canada was selected by the Hutterians as their new home not only because it offered them exemption from military service, but also because it was near their old homes in South Dakota. This made it possible for them to bring their household goods and farm equipment with them. Nevertheless, the move caused a severe reduction in their financial resources. Since they made their preparations to emigrate in great haste, their South Dakota lands were disposed of at depressed prices. At the same time the price of land in Canada was relatively high. As a result the first Hutterian communities in Alberta and Manitoba could not be settled on areas large enough to prevent overcrowding. The new colonies were almost immediately confronted with the problem of finding more land for their excess population.

Leaving their homes in Russia to escape the restrictive policies of the Tsarist government, the Hutterians came to the United States in search of religious freedom and the right to pursue their own way of life. As long as the Dakota Territory was relatively unpeopled they found this freedom in full measure. When the Territory became settled and the price of land rose, many of the new settlers grew envious of them and intolerant of their ways. The tension flared into open hostility at the time of World War I, and significantly most of the intolerance was not religious but nationalistic in form. As in the past, there was also economic antagonism, veiled this time by a patriotic cloak, and receiving considerable support from the legal institutions of the state. Finally the Hutterians had to flee again, this time to Canada, where their farming skills were needed.

IV

HUTTERIAN EXPANSION, A CAUSE OF CONTROVERSY

THERE WAS a slight stir of resistance when the Hutterians arrived in Canada in 1918, but, as indicated in the foregoing chapter, the opposition dissolved almost immediately. The people and their colonies were readily accepted, partly because their thrifty and self-reliant ways were admired and partly because neither the public nor the press showed a sustained interest in a group of immigrants that were quiet and law-abiding. Moreover, after 1923 a steady and heavy stream of European immigrants came to Canada, and this influx diverted interest from the Hutterians.

Between 1918 and 1922 the Brethren established nine colonies in Manitoba and fourteen in Alberta. Partly because additional members arrived from South Dakota, but largely because of natural increase, the number of colonies almost doubled within the next twenty years. Later three Alberta colonies established daughter colonies in Saskatchewan, and a number of the Alberta and Manitoba colonies branched out to the United States. By 1964 Alberta had fifty-six, Saskatchewan thirteen, and Manitoba thirty-nine colonies. The United States at this time had forty-six. (See list in Appendix.)

The Hutterian population increased correspondingly and in 1964 it numbered 10,497, distributed as follows: Alberta, 5656; Manitoba, 3842; and Saskatchewan, 999. There were also 4210 Hutterians in the United States, chiefly in South Dakota and Montana, for a total of 14,707 in the two countries.

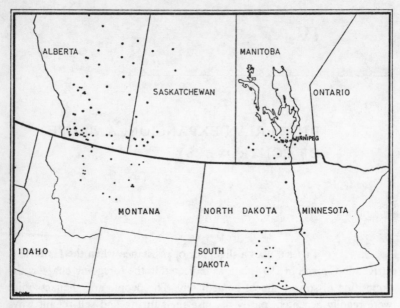

Number and location of Hutterian colonies at the beginning of 1965
Each dot represents one colony

Interwar Years

The expansion of the Hutterian colonies in the early years caused little concern in western Canada. Then came the depression. The prairie region particularly was in difficulties as the national economy plunged into ever deeper gloom. Farmers who wished to leave their homes for Ontario or British Columbia found it increasingly difficult to sell their farms. Merchants lacked cash customers. Municipalities went bankrupt as taxes remained unpaid.

The Hutterian colonies, on the other hand, with their self-sufficient economy, did not feel the economic depression as severely as the rest of Western Canada. "While hundreds of thousands are destitute and on relief," wrote one journalist, "and Ottawa sees a national emergency in the three prairie provinces, there are some Western farmers, rich in money, land and cattle, to whom debts and relief are unknown." [1] These were the Hutterians, and while they were hardly "rich in money," they were sufficiently solvent to buy more land, to patronize business, and to pay their taxes.

Municipalities with Hutterian colonies in them considered them assets and even made efforts to attract additional colonies. This was especially true in Alberta, as the Rockport case illustrates.

In 1934 the Rockport colony in South Dakota showed an interest in moving to the Raymond district in Alberta. There was some difficulty. Faced with widespread unemployment at home, the Canadian government had severely restricted immigration. Alberta farmers, businessmen, and municipal authorities now joined in exerting pressure on the provincial and federal governments to admit the Hutterians to Canada. The Canadian prime minister, R. B. Bennett, who represented a Calgary seat in the House of Commons, received the following telegram from Joseph Card, a businessman: "Owing to prevailing conditions due to several years' losses the entry of Rockport Colony would be of great benefit to vendors, their creditors and all other persons concerned in this district. Anything you may do to avoid further delay will be greatly and personally appreciated." [2]

Another telegram, directed to another Alberta member of parliament, Brigadier-General J. S. Stewart, read: "The Board of Directors of Lethbridge Board of Trade are of the opinion that the Department of Immigration should grant the admittance of about one hundred Hutterites to settle in the Raymond district. The admittance of these people will mean the disbursement of large sums of money to a great many individuals also to the Sugar City Municipality and Provincial Government. These people have furnished evidence that they will be self-sustaining and able to pay their obligations and taxes promptly."

The local school inspector, Owen Williams, submitted a testimonial that "The leaders of these [Hutterian] colonies have always co-operated with the Department of Education in the schools and have invariably supported their teachers." And the mayor of Raymond, W. Meeks, addressed a letter to the provincial premier, J. E. Brownlee, which read in part: "We personally have lived neighbors to a Colony for a number of years and have found them to be good neighbors. They pay their bills and taxes promptly and are honourable in their business dealings. I have not found any group public sentiment against the entrance and location of this Colony near Raymond. Their entrance will be a decided advantage to the vendors and to their creditors."

This correspondence on behalf of Rockport colony would appear to indicate that a mutually satisfactory and even friendly relationship existed between the Hutterians and their neighbors. It continued to exist throughout the 1930's despite the rapid expansion and increase of colonies.

With the outbreak of World War II and in the following years the friendly attitude toward the Hutterians changed into open hostility. The ill-feeling was more marked in Alberta, but was also quite pronounced in Manitoba. The reasons for the antagonism were close at hand. The Hutterians were conscientious objectors, and refused to join any branch of the military forces. Their young men of military age performed alternative service in forestry and public works projects, but to their opponents this seemed hardly enough. Moreover, during the war, farming had again become profitable, and farmers were anxious to expand their landholdings. In buying land they would often be competing with Hutterian colonies. Merchants in small towns joined the farmers in opposing Hutterian expansion because of the Hutterian practice of bulk purchasing in the larger urban centers.

The agitation against the Hutterians began in Alberta and spread to Manitoba. It did not reach its peak until well after the war. Even after steps were taken to curb the growth of the Hutterian colonies there remained a strong and volatile sentiment against them.

Legal Restrictions in Alberta

In 1942 the Alberta legislature passed the Land Sales Prohibition Act, which forbade the sale of land to Hutterians and enemy aliens. When the bill was introduced the Honorable Solon Low stated in the legislature that the act was designed to "allay public feeling which has been aroused to the point of threatened violence." He continued, "They [the Hutterians] are good people generally and have contributed in varying degrees to the war effort. But the right granted them in agreements with Federal authorities that they need not participate in military activity has caused some criticism and opposition to the colonies in wartime." Low stressed that the new act barring sales of land was "not a persecuting measure but one to meet a situation which has developed since the war started." He added that he had heard of "threats of violence" in a few instances in southern Alberta.[3]

The following year the act was amended to include a prohibition of leases of land. When the federal government disallowed the act as it dealt with enemy aliens, a class covered by federal law, the Alberta legislature prohibited land sales and leases to Hutterians only. The act was to terminate one year after the end of the war, but its life was later extended to 1947.

In that year the Alberta legislature set up a committee to study the Hutterian problem. The attitude of a segment of the population and the press strongly in favor of still greater restrictive legislation appeared to have triumphed when the legislature, on the recommendations of its appointed committee, gave assent to the Communal Property Act on March 31, 1947. The original bill began with a definition:

"Colony" means a number of persons who hold land or any interest therein whether as owners, lessees or otherwise, and whether in the name of trustees or as a corporation or otherwise as communal property and includes a number of persons who propose to acquire land to be held in such a manner.

It was almost immediately realized that the legislation could affect monastic orders, the Salvation Army, and Masonic and fraternal organizations, and the act was limited by the addition:

And includes Hutterites or Hutterian Brethren and Doukhobors but shall not include any church or other religious organization or congregation.[4]

The Doukhobors were added for the sake of appearances, although their numbers in Alberta were negligible. The Hutterians felt that the legislation was discriminatory not only in that it specifically checked their expansion but also in that it refused to recognize them as a church.

The restrictive clauses of the act, which is still in effect, prohibit the Hutterian Brethren from purchasing lands within forty miles of an existing colony, and provide that new colonies must not possess more than 6400 acres. The legislation also specifies a ninety-day waiting period during which land must be offered for public sale before the Hutterians can buy it.

At no time has it been deliberate Hutterian policy to settle in bloc settlements. Their communities in Alberta and Manitoba have been described as "a hodge-podge of discrete units, some clustered, others more widely scattered."[5] Yet once a colony reaches its population optimum it must branch out, and in the selection of a location for a new colony proximity to the parent colony can be an important consideration. The implications of the act were explained by L. S. Turcotte, the legal representative of the Hutterians in Alberta:

Take the Sunnyside Colony at Warner for example. This colony has 4,500 acres of land but only 1,700 acres are cultivated. The rest is rough pasture land. This colony has 145 people. In other words between 11 or 12 acres per person. . . .

Unless the Sunnyside Colony can buy more land they will have to leave the country. If such is the wish of the people of this province then I suggest that the Act should say so. It should say that although we welcomed these people in 1918 and as late as 1934, we, the people of Alberta, have changed our minds and we now intend to drive them out of this province.[6]

The Communal Property Act, despite its severity, did not appease the agitators; indeed, the demand after 1956 was for the forcible dissolution of all Hutterian communities. Meanwhile the act and the agitation have affected not only the Hutterians but also farmers who would like to sell their land for the best price possible but are unable to do so because Hutterians are often not permitted to buy it.[7]

Late in 1964 a Hutterian colony, Rock Lake, near Lethbridge, violated the Communal Property Act by purchasing 6240 acres of land without the government's permission.[8] The land, which is to provide the farm base for a new colony, was sold to the Hutterians by four farmers. Rock Lake colony had attempted to buy this land earlier in the year, but the Alberta government had disapproved the purchase. Early in 1965 the premier of Alberta, pressured by organized public opinion, brought charges against Rock Lake colony. Since many Alberta lawyers hold that the Communal Property Act is discriminatory and *ultra vires*,[9] this will provide a test case for the courts.

Developments in Manitoba

In Manitoba, an older province than Alberta with a more established ethnic pattern, the anti-Hutterian agitation took a different form. At no time has there been a danger of violence. One important reason for this is the influence of the two daily Winnipeg papers, the *Free Press* and the *Tribune,* which extends over the entire province. Both of them in their editorials consistently counseled moderation on the Hutterian question. More than in Alberta the agitation in Manitoba appeared to concentrate in a few individuals. The whole atmosphere was relatively free of animosity.

The movement against the "encroachment of the Hutterite colonies," which was later to crystallize into the Community Welfare Association, gained momentum from meetings held in 1947 at Oakville and St. Eustache. These two trading centers lie east of Portage la Prairie. St. Eustache has a population of about 260, Oakville about 150. With the advent of modern transport and improved roads the trade from these and neighboring hamlets has shifted to steadily growing Portage la Prairie. For miles around farmers use the Portage deepfreeze locker plant, which has completely replaced the old familiar "beef-rings," and the traditional ways of the region have been affected in other respects. The protest meetings in these two towns were stimulated by a development in the Manitoba legislature. It had been the practice to incorporate new Hutterian colonies by an act of the legislature. In 1946 bills to incorporate new colonies were rejected by the Private Bills Committee. The members of this committee were no doubt sensitive to public opinion and influenced by political expediency, for the restrictive legislation in Alberta had received widespread popular support. Several cabinet ministers and members of the provincial legislature attended the meetings at Oakville and St. Eustache. The upshot was that soon after the meetings the legislature appointed a select committee "to obtain information regarding the colonies . . . and report and make recommendations upon the same." At least five of the twelve committee members were on record as critics of the Hutterians.[10]

The briefs demanding restrictive legislation against the Hutterians which were submitted to this committee came largely from farmers and merchants from the area between Headingly and Portage la Prairie. But the response of individuals and groups opposed to legislative intervention was much stronger than had been the case in Alberta; among those opposed were the Manitoba Civil Liberties Association, the Manitoba Conference of the United Church, Dr. E. M. Howse of Westminster church in Winnipeg, Dr. Marcus Bach of Iowa State University, who is an authority on small Protestant denominations, and the larger newspapers and the ethnic press. Also one member of the committee, Jack McDowell, legislative member for Iberville constituency, steadfastly opposed not only restriction of the colonies but the investigation itself. It may be noted that Mr. McDowell represented a riding that has the greatest number of Hutterian colonies in Manitoba. If the anti-Hutterian movement had as much public support as its leaders claimed, Mr. McDowell should have had difficulty in retaining his seat in the legislature. Yet in several subsequent elections he successfully contested the riding. Though a few Hutterians did vote, and voted for McDowell, their ballots could not have given him his overwhelming majorities.

After its hearings the committee submitted a report to the legislature.[11] It hesitated to "make any recommendation to the effect that anything be done by legislation or otherwise which will interfere with what may be termed one of the basic fundamental rights of every person — the right to purchase land in Manitoba where and when he pleases." [12] The committee recommended that the legislature appoint a select special committee "to give consideration to the question whether or not appropriate legislation should be enacted which will establish a procedure whereby" anyone leaving the colony will receive an "equitable share" of the colony's assets. This recommendation provided the frame of reference under which proceedings were conducted the following year.

In 1948 the new committee, appointed by the Manitoba legislature, began its public hearings. The main brief against the Hutterian colonies was presented by J. P. Bend on behalf of the Community Welfare Association. It supported legislation that would award an "equitable share" to departing members. Bend's case was that this would be in the interests of the Hutterians themselves, as it would "assist in assimilating" them. Under existing conditions, he continued, Hutterian children "are destined to be farmers; they have no alternative." He intimated that the proposed legislation would be only the initial step: "It is not broad enough, of course, but one problem at a time." [13]

E. A. Fletcher, Q.C., the legal counsel for the Hutterian Brethren, presented the main brief on their behalf. He explained that communal life was an essential element of the Hutterian faith and doctrine, and that it was "not within the province of the Legislature to restrain or control religious practices." Hutterian assets, he pointed out, consisted of farm lands, machinery, equipment, livestock, poultry, and communal dwellings, and their liabilities were in the form of mortgages and doctors' bills. Furthermore, sometimes persons joined a colony bringing in "substantial sums of money or tracts of land which become community property." Under these conditions it would be impossible "to create a formula to establish the individual share of any member." He maintained that churches, clubs, orders, and other organizations have assets "which are the common property of the membership," but individual members do not have any transferable interest in their assets.[14]

An unsolicited brief on behalf of the Hutterians was presented by Mark Long, a Winnipeg businessman. It was important in that it established the point that the legislation would be discriminatory, or, if rigorously enforced, would affect major bodies in the province. An interchange between Mr. Long and Ronald Turner, a member of the committee, pointed to the consequences any legislation of this nature could entail:

MR. TURNER: Would you be good enough to briefly set out your reasons why you think specific enactment of a provision to let departing members take assets with them is bad.

MR. LONG: Because it interferes with the tenets of their religion. A friend of mine joined the Sisters of the Holy Name. She put in $100,000, and she takes a vow of communal poverty. If she leaves she takes nothing. I think this is the core of the question.[15]

During the hearings it was recognized by the Hutterians and by their opponents that the proposed legislation, despite its limited scope, contained a threat to the very existence of the colonies. To project it to an unlikely but not impossible degree, a group of impoverished families or vagrants could join a colony and after a period leave and demand an equitable share of its assets. Similarly, an irresponsible member could alternately leave and return to the colony, taking with him every time he left an "equitable share" of the assets of the community. It should be stated that though a number of former colony members lived in Winnipeg, not one of them appeared before the committee to support the recommended legislation.

In 1948 the committee's original recommendation for positive legislation was moved and defeated on the floor of the Manitoba legislature. Today there is no restrictive legislation but there is also still no provision for legal incorporation of colonies except by act of the legislature. Neither the Company Act, which covers joint stock companies, nor the legal provision for cooperatives is applicable. The first eight colonies in Manitoba were incorporated by provincial acts. The other colonies are not legal entities. Their assets, including land, are held in the names of trustees, that is, Hutterians selected for that purpose by the colonies.

For some years after 1948 the Hutterian question remained dormant, but it came up again at a convention of the Union of Manitoba Municipalities in 1954. A resolution was passed asking the government to restrict both the purchase of land by Hutterian colonies and also their location.[16] During the following three years considerable anti-Hutterian agitation was kept alive in the same regions as in the 1940's. The chief objections to the Hutterian colonies were that (1) they contributed to the disorganization of existing communities; (2) they took no interest in the welfare of the larger community, its schools and social functions; (3) they did not support local business.[17]

Disturbed by the renewed agitation, the Hutterians in Manitoba sought a *modus vivendi*. The provincial government acted as mediator, and the representatives of the Union of Manitoba Municipalities signed what they called a "gentleman's agreement" with the Hutterian Brethren in which the latter acceded to virtually all the demands of the municipalities.[18] They promised to limit the landholdings of new colonies to 5120 acres, and to limit the number of colonies per municipality to two, unless the municipality itself was willing to accept more colonies. The Hutterians also agreed to a clause whereby new colonies would not be closer than ten miles to each other.

Lawrence Smith of Portage la Prairie, an official of the Union, felt that the agreement was a good substitute for legislation: "If everybody lives up to it, the agreement could stand as a permanent solution to the problem." [19] The *Winnipeg Free Press* thought the pact a "feasible solution to years of controversy," [20] and the *Winnipeg Tribune* ended its editorial on the subject on this conciliatory note: "It is to be sincerely hoped that the agreement will put an end to the essentially undemocratic demands which have surrounded the Hutterite question in Manitoba in recent years." [21] It also stated that the agreement was the best possible evidence that the Hutterians were "peace-loving people and anxious to maintain friendly relations with their fellow men."

A few months after this "gentleman's agreement" was signed the Rosedale Colony at Elie negotiated for land in the municipality of Elton, north of Brandon. The Hutterians met all the terms of the agreement: the acreage involved (1280) was well under the stipulated maximum; it was to be the first colony in the municipality; it was many miles away from its nearest neighbor colony. Despite the fact that the provisions of the "gentleman's agreement" had been observed, the municipality asked the government to intervene and block the sale. The government reacted coolly, ignored the appeal, and the colony was established.[22]

The restrictive legislation in Alberta and the agitation in Manitoba contributed measurably to the strengthening of the ties within the Hutterian communities. This was predicted by close observers of Hutterianism. As early as 1924 a sociologist who had spent much time in the colonies wrote: "Persecution from without, if it does not crush out life entirely, always strengthens the bond among those who have endured it in common, and this has been a great factor in Hutterian experience." [23] And C. Frank Steele wrote, "Some day there may come disintegration from within; certainly pressure from without the colonies will not bring it about." [24]

There is some resentment among Hutterians against the Alberta restrictive legislation, though in keeping with their principle of nonviolence they long refused to appeal it. In 1964 the Rock Lake colony, as has been said, finally made a test of the law, and the case is before the courts at the time of writing. According to Mr. Fletcher, the solicitor for the Hutterians in Manitoba, the Manitoba congregation would appeal if restrictive legislation were introduced there.

The Interminable Controversy

Meanwhile the Hutterian controversy continues as it has over the last twenty years. A cursory look through regional newspaper and magazine columns shows how diverse the spectrum of public opinion is on the subject.

W. Metcalfe, of Oakville, Manitoba, a representative of the Community Welfare Association, attacked the press for not supporting the anti-Hutterian cause of his association. He said: "The press of Canada . . . ignores or condones a crude, self-seeking, medieval brand of Communism (Hutterian), which is fast expanding in our prairie provinces. A brand sheltering under the cloak of a few convenient scripture lines, plus a few of its own, apparently with the success of its colonization scheme, 'own the land and rule' its sole objective." He was strongly endorsed by another member of the association, John McAllister, who charged that "Hutterites could undermine Manitoba's industrial economy." A press report quoted McAllister as adding that "the Hutterites have direct access to food store chains as an outlet for their products. The colonies, without having to bid on the market for labor, can undersell other farm communities." [25]

Another leader in the agitation, J. P. Bend, of Poplar Point, Manitoba, in a prepared statement, said he did not think the federal government was aware of "the type of immigrant it was bringing in" when Hutterians were allowed to enter Canada. In the colonies, he declared, there was "no individual family life as we know it." Every colony was "a little government in itself" and "the almighty dollar" was pre-eminent in every act. "The ordinary farmer," he said, "cannot compete with the colony system." He appealed for "protection" against "a way of life that is not Canadian." [26] T. H. Wilson, vice-president of Manitoba Pool Elevators, echoed these sentiments. At a public meeting in Macdonald he said the question "boils down to one thing: are we going to live the Hutterite way, or are they going to live our way?" Describing the colonies as "little empires" within the province, Mr. Wilson said he had no quarrel with the individuals, but he did have a quarrel with their way of life. [27]

In Alberta there were instances of equal hostility. In 1957, when the provincial government approved the sale of a tract of marginal land to the Hutterians, 150 ranchers and townsmen met at Wardlow and demanded that the government block the sale. The government in Edmonton rescinded its approval and ordered the Hutterians to get off their new land or face jail and fines. The protest movement was generated largely by emotional motives. *Time* magazine quoted one Wardlow oldtimer as saying: "They are fine upstanding, God-fearing people, good farmers, good conservationists. But they won't fight for Canada, won't vote, refuse to assume the responsibilities of good citizenship. The people don't want them for neighbors." [28]

This uncompromising attitude was partly stimulated and certainly fanned by a section of the press. An editorial in the *Calgary Herald* is representative of the opposition to the Hutterians. Headed "The Hutterites: A Hard Duty Ahead," it reads:

The government of this province will soon be facing one of the most distasteful and delicate problems in the life of its administration — devising an effective formula for controlling the increase of Hutterite colonies. The job is an unenviable one, but it cannot be sidetracked any longer.

The Hutterite story in Canada begins with an amazingly shortsighted bargain made by our Dominion government. These peaceful and vigorous farmers were guaranteed observance of their belief that bearing arms is sinful, and were allowed to establish communal colonies in the West. In exchange, they forfeited their right to vote.

The government thus created a class of second-rate citizenry, owing nothing to the country except taxes, taking no interest in its political life, and exempt from the primary duty of every citizen of every nation to defend his country in time of peril.

It was an extravagant price to pay for the sake of a few immigrants and a few more carloads of grain for the railways, and now the government must re-examine its position if it intends to serve the interests of the majority which readily accepts all the responsibility citizenship entails.

Perhaps no one could prophesy the rapid multiplication of these people (they have the highest birth-rate of any ethnological group in the country), but the fact is that colony expansion is approaching the point where vast regions of the West will be occupied by people who have, in effect, established quasi-foreign states whose continuance is assured by yearly tribute in the form of taxes.

The question of their religious beliefs has no place in consideration of this problem, although it will inevitably arise. There is much to be said for their way of life: they are good farmers — perhaps, as a group, the best in Canada; they have praiseworthy Christian qualities of kindness and generosity in boundless measure. No one would willingly tamper with such a society if it were in any way avoidable.

Unfortunately, it is not avoidable. The day is coming when national interests will clash head-on with those of people and national interests must take preference.

The Alberta government already has a law forbidding colonies within forty miles of each other, but the Hutterites have found ways to evade the regulation.

In the end, perhaps it may be necessary to insist that future generations of Hutterites be born full-fledged Canadians, and prohibit any more colonies than are needed for Hutterites now living.

As we said before, it is a miserable task, but it must be done.[29]

When the Alberta government set up another commission, in 1958, to hold hearings concerning the Hutterians, their opponents had shifted their ground somewhat. The renewed attack was on the basis that Hutterians deprived their children of "the best education available." R. G. Glover, presenting a brief on behalf of the Lethbridge school division No. 7, said: "They [young Hutterians] are Canadian-born children and they are being left in isolation and denied the education which we honestly believe to be the best for Canadian children." Another brief presented at the hearing in Calgary said: "Hutterite children are of generally high intelligence, have a thirst for higher education and should not be deprived of it because of their parents' religious beliefs." [30]

As the hearings progressed, however, the economic motives surfaced again. G. Davies, of Clyde, Alberta, who attended a session at Warner, said the scene reminded him of a "kangaroo court in an uncivilized country." A spokesman for the Farmers' Union local declared that the farmers "have reached the end of our patience. There is seething resentment which can erupt at any time." And some three hundred people from the area warned they were prepared "to break civil laws in Canada if necessary" if an application by a Hutterian colony to purchase a ranch in the Warner district was granted.[31]

Later in the same year the Farmers' Union of Alberta at an Edmonton convention passed a resolution demanding the "abolition of Hutterite colonies." "To be a farmer in Alberta in 20 years," said one delegate, "you'll have to be a Hutterite. I don't mind one Hutterite for a neighbor. They're friendly, law-abiding people, but I don't want a whole colony of them." [32]

But the Hutterians also had friends. In 1951 a federal bill was passed incorporating the Hutterian Brethren Church. In moving the second reading of the bill, Fernand Viau, Liberal member for St. Boniface, told the House of Commons that although there were about 6700 members of the Hutterian sect on the prairies, "one might search the records in vain to find one of their numbers charged with a major crime." He labeled them "upright, clean and worthy citizens." [33]

In 1954 the Union of Manitoba Municipalities petitioned the provincial government to restrict the purchase of land by Hutterian colonies and the location of new colonies, as we have seen. This time it was a Conservative member of the provincial legislature, Jack McDowell, who said he would put up a "big fight" to prevent restrictive legislation. A story carried by the *Winnipeg Free Press* on November 25, 1954, reads:

> The Hutterites of Manitoba have done great service to Manitoba farmers this year, Mr. McDowell said. Last year the colonies had a poor crop and because they had large flocks of turkeys and many animals to feed they bought hundreds of thousands of bushels of feed grain from Manitoba farmers, he said. The Hutterites in this case provided cash to the farmers that wasn't available from any other source, he said.
>
> In the flood west of Elie this spring, the Hutterites went into the water and plugged the gap, he said. They saved many acres of land from inundation. The army, which was at the flood, wouldn't go into the water because it was "too dangerous," Mr. McDowell said.

Two years later, when the Hutterian controversy bubbled again, a Jewish member of the Manitoba legislature came to their defense and protested attempts to interfere with their "liberty, democracy and personal life." [34] Morris Gray (CCF-Winnipeg) declared that he spoke as a Jew, presumably meaning that the Hutterians and the Jews are both minorities that have known persecution. He went on to say that it was true that "the wives of Hutterites do not wear Paris imported dresses and mink coats. But it is also true that they do not become a public charge on the state or occupy the luxurious hotel at Headingly [the provincial jail]. They pay their way. They produce food for themselves and others. It is true they have large families but who is to say how many children they should have. Would this House legalize birth control for them?"

Dr. R. O. MacFarlane, chairman of the Manitoba Royal Commission on Education, bluntly stated that one of the "big reasons" people disliked the Hutterians was that "they are such good farmers, the others can't compete with them." [35] Another observer, Rev. Nelson R. Mercer, of Westminster United Church, who had visited several colonies in Alberta and Manitoba, thought that the Hutterian life "looked drab," but the "minds are bright." [36] He suggested that the people were happy because of the absence of "fierce competition." Children were loved, "they belong," and if later a man leaves the colony "he is apt to come back. Something draws him."

A rebuttal to the *Calgary Herald's* editorial cited above appeared in the *Winnipeg Free Press* a week afterwards under the title "Hark, the Herald":

If the Hutterites are to be considered "second-rate" citizens, it follows that the same description must apply to Mennonites, Quakers, and other sects in Canada which are opposed to bearing arms. . . . But the Herald is not apparently urging that their numbers be curbed.

It also ignores the fact that the Hutterites came to Canada at a time when skilled farmers were desperately needed on the prairies. That was why the federal Government of that time permitted them to come and not, as the Herald foolishly suggests, "for the sake of a few more car-loads of grain for the railways."

Vague and high-sounding talk about "the interests of the majority" fails to hide that what the Herald proposes is that, against their wish, a group of Canadian citizens should be deprived of basic civil rights and freedoms. And all the crocodile tears shed by the Herald will not wash away the evil of that. [37]

As a rule the Hutterians themselves have avoided being directly drawn into the controversy. Occasionally, however, some of them publicly state their views. Rev. Jacob Maendel, the minister at the New Rosedale colony at Portage la Prairie, was asked, "Do you consider yourselves good citizens?" He replied: "Are industrious people good citizens? Are citizens good if they obey the laws, pay their taxes promptly, produce an abundance of goods, live according to the teachings of Christ? If they are, then we are good citizens, because good fruit cannot grow on bad trees. By their fruits ye shall know them." [38]

On another occasion a Manitoba farmer from Gladstone, Harry Morton, invited a group of municipal and Hutterian leaders to review and discuss the Hutterian problem. When the question of "voluntary" restriction was brought up, the Hutterians rejected it. Copiously quoting Scripture, the senior leader of the Manitoba Hutterians, Rev. Peter Hofer, of James Valley colony, intoned: "Leviticus, chapter 24, verse 22: 'Ye shall have one manner of law, as well as for the stranger as for one of your own country.' Proverbs, eleven, verse one: 'A false balance is an abomination to the Lord: but a just weight is his delight.' " [39]

It is in this spirit that Mr. Hofer, with the approval of the Hutterian ministers, published a 48-page booklet, *The Hutterian Brethren and Their Beliefs*.[40] As its foreword indicates, the brochure is a "defense of the Hutterian colonies, whose natural growth and development is threatened at this time by the [Union of] Rural Municipalities of Manitoba." Hofer's arguments on behalf of his people are usually scriptural texts or analogies drawn from the Bible, their tone and presentation resembling in many ways the polemic writings of the Reformation era.

Perhaps the most trenchant statement of their position was made by two Hutterian leaders in Alberta, Jacob Waldner, of the OK colony, near Raymond, and Jacob Hofer, of the Sunnyside colony, near Warner. In a newspaper interview they said that the whole atmosphere was "repugnant to their sense of values . . . the threats were unbecoming of people who stress democracy and good will." [41] If standard of living was judged by wholesome food, comfortable living quarters, church activity, and satisfied conscience, they said, "then ours is as high as anyone's. If standard of living is judged by cars, television, radios and fancy furniture, then we admit ours is lower." Waldner said that the Hutterians could not be blamed for agricultural trends in which large farms are taking over and small farm families are moving to cities.

Asked for their opinion of the integration of their children with the general community, Waldner replied: "We think that most people who talk about integration are really talking about disintegration. . . . We feel that any person who knows what integration would do to us has no right to ask us to integrate, any more than we have a right to ask him to integrate with us."

The Hutterians and the Changing Rural Pattern

The anti-Hutterian feeling and agitation had its roots and nourishment, at least in part, in developments for which the Hutterians were not responsible. In the two decades from 1931 to 1951 the pattern of rural life on the Canadian prairies was seriously disturbed. First there were the drought and the depression of the 1930's, which drove many farmers from their land. Secondly farm technology, the introduction of combines and power machinery, transformed farm life and threatened the very existence of the small farmer.[42] Both decades saw an alarming decline of the farm population. There was also a shift away from the prairie provinces as a whole, as can be seen from the accompanying figures. In contrast, from 1941 to 1951 Ontario gained in population by 305,000 and British Columbia by 231,000.[43] As the figures indicate, Saskatchewan, with practically no Hutterian colonies, suffered a greater population loss than the other two prairie provinces combined.

	Loss of Population	
Province	1931–1941	1941–1951
Manitoba	48,000	60,000
Saskatchewan	158,000	200,000
Alberta	42,000	7,000

The move away from the prairie farm was only one development. The first result was an increase in the size of the farms.[44] Then farm mechanization and the higher prices for farm commodities during and immediately after the war contributed to a changed pattern of rural life. The farmer on the whole had more leisure. The traditional community socials and sports events were to some extent replaced by commercial entertainment. Automobiles and better roads permitted the farmer to be more selective, and very often he bypassed the small hamlet, which had served his needs in the past, to take his business to a larger center. The inevitable result was that the small towns became smaller and suffered economically, and the large towns became larger and increased their business turnover.

Farm consolidation and the urbanization of rural life were especially marked in Anglo-Saxon communities, as was the departure of many of the young people for the greater monetary rewards and opportunities in larger towns and cities. The result was the "displacement of the less thrifty farmers of British origin by those of other ethnic origins."[45] The influx of new settlers with no ties and loyalties to the old communities and their traditions accelerated the disintegration of these communities.

The Hutterians as well as other ethnic groups infiltrated the older communities. Inevitably, however, the Hutterians, easily distinguished because of their appearance and their cluster-type colonies, were marked as the cause of the trouble. In Alberta and Manitoba the frustrated farmers and small town merchants began to see in the Hutterian colonies a tangible threat to their old way of life and even to their continued existence. The Hutterians were hardly responsible for the deeper forces at work, but, in the words of one observer, they were "particularly vulnerable to retaliation because of their distinctive way of life and success in maintaining it." [46]

The outbreak of World War II with its atmosphere of patriotic fervor accentuated and solidified latent public sentiment against the Hutterians. Its causes were thoroughly analyzed by Harry Halliwell, agricultural editor of the *Winnipeg Tribune*, in an article on May 9, 1955, dealing with one of the numerous farm-protest meetings. The article, entitled "Farm Men Raise Hutterite Bogey," is sufficiently thought-provoking to appear here in full:

This week the Hutterite bogey has been raised again in Manitoba. At a meeting in Portage la Prairie, sponsored by the Community Welfare Association of Portage and Cartier municipalities, about 200 farmers voted almost unanimously in favor of a resolution asking a ban on the purchase of land by or for Hutterite colonies without permission of the government.

This is by all odds the most restrictive law that has been demanded to deal with the Hutterite "problem." It would deprive the Hutterites of any right to purchase land except at the whim of some politician or group of politicians, or at best, of someone appointed by politicians.

A good many pros and cons have been discussed during arguments about the Hutterites during the past few years. Two major theses have been advanced by their critics: that they harm the municipalities in which they settle and injure the nearby towns; and that given their present rate of increase they will, in the not too distant future, overwhelm the "ordinary" Canadians in the province.

The specific charges made against them run much as follows: They take no part in community life generally, but keep to themselves. They do not attend or support regular schools, but have their own. They don't do business with local merchants but buy wholesale in the cities, thus reducing the markets of local businessmen and people who provide local services, driving some of them out of business and so impairing the volume and the quantity of services available to "ordinary" Canadians.

No doubt there is an element of truth in all these accusations, perhaps a substantial element in some. They do not, for example, take part in community activities. In that respect, they differ from a good many ordinary Canadians by virtue of the fact that their refusal to do so is better organized.

Neither do they support regular schools, although this isn't necessarily harmful.

Probably the chief reasons for the restrictions sought against them are the economic ones.

By buying "wholesale" in the cities they perhaps contribute to the trend of business away from the small towns to the larger ones and the cities. Whether or not this is the major cause, or even an important cause, of the decline of business in small towns is another matter.

Small towns throughout the west are suffering from the increase in the size of farms, accompanied by a shift of population from farms and small towns to larger towns and cities. (They are also suffering from better cars and roads, which make it easy for people to go to the city to shop.)

Between 1941 and 1951, the size of the average farm in Manitoba increased from 310.5 acres to 338.4 acres. Despite the fact that the area of occupied farms in the province increased from 16.9 million acres to 17.7 million acres, the number of farms of one acre or more, with income of $250 a year or more, decreased from 54,400 to 52,383. The trend is continuing.

During the same period, the population on Manitoba farms decreased from 407,871 to 392,112 and the urban population (in towns, cities and incorporated villages) increased from 321,873 to 384,429. The increase came in the larger centres.

With three exceptions, no municipality in Manitoba has more than one colony of Hutterites. Cartier has nine, Portage four and Westbourne two. There are 22 altogether.

One of the colonies, incidentally, New Rosedale at Portage, originally comprised 3,100 acres of land purchased from two men. There are about 100 to 125 persons in a colony.

The conclusion from the foregoing facts seems to be that at worst the Hutterites are aggravating a situation that would exist without them, and that they are doing so only at two or three points in the province.

In Cartier, the municipality of greatest concentration, they occupy about 30,000 out of a total of 130,000 acres, or about one-fifth of the land, according to one of the instigators of this week's resolution.

A good many figures have been tossed about purporting to show that in relatively few years, say 50, they will overrun the province.

One man told the meeting in Portage that within that time they could own 10,000,000 acres, or as he claimed, 2,000,000 acres more than the total arable area of the province.

He drew these conclusions on the basis of the rate of growth of the colonies, and excluded immigration, he told the meeting.

A little simple arithmetic seems to show these conclusions are out of line with the facts.

In 1931, there were 10 Hutterite colonies in Manitoba, comprising 31,000 acres, with a total population of 1,064 persons. The latest figures show there are now 22 colonies, with an area of about 85,000 acres and a population of 2,583.

In 24 years the population has increased 2.4 times and the area of land they hold 2.7 times. Say, for the sake of simplicity, that they treble their numbers and the area of land they hold every 25 years.

In 50 years, at the rate of increase in the last 24, there could be about 23,250 Hutterites in the province, holding 765,000 acres of land. This would be about 4.3 per cent of the total occupied farmland area of the province, if it doesn't change from the present 17.7 million acres.

The opposition to Hutterian expansion had some of the same intensity often associated with racial clashes. The problem it presented was expressed by Professor H. F. Angus in writing about the experiences of the Canadian Japanese in British Columbia during World War II: "Even if we decide that our political ideals require that law-abiding minorities should suffer no discrimination on grounds of race, there remains a further question to be answered: How should society deal with intolerant local minorities which say that they are likely to resort to violence if they are not allowed to exclude from their occupations or their neighborhood a group which they dislike?" [47] The Hutterians, although an extremely religiocentric culture group, are racially hardly different from the rest of the Canadian population. Only this saved them from the drastic measures that were taken against the Canadian Japanese.

One of the strictures made about the Hutterian "problem" appears to be valid: their large communal landholdings partly contribute to the disorganization of older communities in which the colonies are established. On the other hand individual farmers quite often farm as much land as an entire Hutterian community without arousing protests from their neighbors. Moreover, it may be said that the Hutterians' emphasis on family life, their care for the young and the aged, the democratic functioning of their communities, their freedom from crime, their refusal to accept state assistance, all are virtues consistent with the highest ideals of the larger Canadian society. As agricultural communities engaged in diverse farm enterprises the Hutterian colonies contribute materially to the wealth of

Canada. The Hutterian emphasis on rural life, frugality, self-sufficiency, and careful business practices is also not inconsistent with Canadian ways. Most Hutterians speak the English language, and the colonies support the public schools in their communities. Though only a few of the Hutterians use their franchise they all cherish the democratic institutions of Canada.

The Hutterian Church has practiced "avoidance of the world" for over four hundred years. There is no evidence that the present leaders and the young generation are prepared or willing to throw their basic beliefs overboard, and these include communal life. Canadians may have to accept the Hutterians for the present and for the foreseeable future as an unusual fragment of their population mosaic.

It is man who makes monarchies and establishes re-
publics, but the community seems to come directly
from the hand of God.   DE TOCQUEVILLE

Part Two

THE HUTTERIAN WAY

V

THE COMMUNITY-CONGREGATION

A PERSON in an individualistic society can be considered as the center of a series of concentric circles. The individual is in the middle, the first circle around him may denote his relationship to the family, the second circle may represent the school, the next one the church, and so on. The Hutterian's life cannot be pictured in the same way. An analysis of the Hutterian way into components such as the church, the community, the family, is an arbitrary procedure employed to portray the role of these institutions in terms of the outside society. More accurately, the entire circle, with the exception of one small arc, is an entity in which the places of the family, the school, the church, are all blended until the demarcations are blurred, or indeed erased. An example may illustrate this. What is in our society a routine function, such as the gathering of a family around the supper table, becomes to the Hutterians an expression of worship as the entire community assembles in the colony dining hall to partake of a meal in almost complete silence. The taking of nourishment to them is more than just that; it is a religious service, a tribute to the glory of the Provider of all.

The one clearly defined segment jutting into the Hutterian circle is the community's formal contact with the outside world and with the public school, an agent of an outside authority. However, the business relationship with the outside world and the public school plays only a secondary role in a Hutterian's life.

The Hutterian's way of life is encompassed by his religion. Religion "permeates all Hutterian thought," says the Chicago sociologist Bertha Clark. She continues, "Twentieth century America knows little of that sort of piety which makes the enveloping atmosphere of all Hutterian life." [1] And the authors of a more recent survey report: "The people as a whole are religious to an unusual degree, and there is hardly a doubter among all the Hutterites." [2]

Faith and Doctrine

There is no distinct church organization within the Hutterian colony. The community is the congregation. In the Hutterian Articles of Association both terms are used interchangeably:

Complete dedication in the work for the aims and objects of the Church is expected from all members thereof. The capital and surplus produce and surplus funds of each individual congregation or community of the Church is to be used by such community for social work to which the Church is constantly dedicated, healing poor, weak and sickly persons who need, ask for and accept this help, especially children, and for the purchase of lands, stock and equipment for the use of such congregation or community in order that the members thereof may maintain themselves and acquire funds for the purposes of carrying out the aims of the Church. [3]

Much of Hutterian church doctrine differs little from that of other fundamentalist Protestant church bodies. [4] Since the days of the Reformation, in common with other Anabaptist groups like the Mennonites and the Amish, the Hutterians have practiced adult baptism, nonresistance, and refusal to take the oath. They also observe strict avoidance of the world. Beyond that and unlike the others the Hutterians practice *Gütergemeinschaft,* the common ownership of goods. This tenet is partly based on the Scripture passage in Acts 2:44: "And all that believed were together, and had all things common." But it also expresses the Hutterian interpretation of the spirit of the gospel as a whole.

With its roots in the social, cultural, and religious soil of the medieval and Reformation world, the Hutterian way may be interpreted as a case of arrested development. Modifications in the social and cultural pattern have been permitted, but at an almost imperceptible pace. Hutterian doctrine itself has remained unadulterated and unchanged for over four centuries. The five tenets of doctrine mentioned above — adult baptism, nonresistance, rejection of the oath, avoidance, and community of goods — may be singled out for particular attention.

Adult Baptism. A careful check which I made of church records at the Hutterian communities indicates that candidates for baptism very rarely are under the age of eighteen, and many of them are over twenty-one. A period of probation and instruction precedes the candidate's admission to church membership. Parenthetically it may be mentioned that the Hutterians have retained the original form of baptism by sprinkling (*Begiessungstaufe*), which takes place in church.

Nonresistance (*Wehrlosigkeit*). During World War I every Hutterian was a conscientious objector; there were no defectors.[5] In World War II about half a dozen of their young men, in most cases not yet baptized members of the Church, joined the Canadian armed forces, but the rest of them performed alternative service. This consisted of forestry work or work in mental institutions. Those who joined the army and returned to the colonies were required to do penance before they were accepted for church membership.

The Oath. The Hutterians reject the taking of an oath. On legal documents an affirmation is substituted for a sworn statement.

Avoidance. Life in the colony, segregated from the outside world, is an expression of their belief that Christians should live separated from "the world." In keeping with "avoidance" Hutterians do not accept public office, and members are discouraged from taking part in municipal, provincial, or federal elections. For the same reason innovations that impinge on colony seclusion, inventions like the radio and television, are rejected. On the other hand, more controllable, utilitarian inventions like the telephone are permitted.

Community of Goods (*Gütergemeinschaft*). An elected steward is installed in every colony to control the common purse. All things are held in common, and when a member dies any articles of use are redistributed. Children may be permitted to retain the parental library, or some family heirloom like embroidery work, or a decorative tool chest made by the father, but these are the exception.

To these salient tenets of the Hutterian faith must be added a general outlook on life which early Hutterian writers termed *Gelassenheit*, a word that is difficult to translate into English but that denotes a deliberate, resigned composure. The belief underlying *Gelassenheit* is that God bestows His gifts freely on man, but man in his wickedness and foolishness refuses to accept and share them. The calm and confident Christian, however, is secure in the hollow of God's hand. Ulrich Stadler (*ca.* 1537) expressed *Gelassenheit* in these words:

Everything should be arranged for the good of the saints of God in the church of the Lord according to time, place, propriety, and opportunity, for one cannot set up a specific instruction for everything. The hearts which are free, willing, unhampered, patient, ready to serve all the children of God, to have everything common with them, yea, to persevere loyally and constantly in their service, shall remain always in the Lord. Where such hearts of grace exist, everything is soon ordered in the Lord.[6]

Gelassenheit, the consciousness that God works in His own way and in His own time, also impels the Hutterians to reject active missionary work. When an outsider, a religious worker, in my presence asked a Hutterian minister why the colonies did not have full-time missionaries, the minister answered by citing St. Paul (2 Thessalonians 3:11): "For we hear that there are some which walk among you disorderly, working not at all, but are busybodies. Now them that are such we command and exhort by our Lord Jesus Christ, that with quietness they work, and eat their own bread." "Besides," the minister added, quoting Matthew 5:14, "'A city that is set on an hill cannot be hid.'"

To repeat, there is no Hutterian church organization distinct from the community, or colony, organization. The latter is the tangible form of the first. The habitat itself is known as the *Bruderhof*, the "community of Brethren."

The Bruderhof

In many ways the Hutterian *Bruderhof*, or colony, is like a cloister, except that it contains both men and women and is self-perpetuating. Half of its people are children under sixteen years of age. Generally, and deliberately, the colony is somewhat removed from towns and from main traffic arteries. The recent relocation of the Trans-Canada Route west of Winnipeg, however, takes the highway within a few miles of several Hutterian communities.

The casual passerby is not impressed with the appearance of a Hutterian colony. While the individual farmer will have his house and lawns facing the road, the Hutterians, almost symbolically as if to turn their back on the world, put their barns and implement sheds nearest the road. The visitor who turns into a colony driveway thus makes his first acquaintance with the most functional and usually least attractive part of colony life.

The community dining hall is the center of the colony. It has two rows of tables and will seat from sixty to a hundred adults. The men eat on one side of the room and the women on the other side. There is a second dining room for children of six to fifteen. Usually the unit housing the kindergarten is not far from the dining hall, and the youngsters from two and a half to five years of age take their meals there under the supervision of their teacher and her assistants.

The community dining hall may also serve as a place of worship, if the school is not convenient for this purpose. Since no ritual aids are required, not even pulpits, either place serves equally well. The dining hall has a tower with a bell. The bell may call the colony congregation together for church service, or call the men at mealtime, or call the women together for work in the garden, or it may send the children to bed at nine o'clock in the evening. More recently a siren has replaced the bell at some colonies.

The kitchen adjoins the dining hall. It has modern equipment, comparable to that of a large restaurant. All colonies have electrical or gas appliances. Near the kitchen are the baking room with its large ovens and mechanical mixers, and the refrigerated coolers and deepfreezes in which great quantities of perishable food are kept. While some colonies have separate laundry houses, others have the laundry unit installed in the basement of the community hall. Since laundry work is the responsibility of the individual family, specific days of the week are allotted to each family for this purpose. The laundry unit will often have an area reserved for baths and may also have showers, which are very popular. Most school buildings have indoor toilet facilities; otherwise old-fashioned outhouses are the rule. Some colonies are heated from a central heating plant.

The family dwellings are spaced around the community dining hall. In Manitoba these are generally frame buildings. The New Rosedale colony southwest of Portage la Prairie, one of the largest Hutterian communities in Manitoba, has the following units: two long two-story buildings housing four families each, one three-family unit, two duplexes and five single-family homes. All units have separate entrances for each family, but none have kitchens, as all food is prepared in the community kitchen. A Hutterian home has a comfortable living room and bedrooms; the number of bedrooms allotted to a family depends on the size of the family.

Beyond the family dwellings are the numerous buildings housing livestock, poultry, ducks, geese, pigs, and turkeys. There are also implement sheds, granaries, carpenter's and blacksmith's shops, the hatchery, the killing plant, and other buildings. There are acres of garden plots that provide vegetables for the community. Somewhat removed from the colony is the orchard, which may have around a hundred beehives in one corner.

In many colonies cement walks from the dwellings lead to the dining hall, the school, and other buildings used by the community. Some colonies may have shrubbery, lawns, and flower beds; at others they are conspicuously absent. The condition of the dwellings varies from colony to colony just as the ordinary farm houses in western Canada differ from homestead to homestead. For while the pattern of life in the different colonies is practically the same, each colony functions as a completely independent economic unit.

The harmonious operation of a complex social organization like the *Bruderhof* is in itself an achievement. Here from eighty to two hundred people live together for a lifetime. Assignments are distributed to occupy them all during all the seasons. Numerous enterprises are conducted on a fairly large scale. The buying of land and farm equipment, purchasing the colony supplies, marketing the surplus produce — all these transactions involve hundreds of thousands of dollars. These activities combine into an intricate administration problem which the Hutterians have solved, if not entirely to their own satisfaction, at least in a manner which assures not only the survival but the prosperous expansion and development of the group.

The Administration of a Colony

The Hutterian administrative system, like British parliamentary institutions, is not regulated by written codes and constitutions but by custom and tradition. It is a system of checks and balances, but not overtly so. The power resides in the adult male members of the church of each colony. All important questions are presented to them; all important decisions are made by them. The administrative superstructure for each colony consists of a council of five or six men who are known as *Zeugbrüder* (literally, "Witness-Brethren").[7] The minister, the colony steward, and the farm foreman are automatically members of the council, and the other two or three *Zeugbrüder* are elected for life by the male congregation. Only a serious offense could bar a member from the council. This does not mean that the composition of it is static. Death, or the election of an assistant minister, or the periodic colony division when branching out, all affect the council membership and lead to the influx of new men. *Zeug-brüder* have no special privileges. Dr. Joseph Eaton reports that in an interview a young Hutterian remarked, "They just got to work harder and worry. I hope they never elect me." [8]

Indeed, no position in the colony entails the right to be exempted from manual work. In many unannounced visits to different colonies I invariably found the ministers working, unless age or illness made this difficult. Visiting five colonies in Manitoba one day I found the ministers all at work: at Riverside changing the bottoms of the cultivator; at Riverdale spraying the potatoes in the garden; at New Rosedale mixing feed grain; at Crystal Spring laying bricks; and at Milltown hauling grain. The colony steward at Milltown was engaged in the rather unpleasant task of cleaning the potato cellar.

The Minister. The minister, known as the *Diener am Wort* (servant of the Word) or simply *Prediger* (preacher), is the spiritual and temporal head of the community, and his election is a combination of human selection and reliance upon divine choice. The procedure was outlined by the minister of Crystal Spring colony, Rev. Jacob Kleinsasser. Asked how the colony would proceed in the election of an assistant minister he answered:

If we required a second minister at Crystal Spring colony we would inform Elder Peter Hofer of James Valley colony,[9] and he would notify all the other colonies that we had applied for another minister. He would set the date, usually a Sunday, when the election is to take place. On that day every Hutterian minister in Manitoba, together with one or two Brethren from every colony, would come to our community. Before that our Brethren at Crystal Spring will already have nominated two or three candidates out of our midst.

On the set date a service is held before the election, and we ask God to guide us in our decision. Then all the Brethren of our colony and the visiting Brethren file past Peter Hofer and tell him which candidate each one favors. It is a verbal vote which our Elder records.

Then the votes are counted. The candidate who received less than five votes is eliminated. The Brethren then kneel down and pray to our Lord that He should show us through lot which one He would see fit for the position. The names of the candidates who receive more than five votes are then placed in a hat and the Elder draws one name. This candidate is the new minister.

He is on probation and may remain so for two, four years, or longer. Then he is ordained. This is done by the laying on of hands by two or three of the senior ministers.[10]

Entrusting the final election to Providence by drawing the name of the minister by lot (*das Los ziehen*) may have had its origin in a practical consideration. Deets suggests that it reduces the chances of partisanship within the community before and after the election.[11] The drawing of names is used only in the election of ministers; all other officials are elected by simple majorities.

A sampling of the Hutterian communities in Manitoba shows that most of the ministers are between the ages of twenty-five and forty at the time of their election. Two ministers are generally found in large colonies or in colonies where the minister has reached an advanced age.

A brief biography of Rev. Jacob Kleinsasser may serve to illustrate the typical background of a Hutterian minister. Kleinsasser was born at the Blumengart colony near Plum Coulee, in Manitoba, in 1922. When the Blumengart colony branched out to establish Sturgeon Creek colony near Headingly, he moved with his parents to the new colony. Here he became the colony carpenter, joined the Church at the age of twenty-three, and married the following year. At the age of twenty-five he was elected assistant minister. His father was the colony steward, and his mother was in charge of the kindergarten. When Sturgeon Creek colony established a new colony at Crystal Spring, east of Ste. Agathe, Kleinsasser went with the new group. Though he is the only minister at the colony he spends much of his time at woodwork and carpentry.

The minister occupies a somewhat exceptional place in the colony. He alone is required to take his meals by himself in his own home. This practice is rigidly observed in all Hutterian communities. While the casual outside visitor will be invited to eat in the community dining room, the respected guest may be asked to join the minister at his table. The Hutterian ministerial conference has gone on record as not favoring the occasional practice of bringing better food to the minister. Generally his food is the same as that eaten by the community members, but as there are quite often one or two sick people in a colony who are served something extra, like chicken soup or pudding, some of it will find its way to the minister. This will occur especially if he is an older man. When I discussed this practice with a group of women in the presence of a minister, I was told by one of them that this was just *ein kleiner Liebesdienst* (a small service of love), and she did not see why the ministers should object to it.

As a minister grows older, or the colony membership increases and the community prepares for a division, an assistant minister is elected. He generally takes a subordinate role to the senior minister, but again, depending on his ability and personality, he may assume the major responsibilities of the ministerial position. In such instances the inculcated respect for age comes into play and he shows due deference to his senior colleague, never proceeding on a course without previous consultation. For his meals the assistant minister goes to the home of the senior minister, and they eat at one table. At the dinner table in the home of Elder Peter Hofer I commented on the absence of the assistant minister. The explanation was that Elder Hofer, who had undergone a prolonged and severe illness, was on a medically prescribed diet. For this reason the colony's two ministers had agreed to take their meals in their own respective homes.

On the whole the Hutterian minister follows the injunction that "a good example by the elder brings forth good followers." [12] He is an understanding leader and has faith in the common sense of the colony members. As a rule he is most unwilling to use coercive measures. Quoting an old German proverb, the minister of New Rosedale colony said, "After all, the horns provided for the leaders are not there to disperse the herd but to keep it together and protect it."

The importance of the minister's position is exemplified by the Hutterian rule that before a colony can branch out it must have two ministers. This is more important than economic considerations or the location of the new colony. One of the ministers must then be ready to transfer to the new *Bruderhof* to provide spiritual guidance and supervise the election of offices. Since the minister, before his election to that position, may have been the colony steward or the head of one of the major colony enterprises, he is usually well qualified to provide leadership in temporal matters as well.

The Colony Steward. It is difficult to translate the archaic German nomenclature into English. To the Hutterians the steward is the *Wirt* or *Haushalter*, which is literally the householder. In the formal relationship with the outside world, as in business transactions where the colony is treated as a corporation, the minister becomes the chairman and the steward the secretary-treasurer. The English vernacular "colony boss," generally used by outsiders and sometimes by Hutterians, has no equivalent in German-Hutterian terminology and its use is not approved by the Church. The connotation of "colony manager," an expression sometimes used for the *Haushalter*, is somewhat too authoritative and therefore misleading. The position of the *Haushalter* has a long tradition in Hutterian history, for the first two stewards were elected as early as 1528, one of them named Jakob Mändel.[13]

Next to the minister the steward is the man most responsible for the colony's welfare. He is elected by the male congregation without any assistance from the members of other colonies. The medium used is the ballot. There are no nominations and there is no canvassing for votes, as this would lead to expressions of "unbrotherly preferences." Every man puts the name of the man he thinks best qualified for the position on a slip of paper, and the one getting the largest number of votes is declared elected. As colony steward he cannot show any favoritism. If in elections of enterprise heads he should voice a preference for any man the steward could be punished. On the other hand, the colony delegates considerable latitude in decision-making to the steward.

The steward keeps the colony's financial records, but the Hutterian ordinances instruct him not to spend too much time on the books. Instead he should be in the workshops and in the kitchen, helping and supervising, and checking that no one receives special concessions or privileges. He must be willing to do himself the most menial tasks he assigns to others.[14] The steward is to check periodically and carefully the work in every enterprise, and in the evening he is advised to consult the farm foreman about work assignments for the following day.[15]

The colony steward thus leads an arduous life. He is intimately familiar with every facet of colony life. Even early on a Sunday morning, when everyone is engaged in the necessary farm chores, he can very often be seen walking through the barns and discussing livestock matters with the cattle-man. From there he may proceed to the poultry houses, the pig barns, the turkey compounds, and by the time church service begins he will have visited a number of the enterprises of the colony.

The steward eats in the community dining hall, usually after the rest of the colony members have finished with their meal. He is joined by the farm foreman and by the chief cook, and sometimes by her assistants as well. This gives the steward an opportunity to check with the farm foreman what work has to be done and discuss with the cook what supplies are required from the farm enterprises and from town. He may voice some comment on the food. The cook in turn may say that her menu calls for roast duck on Sunday. The steward gives his approval and the duck-man is duly informed to keep between thirty-five and forty ducks in readiness. All this is done very informally, as if the community were a large family.

The cook may in fact be a close relative by blood or marriage to the steward; in a few colonies she is his wife.

While the heads of the colony enterprises may each have a competent younger assistant to share their responsibilities and have the counsel of the steward in all matters, the steward himself has no assistant. When the chief carpenter or cattle-man grows old he may delegate some of the work and responsibility to his assistant. If the steward's health or his age should impair his leadership and affect the welfare of the colony, he resigns. Should he be reluctant to resign, the kindly pressure from every quarter, the family, the council, and the community, will persuade him to lay down his task and make way for a new manager.

It should be remembered that each colony member has been conditioned from his childhood to put the common good before anything else. This reduces the difficulty of a problem often quite serious in society at large where leaders sometimes insist on retaining their positions long after their maximum usefulness is past. Regardless of how much drive and initiative a Hutterian steward may have displayed, when advancing age makes his leadership a liability he usually retires gracefully and relinquishes control to younger hands. However, he retains the informal status of a senior adviser and is frequently consulted by his successor.

Invariably the steward has demonstrated some of his qualities, his qualifications, and his ability of leadership long before he is called to his position. A sampling of the ages of the stewards at the time of their election to that post revealed that most of them were in their late thirties or early forties. As a rule the steward, before his election to that post, has headed several of the colony's enterprises in turn. Thus the present steward at James Valley colony, Joshua Hofer, was the *Pferdemann* (horse-man) at an early age. This was before the farm horse became obsolete, and he was in charge of over a hundred horses used by the colony at the time. Later he became the farm foreman, and then was elected steward. He is well read and his library contains some excellent books on early Hutterian history, including Loserth's works,[16] which his father brought back from a trip to Vienna before the outbreak of World War II.

The Farm Foreman. The farm foreman, or *Weinzierl*,[17] is third in rank of the colony administrators, following the minister and the steward. He too is elected by the male congregation. The farm foreman is in charge of agriculture proper and of the colony's manpower. It is he who decides, after consultations with the steward and enterprise heads, what crops should be sown and where, whether land should be broken or left for pasture or haying, when seeding, harvesting, plowing, haying, and so on should take place. He also provides liaison between the steward and the various enterprises in the colony. At harvest time he may muster all hands, including the enterprise heads like the cattle-man and the poultry-man, to help at least on a part-time basis with the work in the fields. No man is ever exclusively concerned with his enterprise. He must be prepared to help the other enterprises as much as his own work permits.

If the turkey-man informs the steward that the turkeys are ready and the market shows a demand, the steward consults with the farm foreman, and he in turn will provide the turkey-man with the necessary help to operate the killing plant. Here the farm foreman, after consultation with the women leaders, would even draw help from the female labor pool.

The farm foreman will also assign the older boys to different enterprises, or use them as operators of tractors or farm machines in the fields. The boys are permitted a choice to some extent. However, it is expected that they will spend at least some time in each colony enterprise in order to familiarize themselves with its operation and routine.

A salient characteristic of the administrative order is its extreme elasticity. One incident may serve to illustrate this flexibility. During the summer of 1957 when I spent some weeks at the New Rosedale colony, the farm foreman fell ill and was hospitalized for a considerable period. His duties were immediately absorbed by the steward. The minister in turn took over some of the regular duties of the steward. There was no interruption in farm operations.

These three men, the minister, the steward, and the farm foreman, invariably make up half of the colony council. Occupationally the other *Zeugbrüder*, or members of the council, may be anyone from the poultry-man to the assistant mechanic.

Distribution of Colony Tasks

To one unfamiliar with Hutterian ways a discussion of division of labor in conjunction with faith and doctrine may appear incongruous. However, according to their Articles of Association "each congregation or community . . . is empowered: To engage in, and carry on farming, stock-raising, milling, and all branches of these industries; and to manufacture and deal with the products and by-products of these industries."[18] A good church member, then, is one who does his honest share of work in the colony in order "to obtain for its members and their dependent minors, as also for the novices, helpers, children and persons in need under its care, without distinction of race, class, social standing, nationality, religion, age or sex, spiritual, cultural, educational and economic assistance based upon the life and mission of Jesus Christ and the Apostles, in the spirit and way of the first Christian community in Jerusalem and of the community re-established by Jacob Hutter in 1533 at the time of the origin of the 'Baptisers' movement' in such a way that the members achieve one entire spiritual unit in complete community of goods (whether production or consumption) . . ." [19]

Since each colony is an assembly of people of diverse ages, skills, talents, and abilities, specialization and division of labor must follow. This is not carried to the extreme of Adam Smith's classic illustration in the manufacturing of pins, but is considerable when compared to the modern mixed farm on which the farmer personally directs every enterprise and very often represents the farm's total labor force.

Specialization begins with the election of the heads of the various enterprises, and their assistants. There is the German teacher, the *Viehwirt* or *Kuhmann* (cattle-man), the *Schweinewirt* (pig-man), the *Hennemann* (poultry-man), the blacksmith, the carpenter, the mechanic, the shoemaker, the bee-man, the bookbinder, the gardener, the turkey-man, and others, each responsible for his own enterprise. If a colony decides to enlarge substantially any one enterprise, like the raising of turkeys, for instance, the turkey-man will get one or more assistants. On the other hand small enterprises may also be combined. The gardener may also be the bee-man, and the shoemaker, whose work today consists largely of shoe repairing, may also be the colony bookbinder.

The system, like most other colony practices, is not absolute and rigid. At one colony recently the elected assistant to the poultry-man found that he was allergic to the smell of eggs and henhouses. With the consent of the community he became assistant to the carpenter. The community realizes that this flexibility may lead to abuse, but it generally assumes that the reasons advanced for a transfer from one enterprise to another are genuine. Moreover, the colony is unwilling to assign a member to an enterprise which he may dislike and which would only deteriorate for his lack of interest. At one colony the carpenter had not particularly liked his work, but he was a young man and the colony encouraged him to "give it a try." "I was the *Schweinewirt* and I liked the work, but we had no carpenter," he said to the interviewer. "Of course I had worked in the carpenter shop before, and after a while I began to like the work. I am not sorry I switched."

Sometimes the colony council may appoint a minor to head an enterprise if the position is vacant and the colony's population is too small to provide an experienced head for it without weakening another department. This occurs quite frequently. A number of current Hutterian leaders were appointed to head an enterprise at the age of seventeen, that is, before they were baptized members of the Brotherhood.

There is also some division of labor among the women. The heads of the departments are elected to their positions by the male congregation of the colony. Heading the list is the *Haushälterin*, also known as the *Küchenfrau* (literally "kitchen-woman," the colony's chief cook), whose major duties concern the planning of meals and the distribution of kitchen chores. There is the *Zuschneiderin* (seamstress), who together with the *Haushälterin* is in charge of the purchase and distribution of cloth for the colony. The *Gartenfrau* is in charge of the gardens and the canning for winter. The kindergarten teacher, known as the *Kinderweib* or *Kinderangela*, or simply *Angela*, is in charge of children between the ages of two and a half and five. Finally there is the *Hebamme*, the midwife, who is kept very busy and usually works in close cooperation with the doctor of the nearest town. As with the men, positions may be combined; at New Rosedale, for example, the midwife is also the *Gartenfrau*.

The daily work of the women is planned jointly by the department heads. A call from the large bell over the dining hall at nine o'clock in the morning assembles the women, and they may be placed under the *Gartenfrau*, who will assign them to work in the garden. The bell may ring again at half past ten, the signal for the *Gartenfrau* to release some of the women for kitchen duty before the men come for their meal. With the women as with the men there is one standing rule, expressed in the German axiom *Der Wirt geht voraus* (the leader shows the way). It is rare for a leader to chide the others for poor or slow work; instead he or she sets the pace.

If a woman is ill or has a sick child at home, or if it is her turn to do her laundry work, she is excused. Group pressure is almost invariably sufficient to prevent misuse of this system. If one member should persist in shirking her duty over a long period of time, and the leader's coaxing is of no avail, the minister may have a word with her. If this fails the member is regarded as somewhat abnormal, and her frailty is borne with patience by the community. The same is true of males. But such cases are extremely rare. Evil talk is not tolerated, and if the offending party persists in it, a visit from the minister is usually a sufficient check.

The groups of colony women at work always appear happy. There is laughter, chatter, and singing as they clean chickens for supper, make soap, or sit at their spinning wheels. More unpleasant tasks are done in rotation. The assistant to the *Küchenfrau*, who has to peel potatoes and do the kitchen chores, changes every week. Automatically the assistant's husband is assigned to kitchen duty for the week. He is required to do the work considered "too hard for women," like chopping or grinding meat, and to supply the kitchen daily with fresh milk and eggs. The colony women do not seem to be overworked. Edna Kells, who spent some time at an Alberta colony, reported, "I came away from this colony with the impression that they do not work as hard as nine out of ten Canadian farm women." [20]

Outsiders who have lived at Hutterian colonies for some time generally leave impressed with the Hutterian attitude toward work. Henrik Infield found their work satisfaction "very high, with pride in [their] unhurried efforts." [21] Bertha Clark wrote, "Love for work and pride in the kind of work they do are two of their outstanding traits; and so contagious are they both that it would seem the problem of idleness is one that has needed very little attention." [22] And Joseph Eaton summarized his impressions in these words: "All work is rated to be of equal importance. The preacher or any other elder will not consider it below his dignity to do the most menial tasks. The Hutterite attitude toward all work — be it skilled or not — as of equal value, and the belief that work is a pleasure rather than a burden, contributes much to the smooth functioning of their social organization." [23]

Since so many of the activities on a Hutterian community are carried on by people working in groups, it is clear that the role of the leaders is of great importance. A penetrating observer of this aspect of Hutterian life says:

The . . . system is well calculated to train leaders. The active part that all the male adults of a community take in determining all matters pertaining to community life both develops leadership and brings it to the general notice. The fact that all leaders are unpaid, that they are in no way relieved of manual duties when they take office, and that there are no special privileges for them has greatly helped to keep out corruption and to keep fit leaders in office.[24]

Another aspect is the democratic fabric of the Hutterian community. No single individual has the authority to make decisions affecting the whole colony. If the cattle-man requires a new truck to haul feed for the livestock he will broach the matter to the steward. If the steward feels that the colony's financial position does not permit the expenditure, he will turn down the request for the time being. If he concurs with the request and agrees that the need is there, he passes it on to the council. Should the council be undecided it may refer the matter to the male congregation. Here decisions are made by a majority vote. Indeed, all larger projects are dealt with not by the colony council but by the members. The erection of a new barn, for example, would require the approval of the male congregation. In very important issues, like the division of the community, the approval of the male congregation at some colonies must be unanimous.

The community-congregation is thus characterized by (a) an attempt to preserve the ideal of early Christianity as interpreted by the Hutterians, in which the practice of community of goods is a tangible expression of Christian love for one's fellowman; (b) the organization of the *Bruderhof* as an isolated habitat in order to strengthen the feeling of *Gemeinschaft* (community) within, and to avoid unnecessary contact with the world outside; (c) a democratic internal organization in which the male congregation is in fact the colony administration; and (d) vocational specialization of its membership and distribution of colony tasks providing full employment for the entire group.

VI

COLONY LIFE

THE HUTTERIANS speak of their group as the *Gemein-schaft*, or *die Gemein'*. The expression defies a simple translation, for its comprehensive explanation implies a community of place, mind, and spirit. With the Hutterians it is also very largely a community by blood, entrenched in religion and tradition.

Sociologists speak of this form of social relationship, which is of course not confined to Hutterians, as an informal, familistic association. Sorokin defines it as follows: ". . . lives are thrown together and organically united into one 'we.' There is almost nothing of the 'it does not concern me,' 'it is none of my business,' 'mind your own affairs' attitude. On the contrary, what concerns one party concerns the other: joy and sorrow; failure and success; sickness and recovery; food, clothing, shelter; comfort, mental peace, beliefs, convictions, tastes of one party — all these concern most vitally the other, and meet concurrence, care, approval, aid and sympathy. It is as though they are bound by so short a rope that one party cannot make a step without pulling the other." [1] In his description Sorokin may have had in mind the self-contained, medieval, rural society, but it also applies to the Hutterian colony *Gemeinschaft* of today.

The Family

One important component of the colony life is the family. In form it is strictly monogamous. However, the Hutterian family differs somewhat from the family in individualistic society in that many functions, like the assumption of family property and support, are transferred or extended to the colony.

Concerning Hutterian marriage Riedemann says it "is the union of two, in which one taketh the other to care and the second submitteth to obey the first." [2] Hutterian Church regulations do not permit marriage unless both partners are baptized. Since most Hutterians are baptized after the age of nineteen, teen-age marriages are extremely rare. Usually the Hutterian men marry between the ages of twenty and twenty-five, and the women on the average are about one year younger. A survey found that among the Hutterians "the average age at marriage is slightly above that of the United States population." [3]

An inspection of the marriage records of five colonies revealed that though the groom is usually older than his bride, the reverse occurs rather frequently. The accompanying list shows all marriages in the Sunnyside colony in Manitoba over a period of sixteen years, with the exception of one which was a second marriage. Sunnyside was established in 1942. Five men selected their mates from the home colony and nine men selected their mates from other colonies. During the same period (1942–1958) ten brides left Sunnyside colony to live with their husbands at other colonies, for Hutterian society is strictly patrilocal.

Among the Hutterians aged forty-five years and over 99.4 per cent of the men and 98.7 per cent of the women are or have been married.[4] Unmarried life is considered almost abnormal.

At one stage of Hutterian history, about 150 years ago, in Russia, marriage partners were matched by the colony leaders. This practice was not popular, especially among the young people. When a young girl appealed

Groom's Name and Age	Bride's Name, Age, and Colony
David Hofer, 25	Barbara, 21, Rosedale
David Hofer, 22	Rebecca, 22, Riverside
Georg Hofer, 21	Maria, 20, Sunnyside
Joseph Hofer, 27	Anna, 37, Bon Homme
Michael Hofer, 20	Dorothea, 22, Bon Homme
Edward Kleinsasser, 26	Rebecca, 20, Sunnyside
Joseph Kleinsasser, 22	Susanna, 22, Sunnyside
Zack Kleinsasser, 24	Maria, 18, Waldheim
Jacob Waldner, 21	Katherina, 20, Blumengart
Jacob Waldner, 19	Maria, 21, Sunnyside
Joseph Waldner, 25	Marie, 22, Sunnyside
Michael Waldner, 21	Sara, 21, Maxwell
David Wollmann, 22	Maria, 19, New Rosedale
Michael Wollmann, 19	Barbara, 20, Blumengart

to Cornies, a Mennonite administrator in charge of the supervision of "foreign" colonies, the latter advised the Hutterians to discontinue the practice.[5] It was dropped and has not been revived. Parental approval to a marriage is required, and the colony's consent is requested. When one colony woman was asked whether she approved of all the marriages of her children, she shrugged her shoulders and said, "It is really very much like with you people in the outside world. I did not like to see one of my daughters marry into a particular family and had my reasons, but she had her heart set on the man. What can the mother do in such a case but consent in the end?" Since both the marriage partners must be church members in good standing the colony generally raises no objection.

Members of the *Schmiedeleut'* generally marry within that congregation, and members of the *Dariusleut'* and *Lehrerleut'* within their congregations.

Numerous intercolony visits indirectly serve the purpose of acquainting the young people with one another. It is rare for a Hutterian individual or couple to visit another colony alone. Usually the man drives the colony's panel truck, which is remodeled to serve as a small bus, and he takes with him as many members of his family and relatives as can find room in it. It is on such social calls that young people get to know one another.

There are also other ways. A young "cat-man" (an operator of a caterpillar Diesel) at the New Rosedale colony related his courtship: "I was born at the [Old] Rosedale colony and my wife was born at the Iberville colony. The two are only three miles apart. She had relatives at Rosedale and was visiting there off and on. That is how I got to know her. Later she moved with her parents to Rock Lake. Our colony had rented some land out there, and we had to go there to work the land. So I often called at Rock Lake. Later when Rosedale branched out to New Rosedale in 1944 I moved there with my parents. I joined church at the age of twenty-one, and got married when I was twenty-five." [6]

Parallel marriages in which brothers marry sisters, or a brother and sister marry a sister and brother, are very common. One colony's German teacher illustrated this as follows: "My wife came from the James Valley colony. My oldest sister was married to her brother and we visited them and they visited us quite frequently. It was almost inevitable that we should get to know each other. Later we married."

Physical attractiveness is not ignored, but it plays a secondary role. The girl who is good at housework or at managing children and the man who shows initiative at his work are respected by the community; they are considered the most desirable mates. Courtships are generally brief, though prolonged courtships of two and three years are not rare. The wedding invariably takes place at the groom's colony. Formerly, when there were fewer colonies in Manitoba, everybody was welcome at weddings. More recently invitations are confined to the bride's colony, the groom's colony, where the wedding takes place, and the last branch colony of the groom's community. In other words, Hutterian expansion has reduced the primary social contacts between the communities, and a wedding has become almost a family occasion. The preparations for the wedding are entirely in the hands of the groom's community.

The wedding is generally held on a Sunday after the morning service. The ceremony itself differs little from the customary Protestant ritual. The occasion is highlighted by a special meal consisting of many courses. Wine is served freely. In the afternoon there is much visiting and singing. German and English hymns, interspersed with gospel songs, are very popular with the older group. The younger group, boys and girls not yet baptized and thus not formally church members, may slip in an occasional Western or cowboy song. Most folk songs are labeled *Buhlenlieder* (songs of wantonness) because their themes are often romantic or illicit love. For this reason some of them are taboo; the more innocent ones, however, are sung. During the afternoon and evening refreshments are served. These may consist of ice cream, apples, oranges, peanuts, beer, wine, and soft drinks. Soft drinks are reserved for children and for women who prefer them to stronger stimulants.

The groom will wear his best Sunday clothes. The bride may dress a shade more colorfully than colony regulations usually permit. All her clothes are new and of a finer quality than the ordinary. Her dress is of fine cloth, often blue satin, adorned with the traditional *Kleidschürze* (dress-apron). The colony women take great interest in the bride's costume and often help in its making.

In keeping with Hutterian plain living, which bans all jewelry, there is no exchange of rings. The gifts, if any, are homemade articles for use around the house. One common practice is the presentation of a Bible and one of the Hutterian chronicles to every newlywed couple. This is done by the minister on behalf of the church.

There is no honeymoon. The bride moves to her husband's community. However, the informal Hutterian approach to exceptional cases permits a husband to move to his wife's colony on "compassionate" grounds. This happens very rarely. In one instance the bride was the youngest member of the family and found it difficult to be away from her mother. In a more recent case the groom expressed his preference for his wife's colony. He applied for admission and it was granted on condition that his own community release him. When the home colony promptly consented to the transfer the other colony rescinded its ruling because it felt the member could not be very useful.

The Home

The newly married couple is assigned a separate dwelling unit. If there is a housing shortage in the colony the home may be quite small, consisting of a living room and one bedroom. The living room has in it a sturdy table and chairs, one or two cupboards, and shelves. The bedroom has a bed, a bookshelf, and the chests which the young man and his bride received at the age of fifteen from their respective parents. These contain personal articles and clothing. Without exception the Manitoba colony home will also have a sewing machine, which is the wife's dowry from her colony. The conservative Hutterian home will have no wallpaper, no mirrors, no pictures, except possibly calendars, and sometimes no curtains. The unit has no kitchen.

As the family grows larger the couple will move into a home with more rooms. The vacated home may be reassigned to a retired couple or to newlyweds. These arrangements are made by the colony. A typical home of a large family is the single-unit dwelling of the German teacher at the Rock Lake colony at Grosse Isle. The man is also the colony's shoemaker. He has twelve children. The second floor of his home has three very large bedrooms and there is a spacious master bedroom downstairs. For visiting the family gathers in the living room, and there light lunches, prepared in the community kitchen, may be served when outsiders visit.

Describing an Alberta household Edna Kells says: "Furnishings of a Hutterite home are simple and most of the furniture is homemade. A bed with a huge feather tick, feather comforter, wool comforter, and a light spread overall, a table, couch, sewing machine, two or three chairs, a cupboard, perhaps a chest, a shelf with a few simple treasures, and a cradle where needed" make up the interior of the home.[7]

Edna Staebler, also reporting on the Alberta group, wrote:

. . . when a girl is fourteen she is given a chest for clothes, a rolling pin and a spinning wheel. When she's married she gets a sleep couch, a sewing machine, a wall clock, table and chairs and the big books of Hutterian History . . . The hardwood floor shone like a table top. The furniture around the gleaming white walls was the color of wheat, doweled and dovetailed without the use of a nail; flowers were painted on the big feather bed and chests. The counterpane and wall mottoes were embroidered in colorful cross-stitch.

The man demonstrated the sleep bench: like a chest with arms and back, the lid lifted up and the front pulled out making room inside for children to sleep on plaid-covered feather-filled bedding. The wife showed me a chest full of lengths of cloth: black satin brocade for Sunday, gabardine for her man's suits, figured flannelette for underwear and little girls' dresses, bright prints for pillow slips, curtains and bonnets, soft silk for neckerchiefs, dark sprigged goods for her vests, skirts and jackets.

"The styles haven't changed in four hundred years," the man said. "If a woman's not hard on her clothes she can have an awful great many." [8]

In Manitoba there are considerable differences in the appearance of the homes as there are also differences in the appearance of the colonies themselves. A woman visitor who accompanied me to several colonies wrote this account of one of the most attractive communities:

The yard was beautifully laid out. There were willow hedges and trees in whose shade newly painted green garden benches, chairs, and tables invited the colony folk to relax. The summer-shed behind one house was painted and had a mass of well-trimmed wild cucumber vines climbing up its walls. There were flower beds everywhere around the walks, and spacious grass plots. Around the houses were tall dahlias and hollyhocks. On the line were some artistically designed patchwork quilts. Two sisters invited us to their mother's home.

The entry to the home was scrupulously clean. The water was in a pail which was set in a platter of Blue Willow. The door was screened. The windows in the meticulously kept sitting room had white curtains. In the adjoining bedrooms the two double beds had white chenille spreads. Each bed was adorned with a white satin cushion hand-painted with tube colors. There were beautiful chests for garments and linens. Each girl had a footstool covered in needlepoint done by the girls themselves, all in harmonizing colors. There were rows and rows of china and porcelain on the shelves. The teapots were decorated by hand in enamel paints. The whole atmosphere in the home was cheerful and happy.

All this was in sharp contrast to the appearance of a household in a neighboring colony which the same visitor described as follows:

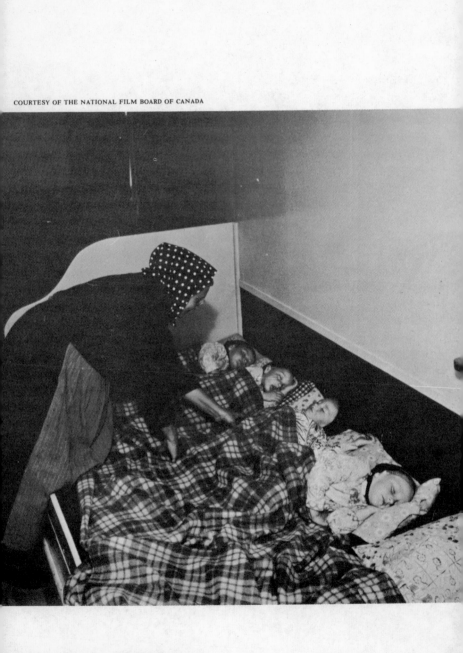

COURTESY OF THE NATIONAL FILM BOARD OF CANADA

COURTESY OF THE NATIONAL FILM BOARD OF CANADA

I was rather shocked at the interior of Sara's [the name is fictitious] home which was such a contrast to the other Hutterian homes I had visited. Right in the entry there were stacked some dirty dishes in close proximity to a water pail with a mug dangling at its edge. The floor of the living room was grimy and dull-looking from careless washings. On the floor under a chiffonier of a kind stood a basin containing slabs of white cake. There were several untidy children around, as well as a number of somewhat unkempt teen-age girls.

Sara was sewing her sons some trousers out of some fine black wool material. They were Sunday garments. She used an electric sewing machine. Each family at this colony had one. The trousers had no cuffs and were hemmed by machine. Sara told me that the women made their own foundation garments, and that this was a general practice at all the colonies.

While this account depicts two extremes it is fair to say that the second description is further from being that of a typical household. The interior of most homes is austere but spotlessly clean.

Parents and Children

The Hutterian family relationship is generally excellent. Lee Emerson Deets states that there are no family quarrels.[9] On two or three occasions I witnessed differences of opinion between man and wife, but these were discussed and then the subject was dropped.

The families are very large, averaging nine or ten children. The chronological order of a completed family may be illustrated with the David Hofer family of the Bloomfield colony, at Westbourne, Manitoba. The husband is fifty-five years of age and the wife is forty-eight. The names and ages of the thirteen children are: Samuel, 27; Jonathan, 25; Anna, 24; Rebecca, 22; Marie, 20; Peter, 17; Joseph, 15; Darius, 13; John, 12; Michael, 10; Timothy, 7; Sara, 6; and Karl, 3. All the children are still unmarried.[10] Perhaps one reason for some late marriages among the Hutterians is the happy and devoted relationship under the parental roof.

In early Hutterian times mothers took their infants to special nurseries, where colony women took care of them (see Bunin's description in Chapter II). The infant nurseries were maintained partly for practical reasons and partly, as one Hutterian explained it to me, to prevent excessive parental care. These nurseries were discontinued before the Hutterians came to America. Today parental control over children is strong. While the influence of the numerous playmates and the kindergarten is also strong, it does not supersede the influence of the home. Hutterians love their children but rarely suffer from the inhibiting fears of modern parents that they may "scar the child's psyche" or create "a feeling of rejection" in the child. Eaton bluntly states, "Permissiveness in child rearing is not a Hutterite virtue; it is regarded as a vice," [11] and quotes from Ehrenpreis's *Ein Sendbrief*, the 1652 book which is still used as a primer in every Hutterian home. The passage reads:

Just as iron tends to rust and as the soil will nourish weeds, unless it is kept clean by continuous care, so have children of men a strong inclination towards injustices, desires, and lusts; especially when children are together with the children of the world and daily hear and see their bad examples. In consequence they desire nothing but dancing, playing and all sorts of frivolities, till they have such longing for it, that you cannot stop them any more from growing up in it . . . Now it has been revealed that many parents are by nature too soft with their children and have not the strength to keep them away from evil. So we have a thousand good reasons why we should live separated from the world in a Christian community. How much misery is prevented in this way. For do we not hear it often said: How honest and respectable are these people; but look what godless children they have brought up . . . Sometimes father and mother have died long ago and nothing is left of their earthly remains, but their bad reputation still lives among the people who complain that they once neglected to discipline their children and brought them up disgracefully.

When a number of teachers in public schools assigned the composition topic "What I Would Like to Be When I Grow Up," almost all the Hutterian youngsters indicated in their essays that their ideals were their fathers and mothers and their respective occupations.[12] This parental attachment is carried on through life, and when one of the parents dies the survivor will usually move into the home of one of the children. Remarriages are rare, especially among women. One source states that only 5 per cent of the widowed women marry a second time. The same source maintains that there is only one divorce on record for the Hutterians of North America.[13]

Death

Death is accepted by the Hutterians as the normal course of nature. It is the transition between this life and life eternal. All believers will be assembled in heaven, but on the day of judgment, as one minister put it, "God will expect more from a Hutterian because he has been taught to live more closely in the ways of Jesus." Excessive grief is regarded as showing a lack of faith in God's ways to man, for "The Lord gave, and the Lord has taken away; blessed be the name of the Lord."

At the recent death of a young girl a group gathered in the home of the parents and prayed and comforted them. Then the women prepared the body and put it on ice. The carpenter took the measurements and made a plain coffin. The farm foreman sent two boys out to the burial plot, which was not far away from the colony, to dig the grave. The funeral, two days later, was simple and dignified. The community and close relatives from other colonies gathered for a two-hour service. One hymn of many verses was sung and the text of the service was "So teach us to number our days that we may apply our hearts unto wisdom."

The care of the *Totengarten* (cemetery; literally, "the garden of the dead") is not assigned to anyone in the community. Such is the informal nature of the organization that the colony can usually rely on one of the older women to take charge of it. Generally the cemetery is well kept, with wooden markers or concrete slabs designating the final resting places. At one colony the *Totengarten* was a profusion of lilies, and the oval mounds were bordered by whitewashed bricks. The farm foreman explained that there was no particular reason for the shape of the mounds. The teen-age girls, on their own initiative, had assumed the care of the cemetery and "they liked the graves that way."

The tombstones are made by the women. Again this is not a colony-assigned task. A woman who has lost a son, or husband, or father may decide that the place should have a marker. One or two men, usually of the immediate family, will help her with the more strenuous work. At the Crystal Spring colony I was taken by an elderly widow to a small room where she was working on two tombstones, one for her husband and the other for her father-in-law. Her sons had made the molds and she had poured the concrete. She was then engaged in painting in the chiseled lettering.

Riverside colony has a *Totengarten* which with its shrubs and flowers, all surrounded by a high hedge, looks like a little park. Here one concrete slab carries these words:

> I am distressed for thee. Very pleasant hast thou
> been unto me; thy love to me was wonderful.
>
> Barbara.[14]

The story behind this Scripture passage (2 Samuel 1:26) was that twenty years ago an accident proved fatal to one Peter Waldner, and his young bride scratched these words into stone. The minister mildly disapproved of them because they showed too much attachment to things temporal. Barbara, employed in the kitchen and known affectionately by the whole colony as *Barabäsle*, has not remarried.

Hutterian Names

The average number of families per colony is seventeen. Spring Valley, near Brandon, has nine families. The Elie colony of Rosedale, which has reached its population optimum, has twenty-six. Lakeside colony, at Headingly, has a typical patronymic pattern: Hofer, 7; Wipf, 5; Wollmann, 2; Gross, 2; Waldner, 1. The patronymic makeup of a colony is not necessarily indicative of the blood relationships of its members. Bearers of the same name may have a common ancestor generations back but be otherwise unrelated.

The old Hutterian patronyms are all represented in Manitoba. The most common surnames are Waldner, Hofer, Wollmann, Maendel, and Kleinsasser. These are followed by Gross, Wipf, Wurz, Stahl, Glanzer, Tschetter, and Walter. Least common are Dekker, Entz, and Knels. While these fifteen names, found in the United States and Canada, exhaust the old Hutterian patronyms, their frequency in different areas varies.[15] A few new family names are found in Manitoba, the result of the admission of converts: Baer, Dorn, Georg, Randle, and Suess.

A check of six school registers indicated that the most popular given names are those found in the Bible. The eleven most common names for boys are Joseph, Jacob, Samuel, John, David, Paul, Andrew, Peter, Michael, Zacharias (Zack), and Joshua, in that order. The eleven most common names for girls are Susanna, Maria, Katharina, Anna, Sara, Rebecca, Elisabeth, Barbara, Margaret, Rachel, and Dorothea. However, it is not mandatory for parents to select Biblical names for their infants, as some of the names for girls just mentioned prove. School and church registers show that there always has been a liberal sprinkling of other names.

Communal Interdependence

The Hutterian family unit is patriarchal in form, but it is not authoritarian in practice. Family life is characterized by an intimate companionship in which the husband, the wife, and the children play their designated roles. As one of the main pillars of the *Gemeinschaft* the Hutterian family appears unusually stable and functional.

Moreover, the community of blood, the intimate familial relationship within the entire Hutterian group, is so strong that children and adults address all grown-ups as *Vetter* or *Base*, the German terms for male and female cousins. Every Hutterian knows that *der Samuelvetter* at Sturgeon Creek is Reverend Samuel Kleinsasser, and that *der Petervetter* is Elder Peter Hofer of James Valley colony.[16] In the wider sense and in the sense of family functions a colony constitutes almost a family. (Indeed, the English Quakers of the seventeenth century called the *Bruderhof* colonies "Hutterisch families." [17]) Though the Hutterian family, made up of parents and children, is a distinct institution, the communal meals, where the men and women eat a separate tables and the children in separate dining rooms, are only one indication of the extent to which family functions are transferred to the colony.

The Hutterian colony in practice assumes the responsibilities of an extended family. It provides its members with complete economic security. Furthermore, it extends this security to a member's relatives even if they do not belong to the Church. This is clearly outlined in their "Rules as to Community of Property":

The members of a congregation or community shall be entitled to and have their husbands, wives and children who are not members thereof, reside with them, and be supported, maintained, instructed and educated by that congregation or community, according to the rules, regulations and requirements of that congregation or community, during the time and so long as they obey, abide by and conform to the rules, regulations, instructions and requirements of that congregation or community.[18]

The solicitous care of the community extends over the entire life span of its members. The woman expecting a child is excused from all strenuous work. Indeed, she is permitted to set her own schedule. She is attended by the colony midwife and by the physician of the nearest town. Some colonies in the Elie district of Manitoba have no midwife, but use the services of Joseph Gross, a chiropractor, and his wife of Iberville colony. After the birth of the child the mother is again excused from all work for a period of four to six weeks. She is treated as a colony patient and takes her meals at home. A nurse, a position sometimes assigned to the midwife but as a distinct charge, will see that she gets the proper diet.

An older woman usually has daughters who will look after the home and the laundry during any illnesses. A younger woman may have sisters, her mother, or an aunt to take care of the household duties. If the patient's original home was some other colony, one of her close relatives, perhaps the mother or a sister, may come over for an indefinite period.

Up to the age of two and a half the Hutterian children remain at home, spending much of their time playing outside. Usually their mothers or their older sisters, called "baby-minders," take care of them and bring their food to the house. When visitors arrive these girls usually volunteer to act as guides. Newspaperwoman Edna Staebler found them most communicative, and gave this description of them: "Dressed like the grownups in long skirts and plaid aprons, their hair severely drawn under tight bonnets and white-dotted black kerchiefs, the baby-minders looked as if they were playing mother." [19]

The next three years are spent in the kindergarten, known in the colony as the *kleine Schul'*, where an older woman and her assistants are in charge. The children have their meals there, and, like their elders, the rows of little men and women recite a long prayer before and after each meal.

The transition from childhood to adulthood is gradual. The child is never out of reach of the colony influence. At home, at the kindergarten, at school, at church, in the dining room, at work or play, the colony atmosphere envelops him. However, such is the nature of this conditioning process that it makes anything but robots out of the children. Reporting on Hutterian teen-agers, Bertha Clark wrote: "They are extremely acute observers, are independent in the conclusions they arrive at, and are fluent and sensible in conversation, discussing matters with the sobriety and earnestness of adults." [20] Young people shoulder much of the work, but the older men and women assume the responsibility and provide the guidance. One minister pointed out that Christ was thirty years of age before he began his life's important task, and that young people should not be pushed into responsible positions too early: *Sie müssen reifen wie die Frucht am Baum* (They have to ripen like the fruit on a tree). As the young Hutterian grows up he almost invariably has a strong attachment to his family and loyalty to the colony and community ideal.

The colony assumes all financial obligations, and the parents are free to enjoy their familial bliss. Their state is literally utopian, for it was Thomas More who wrote: "For what can be more rich than to live joyfully and tranquilly without any worry, not fearful for his own livelihood, nor vexed and troubled with his wife's importunate complaints, not dreading poverty to his sons, nor anxious about his daughter's dowry? But instead to be secure about the livelihood and happiness of their wives, children, grandchildren, and their posterity which they handsomely assume will be a long time." [21]

Perhaps the greatest privileges in the colony are enjoyed by its senior members. The informal retirement age is around forty-five, and from then on the amount of work Hutterians do is left entirely to them. Yet most of them easily earn their keep. I repeatedly encountered men seventy-five years and over at some useful occupation, and women of sixty still in full charge of the kindergarten, or some other work. At New Rosedale the oldest man of the colony spent several hours every day candling and crating eggs at the poultry house. There was no compulsion; he left his work whenever he felt the urge to leave. At one of the colonies near Headingly a man well over eighty had a comfortable chair in the carpenter's shop. He had been the community's head carpenter before his retirement, and the position was now held by his son. But the old man was still repairing furniture, including some chairs brought in by a neighboring farmer at the time of my visit. Similarly the older women may be seen helping in the kitchen, or at their knitting and mending, or sewing for their grandchildren.

A visit to an old widower who occupied one spacious room in his son's house revealed the usual household furniture: table, chairs, bed, cupboard, shelves, and washstand. The guest and host had barely sat down when a granddaughter came with fresh water and towels and remained available to run errands. After the old man and his guest had washed up, the former went to the cupboard for some fruit and a bottle of homemade wine. Such extras are rationed out to every family every week or month, depending on the perishable nature of the article. As the old man set the heavy tumblers on the table and poured the wine he said: "Sometimes when I am by myself I think of the old people in the world. They spend their time in loneliness in old folks' homes and in poorhouses, away from their children and from their work. Then I am thankful that I live in a colony."

Leisure and Recreation

Communal life provides considerable leisure for its members. "I work a lot harder here than I ever did on the colony," said Samuel Kleinsasser of Winnipeg, one of those who have left the colony. The most common form of recreation enjoyed by young and old is visiting. At the end of a day's work the people visit each other at the colony. Since doors are never locked, and the practice of knocking is not observed, visitors walk in and out as if they were at home.

Usually intercolony visits take place on Sundays. The buslike panel truck may take its passengers to any colony in Manitoba. Several families may go for an extended trip to South Dakota or Alberta. The mothers of small children, knowing that these are in good hands at the colony, do not hesitate to leave them at home. These vacation trips may last up to three weeks.

When visiting another colony the men sit in groups and talk shop. Their long discussions are interrupted by walks to the new "milking parlor," which is critically inspected, or to the hog barns, where the "hog-boss" may have experimented with a new insecticide. Information is exchanged on feeding practices, use of new machines and techniques, marketing of livestock, and on a host of other subjects. The women will be similarly occupied. The Hutterians have retained one characteristic of the southern Germans: they are good conversationalists. Everywhere there is a good measure of joking and teasing.

Reading is a popular pastime. Hutterians publish no periodicals or newspapers of their own, but they subscribe to a few German Mennonite newspapers, and these are passed from home to home, indeed sometimes from colony to colony. Of these the *Mennonitische Rundschau*, published in Winnipeg, is the most popular. Most colonies in Manitoba take either the *Winnipeg Free Press* or the *Winnipeg Tribune*. Some colonies subscribe to them, others buy these dailies in Winnipeg and bring them home. The *Prairie Farmer* and the local town paper are found at many of the communities. The *Red River Echo* in Altona even has a contributor at the Blumengart colony. In isolated cases one may find *Reader's Digest*, *Time*, or *Newsweek*. The various enterprise heads subscribe to poultry, hog, cattle, and farm reviews and magazines. Occasionally a Hutterian may purchase a book, in English or in German. Many adults make extensive use of the public school library. The books written by Hutterians, the old chronicles, the hymnary, and the Bible are of course in constant use.

Cameras, television, radios, musical instruments and dancing, and playing cards are not permitted. The taking of pictures is not only regarded as a sign of vanity but also as a violation of the Biblical injunction "Thou shalt not make unto thee any graven image." The ban on radios and television sets was explained by Rev. Jacob Maendel, of New Rosedale colony: "As soon as you permit them you are no longer master of your own home. You invite alien and un-Christian influences into your living room."

Boys and girls have few recreational outlets; they may meet at one of the homes and sing. Girls especially have a large repertoire of religious songs. Boys still not baptized may compromise their conscience and sing Western or cowboy songs to the accompaniment of a mouth organ. Some may even have a radio hidden in their room. These are exceptions, however. A number of public school teachers and several young men who had left the colony maintained, when interviewed, that baptized members rarely violated colony regulations.

Though the recreational outlets are few, the atmosphere in a Hutterian colony has little in common with the stern austerity we associate with the Puritan commonwealth. A closer analogy in many ways would be the simple life and pleasures of Thomas Hardy's heath dwellers. On one occasion I even saw a re-enactment of the haircutting scene. It was a beautiful midsummer Sunday morning. All week the men had worked on the fields. The junior minister had left on a trip, and the senior minister suddenly fell ill. Since Hutterians do not readily delegate to unordained men the right to read the sermon, there was no church service in the colony. Instead there was the tonsorial harvest. In about a third of the homes men and boys gathered and had their hair cut. One young Hutterian commented critically, "About one out of every three men is a barber, but some don't make a good job, and that's for sure."

One may summarize and describe the fabric of the Hutterian colony life, the pattern that prescribes the individual's activities at work or at play, his functions in the family and in the community, as totalistic. Beginning with the family, every part, every office, every activity carries with it the religion-sanctioned approval or disapproval of the *Gemeinschaft*, the community. Once this totalistic pattern is accepted, however, the colony regulations become quite elastic and flexible, permitting adjustments and interpretations which in turn allow considerable freedom to the individual.

VII

THE COMMUNAL ECONOMY AND
COLONY DIVISION

THE OLD, slowly vanishing European rural communities
generally were tightly knit, cohesive social and economic entities in which
"there were no loose, disorderly ends," as Handlin remarks. Modern commercial industrialism has contributed to the disintegration of such communities, and has in a sense urbanized all sectors of society. The Hutterian
colony, on the other hand, has preserved the self-sufficient social and economic independence of the Old World rural community. In its setting and
operation Hutterian communal life follows a pattern which contrasts
fundamentally with the pattern of society that surrounds it. In Canada
perhaps the closest parallel to the Hutterian outlook can be found in the
rural parishes of Quebec.[1]

Agriculture as a Way of Life

Agriculture to the Hutterians is more than an occupation, a way of making a living; it is a way of life sanctioned and indeed sanctified by religion.
This way of life has little in common with commercial farming, in which
work is regarded as a means to the end of money or profit. To the Hutterians work itself is a purposeful ingredient of life, and idleness is almost
sinful: *Müssiggang ist aller Laster Anfang.* Adam worked in the Garden
of Eden. The curse was not the introduction of toil but its consequences
of greed and avarice. The whole Hutterian philosophy of work is rooted
in this medieval school of thought. "Dig and sow that you may have where-

with to eat and drink and be clothed, for where sufficience is, there is stability, and where stability is, there is religion." [2]

This Hutterian attitude is not the consequence of a slavish reverence for the past. Instead, the Hutterian dedication to farm life is motivated by a conviction that for them this way of life is most pleasing in the eyes of God. As a result they have no alternative. "Agriculture," says a Canadian writer, "is fundamental to the Hutterian way of life: to deprive them of the right to buy land would eventually force them to migrate." [3] This Hutterian stand has a tradition of centuries behind it. Over four hundred years ago Riedemann wrote:

We allow none of our number to do the work of a tradesman or merchant, since this is sinful business; as the wise man saith, "It is almost impossible for a merchant or trader to keep himself from sin. And as a nail sticketh fast between door and hinge, so doth sin stick close between buying and selling." Therefore do we allow no one to buy to sell again, as merchants and traders do. But to buy what is necessary for the needs of one's house or craft, to use it and then to sell what one by means of his craft hath made therefrom, we consider to be right and not wrong.

This only we regard as wrong: when one buyeth ware and selleth the same again even as he bought it, taking to himself profit, making the ware dearer thereby for the poor, taking bread from their very mouths and thus making the poor man nothing but the bondman of the rich. Paul saith likewise, "Let him who defrauded, defraud no more." . . .

Neither do we allow any of our number to be a public innkeeper serving wine or beer, since this goeth with all that is unchaste, ungodly and decadent, and drunken and good-for-nothing fellows gather there together to carry out their headstrong wills. This they must permit, and listen to their blasphemy. For this reason we believe not that it is something that one who feareth God may do; namely for the sake of money listen to such blasphemy, allow it, and make themselves partakers of their sins. . . .

But this we do, and regard it as doing right: if one cometh over the pasture land and can go no farther, and cometh upon one of our brothers, he receiveth him and lodgeth him, serveth him and doeth him all the good he can; but not for money, but freely, for nothing. For we find that thus also did the saints, and that they were given to hospitality. [4]

Thus barred from other occupations, the Hutterians confine their pursuits to farming. Furthermore, a widely diversified agriculture enables them to make use of their manpower in such a way that even children and old people become valuable economic assets. This is in sharp contrast to our individualistic urban and even rural society where the aged and the children are becoming increasingly an economic liability. [5]

The Farm Enterprises

The colony farm provides the basis for the communal economy. On it is the *Bruderhof*, a cluster-village type of settlement which takes up several acres, and around it are the various enterprises, each an integrated component of the communal economy.

The Colony Farm. The productivity of any farm economy is determined by the factors of labor, capital, and land. The Hutterian communities have a fair supply of labor, reasonable assets and cash income, but they generally lack sufficient land. The average Manitoba colony owns less land but has a larger population than the average Alberta colony. The average colony in Manitoba has a population of about 120 and owns about 4000 acres of land. In Alberta the average colony has a population of 100 and farms about 6000 acres of land. In addition a number of Alberta and five Manitoba colonies lease land, in some instances on Indian reservations.

Invariably the colonies find it difficult to buy large parcels of land. They buy some land to establish the colony and then make additional purchases as land comes up for sale. The expansion of Waldheim colony in Manitoba may be regarded as typical in this. The colony began with fourteen families and 1200 acres of land. Subsequently it bought 240 acres in 1936, 320 acres in 1937, 240 acres in 1940, 560 acres in 1942, and 240 acres in 1943. It is evident that as the population of a colony increases and its acreage remains constant or does not increase in proportion, the law of diminishing returns becomes operative. This in turn forces a colony to intensify its farm diversification until more land can be found.

Hutterians prefer to settle near a stream or a creek. This assures them of a water supply for their geese, ducks, and stock but also means that much of the land includes waste, pasture, and hayland. On the whole Hutterian farm practices do not differ materially from those of their farm neighbors. However, little wheat is seeded, and practically no row crops are planted except potatoes. Rather the emphasis is on feed grains and fodder crops. Since the limited colony acreage generally does not produce enough grain and fodder to meet the requirements of the colony's enterprises, additional grain is often bought from the farmers in the district. One consequence of their farm diversification is that the Hutterians rarely have marketing problems with surplus grains. Government quotas on grain shipment hardly affect them.

For their farm operations Hutterians use the most modern implements and machinery available. Outsiders sometimes claim that Hutterians over-capitalize in farm machinery. It has been suggested that this indulgence in purchasing new machinery provided an emotional outlet for them. Though the Hutterians take great pride in their modern farm equipment, the facts demonstrate that here they observe sound business practices. The average value of machinery invested per crop acre in all of Manitoba for 1956 was $29.18. The figure varies of course from district to district: for the Altona area it was $33.21; for the Minnedosa area, $27.09; and for the Carman area, $22.29.[6] The average value of machinery invested per crop acre for 1956 on the Hutterian colonies, however, was between $9 and $10. At the same time their crop yield per acre approximated that of the neighboring farmers.

There are a number of reasons for this great difference in machinery investment. One reason is that the Hutterians do not plant row crops, which account at least partly for the heavy investment in farm implements in the Altona area. Another reason is the Hutterian practice of buying a large number of machines or tractors at one time. This enables them to bargain for considerable discounts. Sometimes used machines are bought and repaired at the colony's blacksmith shop at little cost to the colony. A substantial saving is also gained by doing practically all the repair work at the colony. More important, modern farm technology favors the larger farm unit. The steep decline of the number of family farms on the prairie provinces may be attributed at least partly to the almost prohibitive cost of farm machinery.[7] It is logical that the consolidated and compact community farm operated by the Hutterians makes a more economical use of machinery possible.

A number of factors combine to make it extremely difficult to present a clear composite picture of the economic status of the Hutterian communities compared with individual farm enterprises.[8] While the average total acreage per family in Manitoba stands at 450, and goes down to 288 acres per family in the most intensive farming area in the province, the Altona district,[9] the Hutterians own only 240 acres per family. Since their families are very large the Hutterian per capita acreage is very low, less than thirty-five. Furthermore, no two colonies are alike. Some colonies farm on sandy, marginal land in eastern Manitoba, others, west of Elie, have land in the better farming areas of the province. Some colonies, and this depends partly on management, have considerable assets, extending interest-free loans to other colonies; other colonies, again, operate on an extremely small margin. On the whole, however, the credit of the Hutterian communities at the banks and with feed companies is better than that of the average individual farmer. The prospective creditors realize that the stability of the colony is much greater than that of individual operators, where a sudden death or illness may threaten the continued operation of the farm. Moreover, though each colony functions as an autonomous economic unit the colonies would not stand idly by if any one of them were in serious financial difficulties.

As mentioned earlier the colony farm is the direct responsibility of the farm foreman, known by outsiders as the "farm-boss." He, even more than the other heads of the various colony enterprises, must show considerable ability in his field before he is elected to his post. The farm foreman and the enterprise heads have years of apprenticeship behind them; they also exchange information and experiences with their counterparts at other colonies, and periodically attend courses provided for farmers and poultry and livestock raisers by the University of Manitoba. They also make extensive use of farm bulletins issued by provincial and federal departments of agriculture.

On the whole the colony men in charge of the enterprises show initiative and even a readiness to experiment. Some years ago a staff member of the Department of Agriculture of the University of Manitoba on a visit to the United States observed that an increasing number of midwest farmers grew canary seeds. He returned to Manitoba and after a study concluded that the province had the necessary climatic conditions and the market to make canary seed growing possible. Then he discovered that the Blumengart colony at Plum Coulee already had fifty acres of this crop.

Again, the main purpose of the colony farm is not to provide cash income but to sustain the other colony enterprises. The total cash income of one average colony in 1960 as the result of sales in grain, seeds, and potatoes was $9120.59.

Livestock. All the farm enterprises vary in size from colony to colony. However, generally the hog industry brings in the highest cash income. In the colony just cited it grossed $51,384.93 in 1960. The average community may have eighty brood sows producing up to three litters in fourteen months. In feeding and the cleaning of barns automation has largely replaced manual labor. A representative of a Winnipeg feed firm maintained when interviewed that the colony hog industry was managed on the most scientific lines and that hog production was high. Hutterian hog-men, like their farm foremen, will not only introduce the newest methods but sometimes will experiment. At New Rosedale colony the hog-man conducted an experiment, apparently with success, with a new insecticide.

At one time the Hutterians kept "some of the finest stock," [10] but since their settlement in Canada emphasis on this enterprise has been downgraded for unknown reasons. Some colonies keep as few as forty-five cows, others as many as two hundred. In addition there are steers and heifers for the market. Cash income for these at the same average colony in 1960 was $2801.45. Livestock is generally marketed in Winnipeg. Many Manitoba colonies have milking parlors, huge structures with plastic skylights. The milking parlors, which like all other colony buildings are erected by their own carpenters, permit the cows to roam around freely. Most colonies have milking machines.

Many colonies use hay balers, but some have discarded them. "Baled hay is inferior in quality and too costly," explained Sam Maendel, the *Viehwirt* (cattle-man) at one of the colonies. Now they have stackers that stack the hay, and in winter bulldozers are used to push the haystacks to the feeding places.

The raising of sheep, formerly an important industry in every colony, useful for the mutton and especially the wool, has been discontinued in all but one of the colonies. The Hutterians feel that the initial cost of land and the high taxes on it make sheep raising unprofitable. Wool is bought in bulk in the city for making clothing.

Horses are no longer used; they have been replaced by mechanical power. A few are kept for winter travel and as riding horses for the boys.

Poultry. Great attention is given to poultry raising. Most colonies have chicken flocks of 4500 to 6000 birds. The chicken houses are usually very modern, with roll-out nests and automatic feeding. Some colonies have won prizes for their eggs at the Toronto Canadian National Exhibition. The cash income at an average colony for chickens and eggs amounts to about $3000.

The colonies also keep ducks and geese. One of the larger colonies had an income of $16,391.32 from its ducks and geese, and in addition sold $4320 worth of feathers. Down is used extensively for feather ticks sewn by the colony women. Hutterians are very fond of fowl and a great number of them are consumed at the colony, especially on Sundays and holidays. A colony's financial statement of course does not include as income the eggs and meat used by the communal kitchen.

To illustrate the management of an enterprise the turkey industry may serve as an example. All Manitoba colonies have introduced it, though the flocks vary in size; in 1957 the Crystal Spring colony had 9000 birds, Rosedale had 15,000 birds, and New Rosedale had 27,000 birds. The turkeys at the New Rosedale colony were distributed in three compounds. Fred Maendel, the turkey foreman, preferred to import turkey eggs from California. "They have a longer green season out there, and the result is that the fertility of their eggs is about 50 per cent higher than ours," he explained. "We have all the eggs shipped by air. Even at this, if refrigeration is not carefully maintained the eggs will be spoiled. Transportation decreases fertility by about 20 per cent," continued Maendel. "However, that still makes the California eggs superior to the eggs produced in Canada, especially since they are inoculated against more diseases." The colony paid thirty-four cents per egg, plus duty. The birds are scientifically fed on a protein pellet diet.

Many colonies have their own eviscerating plants, and in the fall the birds are prepared for the market. A community killing plant, operating in an assembly line manner with the suspended carcasses moving from rails, has an output of about a thousand birds a day. The work is demanding and the colony men and younger women are heartily pleased when the killing season ends. Here as in the other enterprises all the work is done by the colony people; no outside help is hired.

The New Rosedale colony holds membership in the Turkey Breeders' Association, to which it contributes on a pro rata basis. The gross income from the turkey enterprise at this colony was several hundred thousand dollars.

Other Enterprises. To the major community enterprises already listed must be added a host of other activities that either effect a saving for the colony by supplying its needs or produce a cash income. The blacksmith's shop and the carpenter's shop may also do repair work or custom construction for neighbors. All such earnings are deposited with the steward, who keeps the colony books. In the winter the older men sometimes bind brooms for colony use. Overproduction in such minor side industries is marketed in neighboring towns.

Within the given frame there is indeed no limit to colony specialization. For many years the Blumengart colony blacksmith, who had taken courses in dentistry, was also the community dentist and many outsiders used his services. Similarly, Joseph Gross, the Hutterian chiropractor at the Iberville colony, known for miles around as Doctor Gross, has an income that would compare favorably with that of a rural medical practitioner. On Saturdays he keeps office hours in Portage la Prairie. When more remote colonies use his services and *der Josephvetter* must visit them, they pay the Iberville colony $10. When I visited the Iberville colony I saw some cars in front of Gross's bungalow. A young woman in one of the cars explained that she did not go to see Gross, but her father "swears by him." "Most people think he is very good," she concluded. All the earnings are of course turned over to the colony steward, and, said Gross, "I would not have it otherwise."

Years ago the milling industry was an important communal enterprise, and much custom milling was done for neighbors as well.[11] But the industry could not compete with modern mills and today the colonies buy their flour.

The annual operating expenses of an average colony may total around $200,000. Again, the accounts vary from colony to colony, depending on the diversity of the enterprises, the size of the community, and other factors. The chief items of expense are feed concentrates (which may amount to over $50,000); the purchase of young livestock and poults and chicks; seed and feed grains; gas and oil; lumber, cement, and gravel; debt retirement and taxes; machinery, repairs, licenses; doctors, hospitalization, medicine, and glasses; groceries, dry goods, and hardware; fertilizer; clothing; and meals at restaurants and cafés. Lesser items include telephone, electricity, propane, bee equipment, insurance, and fuel. A further breakdown of these entries sometimes throws an interesting sidelight on colony life. On one account under dry goods is listed the item "131 fur caps." Under machinery another account lists, besides diesels, tractors, meat stuffers, and clothes wringers, "five sewing machines, used." All colony accounts also list *Zehrgeld*, a small weekly allowance in cash to every adult and child.

Practically all the gas, oil, and machinery used by the Hutterians is bought in the nearest towns or villages.[12] Groceries are also usually bought locally, but dry goods are purchased in bulk in Winnipeg. An inspection of the Hutterian accounts also indicated that colonies close to Winnipeg rarely used local doctors but went to the city instead. Colonies farther away from Winnipeg patronized local doctors, drugstores, and hospitals. Small items or services are generally paid for in cash; larger accounts are paid by the colony steward, usually by check. Feed companies extend substantial credit to their colony customers in spring and are paid in the fall when poultry and livestock are marketed.

The colonies also have a detailed internal accounting system. Every year the colony ministers and stewards from all the *Bruderhöfe* meet in conference and plan how many shirts, trousers, jackets, shoes, dresses, aprons, and other items of wearing apparel should be allotted to each colony member. Each colony then credits every adult and child with these items, but should he not require some of them because he has enough shirts or shoes from previous years he could ask for other articles of which he is in need, or he could even ask for an equivalent in cash. This money he would be free to spend on clothing but only of a cut and color that would not violate colony regulations.

Medical expenses, glasses, meals eaten in restaurants in town when on colony or personal business, and similar items are paid for by the colony. Thus, for example, a man taking a truckload of egg crates to the city would ask the steward for five or ten dollars, and would later account for how the money was spent. If the man incurs unexpected expenses, like a police ticket for illegal parking, he will be required to explain the irregularity. The colony council may accept the explanation or may find the member guilty of neglect and bar him from going to town for a time.

Woman's Work: Making Clothes

The Hutterian woman's contribution to the self-sufficiency of the colony economy is considerable. Practically every Hutterian wife and many of the girls have sewing machines. Purchases of cloth for the colony are made from wholesalers. Responsible women like the *Küchenfrau* (the head cook) and the *Zuschneiderin* (the woman in charge of distribution of cloth) make the purchases after consulting the colony women as to their preference in type of material.

Each woman sews for her family. All women's clothes and all underclothes are homemade, and so are most of the men's shirts. Men's suits too are made at home after a plain pattern. Buttons for shirts and blouses are bought, but dresses and men's suits are fastened with hooks and eyes made by the men. At Lakeside colony the minister makes them. While it is mandatory for Manitoba Hutterians to use hooks and eyes on their suits, the rule has been relaxed in many colonies farther west.

Most households have motor-operated spinning wheels. The wool is bought and then spun at home. Even girls nine and ten years old have little metal pails in which they carry the socks which they are knitting.

Woman's Work: The Kitchen Economy

The colony women take great pride in their vegetable garden, which invariably covers many acres. While the men cultivate the garden and do the insect spraying, the women do the planning, the planting and seeding, the hoeing and the "harvesting." Sometimes the garden may be some distance away from the colony and the women are taken there in a canopied wagon known by the Hutterians as the *Weiberwagen*. In case of rain or excessive sun the women can take shelter under the canopy.

Some of the food, like breakfast cereals, is bought. Other food items, like meats, sausages, canned fruit or even vegetables, are bought occasionally. Bread is baked at the colony and is bought only in emergencies. Flour is bought wholesale in hundred-pound bags, and each baking requires about a bag of flour. The kitchens are equipped with electric automatic mixers and automatic ovens. Bread is baked three times a week.

The meals are wholesome and well balanced. Breakfast usually consists of toast and one of the following: cornflakes, pancakes, eggs, or porridge. The choice of milk or coffee or tea is customary at every meal. Dinner, the main meal of the day, is served at 11:30 A.M. Supper is a lighter meal usually made up of cold meats and fried potatoes. Between dinner and supper a snack consisting of a beverage and pastry is served.

The meals vary from colony to colony, but the following weekly dinner menu for one colony of 126 adults and children may be regarded as typical for all colonies:

Monday: Soup; *Knödel* (dumplings) and homemade sausage (made of equal parts of beef and pork); gelatin pudding (40 packages).

Tuesday: Borsch (made of 40 pounds of beef, pork, or mutton, the equivalent of 12 tins of tomato juice, 12 to 14 heads of cabbage, "a bit of onion and lots of cream"); cake, cookies, fresh or canned fruit.

Wednesday: Eiernudeln (egg noodles, with dough made of 120 eggs, flour, and water rolled out thin, cut very wide with cutting machine); roast beef; choice of pie (about 40 pies).

Thursday: Soup; fried potatoes or pureed beans; sausages or bacon; fresh or canned fruit.

Friday: Grüne Bohnensuppe (green bean soup; ingredients: 5 pails of beans, fine-cut, 1½ pails of potatoes, 3 hams, 4 gallons of cream added to water); choice of pie.

Saturday: Soup; mashed potatoes, fried onions, and sausages; fresh-baked buns or cinnamon rolls.

Sunday: Noodle soup; roast beef or roast duck, chicken or other fowl (35 large ducks or 40 smaller ones; ducks are first boiled until tender, then roasted in oven in baking pans until browned), served with peas, beans, or cooked beets, and *Süsskraut* (sweet cabbage: 4 heads of cabbage, fine-cut, cooked till tender, a *Fäustel Salz*, and sauce made of lard and flour, cooked until browned, sugar added and mixed with cabbage); wine served with the meal; fresh or canned fruit, or choice of pie.

From this weekly menu, which also invariably includes vegetables, it can be seen that the can opener and the grocery store are much less used by the Hutterian kitchen economy than by the best home economists of individual households. Because of the simple table settings there is also a corresponding saving in cutlery, dishes, kitchen utensils, dishwashing soaps, and manual work. The economic success of the Hutterian colonies can be attributed in no small measure to the efficient organization and planning of their kitchen economy.

The Division of a Colony

On the whole most colonies prosper economically, but none of them are wealthy, chiefly because of the rapid population increase, which forces every colony to divide and establish another colony about once every twenty years. The high cost of land to found a new colony and the heavy additional investment in farm machinery generally not only exhaust the old colony's financial reserves, but also place the old and the new colony in debt. By the time the debt is liquidated and new reserves begin to accumulate each of the two colonies is again ready for another division.

A new colony with a population of about one hundred will have an adult labor pool, discounting the minors and the aged, of about thirty men and women. Approximately fifteen of them will be male, which means that almost all of them will be in charge of an office or an enterprise; practically every Hutterian is a "boss" in one field or another. As the colony population increases there are duplications in the various enterprises. The cattle-man, the hog-man, the carpenter, and the others down the line get assistants.

The larger population begins to pose administrative and social problems. The intimate relations in the group become more formal. Cliques begin to form within the colony, supervisory duties increase, and these developments weaken the familial atmosphere of the *Bruderhof*. For these reasons Hutterians do not like to see a colony grow much beyond 150 in population. At this stage the men begin to talk about the necessity of branching out and founding a new colony. The leaders scout for available land, preferably not too far removed from the parent colony. But proximity is only one consideration; the price of land and its location also play a role. The purchase of the land, the vast building program on the new site, and the investment in additional farm implements are basically the responsibility of the mother colony, although other colonies may sometimes advance interest-free loans to assist in the setting up of the new colony.

Though Manitoba colonies have branched out as far as one hundred miles and more, a nearby location offers distinct advantages. With land bought in the neighborhood the parent colony can carry on farming operations from the home base with its available manpower and machinery until it is in a financial position to begin with its building program. A new colony is not launched until the main dwelling units and barns and farm enterprise buildings are completed or at least well advanced toward completion.

The actual division of the mother colony follows no rigid pattern and the process may best be illustrated with an example. The division to be described was outlined to me by Rev. John Hofer, the minister at Riverside colony.[13] The Riverside colony at Arden, in Manitoba, was founded in 1933. Twenty years later the community found it necessary to branch out. In 1953 it bought land near Westbourne, about thirty miles away, which it cultivated for three years despite its distance from the home colony. By 1956 the building program at the new location had advanced to a stage where the move could be made, and the establishment of Bloomfield colony began.

As indicated earlier, when a colony prepares to branch out one prerequisite is that it have two ministers. Riverside had two ministers, and these men now prepared two lists of all the families in the community. Care was taken that the heads of families who worked in the same enterprise, with the poultry, or with livestock, or in the carpentry shop, should appear on separate lists. Similarly the size of the family would be considered; each list contained small and large families. An approximately equal number of young and old couples were included on each list. Once completed, these two lists were submitted to the community-congregation for possible adjustments. If any family felt there was a good reason to transfer from one list to the other, it could apply for such a transfer. If the community thought the reason was valid it in turn would approve the transfer.

As soon as the congregation was in general agreement that both lists were about equal in all respects the lists were placed in a hat and *das Los*, a drawing, decided which group was to remain on the home colony and which one was to leave for the new colony. Since the two colony ministers were responsible for drawing up the two lists, their names on either list could indicate a preference for one particular group. To avoid giving the impression of such a preference the two ministers then drew lots to see which one would remain and which one was to join the new colony. The two ministers at the Riverside colony were father and son, and *das Los* decided that the senior minister move to Bloomfield, and the younger remain at the mother colony.

A careful statement of all assets and liabilities was also made before the drawing. The total assets amounted to about half a million dollars. Since there was a slight population difference between the two groups, the assets were divided on a per capita basis.

In all such colony divisions the relationship between the parent colony and the new colony remains very close. This intimate relationship continues until both colonies are ready once more to subdivide.

The carefully planned divisions of their communities help preserve the *Gemeinschaft* relationship and vitality of the Hutterian colonies. In individualistic society a disproportionally large number of young people leave rural communities either to move to urban centers or to take up farming elsewhere. This migration tends to upset the age composition of the population remaining behind. A demographic study of Hutterian colonies, however, indicates that the age grouping of new and old communities remains constant.[14] This contributes directly to the social and economic stability enjoyed by the Hutterian colonies.

In evaluating the Hutterian communal economy the following observations may be made: the Hutterian communities are relatively well-to-do, but this is partly because their living needs are modest and partly because they practice a self-sufficient economy to a much greater degree than their neighbors; the economy provides diversified and full employment; the work pace is satisfactory but is not a maximum pace; the productivity of the communities may not equal in some cases that of the best farmers, but it is greater than that of the average prairie farmer; the large-scale farm and enterprise management offers distinct advantages to the communal operations; the colonies follow sound marketing practices; the communal economy at all colonies appears to be sufficiently healthy to provide complete economic security for all its members; finally, the familial organization of each colony is preserved by the periodic division.

VIII

THE CULTURAL HERITAGE

THE HUTTERIAN BELIEF and institutions are buttressed by a spiritual and cultural heritage that is not only a solid link with the past but also a dynamic directive to each succeeding generation. There is first and foremost that familiarity with the Bible that colors even the vernacular of the colony. Then follows the distinctively Hutterian heritage, consisting of their chronicles, devotional writings, a rich hymnology, the story of the lives of dedicated Hutterian leaders, and a solid educational tradition. Because this heritage pervades the life of every colony, a knowledge of the books generally found on a Hutterian bookshelf and an examination of the school system, aside from the public school, are necessary for an understanding of the group. Their cumulative effects have molded the Hutterian personality and the character of Hutterian institutions to this day.

Hutterian Chronicles

The story of the Hutterians is told in their own chronicles, which for centuries were preserved in the form of hand-copied manuscripts. To these were added the polemics of the Reformation period, and more recent literature, like Peter Hofer's *The Hutterian Brethren and Their Beliefs,* which was published in 1955 as an answer to the anti-Hutterian agitation in Manitoba. The chronicles are typical late medieval annals, narrating events year by year.

The oldest chronicle, known to the Hutterians as the *Gross-Geschichts-*

buch, was begun by their leader Peter Walpot, who asked Kaspar Brait-
michel (*ca*. 1565) to begin a chronicle of the times in which all events in
the history of the communities were to be recorded. Its entries end with
the year 1665. These annals were repeatedly copied in the early years of
the Brotherhood, and the copies were distributed among the various Hutterian communities. Some of these copies were discovered by an Austrian
scholar named Josef Beck (1815–1887), who assumed that the originals
were lost. In fact, Beck thought that Hutterianism itself had been blotted
out during the Counter-Reformation of Empress Maria Theresa. He incorporated the copies he found in his extensive study of the Anabaptists,
which was published in Vienna in 1883.[1]

The *Gross-Geschichtsbuch* has little historical perspective. The first
twenty-five pages recount the story from the Creation to the birth of
Christ. The next seventeen pages summarize the work of Jesus and the
Apostles, the rise of Islam, the merging of the state and church, the corruption of the papacy and clergy, and the rise of Luther and Zwingli. What
follows from that time on is a minute account of the origin of the Swiss
Brethren, and the diffusion of their teachings through all German lands of
the Empire. The simple vernacular of the chronicle often becomes a moving narrative relating stirring tales of heroism and suffering. The annals
contain details and names of places where the early 2100 Hutterians suffered martyrdom. They are recorded in a special "Martyrs' Register"
(*Martertafel*).

The smaller chronicle is known as the *Klein-Geschichtsbuch*. It is
chiefly the work of Elder Johannes Waldner (1749–1824). In almost two
hundred pages Waldner summarizes the older chronicle, but it is much
more than a mere précis. Waldner's sense of history gives the narrative
perspective. There is an attempt at "organization and interpretation," as
Zieglschmid remarks. Waldner tapped many sources and drew from his
own eventful life's experiences. Born in Austria, young Waldner, together
with his parents and other Lutherans, had taken part in the forced transmigration from Carinthia to Transylvania. Here the Waldner family had
joined the Hutterian Brotherhood. As a youth Waldner shared the vicissi-
tudes of the trek to Wallachia and to Russia. One of the great Hutterian
examples of loyalty and devotion, Waldner died at the Radichev colony
and was buried on the banks of the Desna River. The major portion of the
Klein-Geschichtsbuch is his lasting monument. Other Hutterians took up
the work where Waldner stopped and continued the annals at intervals.

After the Hutterians left Russia and settled in the United States in 1874 there was little interest in continuing this record. The growth and geographical distribution of the communities also made it increasingly difficult for an untrained person to write their history. It was not until Elder Elias Walter (1862–1938), of Alberta, began his work at the beginning of the present century that a renewed interest in Hutterian history became evident.

Walter was born in Russia, and moved to South Dakota during the Hutterian exodus in the 1870's. As a young man he was elected colony steward, a position he relinquished when he was elected and ordained minister in 1900. He was the spiritual head of the short-lived colony established near Dominion City, in Manitoba, at the turn of the century, and headed the first Hutterian colony in Alberta, in 1918. In 1902 Walter had Riedemann's *Rechenschaft* printed, in 1914 the Hutterian hymnary, in 1919 the "small" songbook, which he also compiled, in 1920 a selection of the writings of Ehrenpreis, and in 1923 the *Gross-Geschichtsbuch*. All these books were distributed among all Hutterian communities. In addition Walter wrote forty booklets of sermons and introductions to sermons (*Vorreden*).

Up to 1923 the Hutterian chronicles existed only in manuscript form. Painstakingly they had been recopied again and again. Walter alone had copied the *Gross-Geschichtsbuch* three times by hand, in 1889, in 1890, and in 1892. It may be mentioned that Walter was by trade a bookbinder, and bound the hymnary for all the colonies.

In 1923 Walter, then head of Stand-Off colony in Alberta, at the request of the Hutterian congregations commissioned the Viennese scholar Dr. Rudolf Wolkan to prepare and publish the Old Chronicle. Walter asked Wolkan to modernize the language of the archaic, dialectal German original. This entire edition was bought up by the Hutterian communities.[2] In 1943 Dr. A. J. F. Zieglschmid of Northwestern University, with the financial assistance of the Carl Schurz Memorial Foundation and the American Council of Learned Societies, published the Old Chronicle in its original form as a contribution to linguistic study.[3] Because of its outdated language this newer edition, which runs to over one thousand pages, is not popular among the Hutterians. Zieglschmid was then approached by the Hutterians with a request to prepare for publication the newer chronicle, the *Klein-Geschichtsbuch*. He was asked to add the Hutterian regulations, diaries, and some correspondence and relevant documents. This was done by Zieglschmid, whose very extensive use of the non-Hutterian sources in footnotes provided continuity to the chronicle.[4] Its publication in 1947 was assured when the Hutterian communities ordered in advance 4000 copies of the book. Like the older chronicle this one is available only in German.

The religious disputations of the Reformation era, in which the Hutterians participated freely, produced a rash of polemic writings. Some of them are still found in the colonies. One of these dates back to 1557, when Catholic and Protestant theologians met at Worms in Germany with the purpose of reconciling their differences. They failed to reach an agreement except on one point. Both sides were prepared to recommend to their governments "a sharper treatment of the Anabaptists." In reply the Hutterians issued a brochure, *The Defence against the "Prozess" at Worms-on-the-Rhine in 1557*. The booklet outlines Anabaptist doctrine and was regarded as important enough by the Hutterians of Alberta to be translated into English and published.

Devotional Writings

The outstanding authors of Hutterian devotional and doctrinal writings are Peter Riedemann, Peter Walpot, and Andreas Ehrenpreis. Riedemann's *Rechenschaft*[5] was written in 1540 "in the Hessian jails of Marburg and Walkerdorf," as Heimann said. It was printed in 1545, but of this edition no copies exist today. There are five copies in existence of the 1565 edition, one copy at each of the following places: the British Museum in London, the Berlin State Library, the library of the University of Chicago, the Museum at Brünn, Czechoslovakia, and the Rockport colony in South Dakota.[6] The British Museum copy was used by Kathleen Hasenberg for her excellent English translation, published in England in 1950 under the title *Confession of Faith*. The subtitle reads "Account of Our Religion, Doctrine, and Faith, Given by Peter Riedemann of the Brothers Whom Men Call Hutterians." The *Rechenschaft* is not only very readable but also provides a very clear and concise outline of the Hutterian faith. To this day the Brotherhood has not found it necessary to initiate any changes or modifications in the basic interpretations of Christian ideals presented by Riedemann.

To Walpot are attributed the *Fünf Artikel*, which were regarded as important enough by the Hutterians for inclusion in the Old Chronicle. More recently an English translation of the Third Article, *True Surrender and Christian Community of Goods*, has established its place on colony bookshelves.[7]

Andreas Ehrenpreis's *Ein Sendbrief* ("An Epistle") dates back to 1652, and was published by the Hutterians in 1920. It breathes a firm but gentle conviction and is universally popular among the Hutterians. The simplicity of the language in *Ein Sendbrief* is reminiscent of *Pilgrim's Progress*; indeed, Ehrenpreis and Bunyan were contemporaries.

Hymnology

To this literature must be added Hutterian hymnology. Its purpose serves the same end, as is expressed on the title page of the hymnary: "Remember them which have the rule over you [in German: "Remember your predecessors"], who have spoken unto you the word of God: whose faith follow, considering the end of their conversation" (Hebrews 13:7).

Manuscripts of Hutterian hymns, copied many times over, can be found at every Hutterian colony. The sources for the Hutterian hymnary *Die Lieder der Hutterischen Brüder*,[8] an 891-page volume, are three major codices of about four hundred hymns composed in three distinct periods between 1500 and 1660.

Hutterian hymns contain up to eighty stanzas, and as has been pointed out, they are not intended to be sung in full. Many of them may almost be termed epics, narrating the sufferings of the early martyrs. Most of them are prefaced by a few biographical lines on the writer. The first hymn in the hymnary is by Felix Mantz, one of the first Swiss Brethren, "condemned to death by drowning at Zurich on account of his faith, January 5, 1527." Hymns two and three were written by Georg Wagner, who on account of his faith "suffered death by burning at Munich, February 8, 1527." The next hymn was composed by Elder Andreas Ehrenpreis "in memory of Michael Sattler, burned alive at Rottenburg-on-the-Neckar on May 21, 1527, after the executioner had cut out his tongue, riveted him on a cart, and torn his body with glowing tongs . . ." These constant reminders to the reader of early Hutterian martyrs must be regarded as a powerful source of indoctrination.

Another songbook used by the colonies is a miscellaneous collection of hymns and songs of varied origin, several of them written by contemporary Hutterians. Published by the Hutterian communities in Canada, it has appeared in four editions since 1919. This collection, known as the *Gesang-Büchlein*, is used extensively in the German school and in the homes.

Before his untimely death in 1950, Zieglschmid, who spent much of his life in Hutterian research, collected a volume of Hutterian hymns in manuscript. This material is deposited in the Mennonite Historical Library at Goshen College, in Indiana.

Church Services

Perhaps no other aspect of Hutterian life has seen as little change from traditional ways as Hutterian worship.[9] A half-hour service, the *Gebet*, is held daily at every colony, in winter before supper, in summer after supper. The Sunday service, which may last for two hours, generally begins shortly after nine. While on weekdays breakfast is served at seven, on Sundays it is served an hour later. By that time all the farm chores have been done and the families are ready and assembled in their homes. They wait until they see the minister step out of his house and then follow him. The husband goes first, followed by his wife and then by the children.

The men wear their black homemade suits. The women and children wear dresses of various dark or at least subdued shades. Women and girls always have a head covering.

The hymnary, which is used chiefly for devotional reading at home, is not brought along for the worship service; instead the minister announces the hymn and reads one or two lines at a time, which the congregation sings. Generally the minister also intones the hymns. In keeping with Hutterian conviction the emphasis is not on artistic singing, which they regard as an expression of vanity, but on the content and message of the words. Like the folk songs of old the tunes of Hutterian hymns are passed on by tradition. There is no notation of tunes in the hymnary and no musical instruments are used for accompaniment. The singing is followed by a short prayer and by a *Vorrede,* or introduction. The *Vorrede* as well as the main sermon which comes after it are read out of special books. After the sermon there is a long silent prayer, for which the whole congregation kneels, and this is followed by another hymn.

The introductions and sermons have not been written by the ministers who read them. They date back to the early days of the Brotherhood. These sermons have been repeatedly copied by ministers or other men, and still are to this day. Various colors of ink are used, green, black, or blue, with embellishments in red or purple. Such collections are then bound in strong and sometimes very attractive bindings. This is the work of the colony bookbinder, who takes considerable pride in his craft.

Arts and Crafts

The early Hutterians were skilled in many arts and crafts. Of their Moravian period the Austrian historian Dr. Loserth writes: "Anyone who carries on research in the archives of Austria, Moravia, and Hungary, finds notices of the industrial activity of the Hutterian Brethren, and one who roams through the museums of those countries finds products of their industry which today attract attention, as did the pottery exhibition at Troppau in 1924. The catalogs list precious 'Hutterian knives,' and the old manuscript hymnals are not only written in fine penmanship, but are also distinguished by the solidity of their binding. . . . The wool-weaving craft was on a high plane with the Hutterian Brethren; their products were so highly prized, that after the expulsion of the Anabaptists the government sought to fill their place by skilled Belgians . . ." [10] And describing Hutterian ceramics Robert Friedmann states that "their pottery ware reveals a taste for the shapely and aesthetically appealing which made them stand out in this craft and true competitors of the Italian, later also of Dutch, fayence or majolica ware." [11]

These crafts, part of the rich Hutterian cultural heritage, have almost been lost through persecution, forced migrations, and cultural isolation. Scarcely a trace of them lingers at the Hutterian colonies of today. On occasion, however, evidence of artistry and skill still can be found. Manuscript copying, decorative lettering, and bookbinding have already been mentioned. Again, at many colonies the children play with tin cans and honey pails on which the girls and women have painted very colorful floral designs. Spinning is a well-preserved art taught to girls at an early age. A girl's hope chest generally contains a wealth of delicate needlework. The patterns and the lettering are usually copied from samplers, though some of them may be original. I saw some of the finest embroidery and cross-stitch work at the Old Rosedale colony, done by the late Mrs. Anna Hofer. When I commented on the artistry of the work, her husband said, not without a touch of humor and pride, that it had been done at the expense of more useful work.

The men are excellent carpenters and usually make the colony furniture. Woodwork finds its highest expression in keepsakes handed down to members of the family. Strictly speaking they are colony property, but they remain in the family. There are beautifully carved spinning wheels and highly polished rolling pins with the daughter's or sister's name inlaid. The quality of the chests with their inlay work also bespeaks skill and workmanship.

An intimate knowledge and appreciation of their religious and cultural heritage in the form of the printed word is instilled into Hutterians at a very early age. The potency of this inculcation is attested to by "the fact," as Infield says, "that the young man or woman of seventeen is, as a rule, not tempted by the teachings of the elementary public school and emerges as a faithful member of the community." [12] The conclusion that the young Hutterian is almost immune to the influences of the outside world is validated by the continued strength of the colonies themselves. The Hutterians also have an artistic heritage and part of it has been transmitted and preserved. However, because all show and ostentation is carefully avoided the outsider hardly ever becomes aware of it. The emphasis in skills and crafts is on usefulness. The artistic element in them is discouraged as an expression of vanity.

IX

HUTTERIAN EDUCATION

THE PUBLIC SCHOOL is an outside institution which is accepted by the Hutterians. Its place and function are discussed in a separate chapter. Here we are concerned with the Hutterians' own educational heritage and practices.

The Hutterian communities very early in their history realized the importance of a sound elementary education for their members. The motivation was utilitarian. Since the gospels alone were accepted as a Christian's guide, it followed that the convert had to be able to read to get the message from the printed page directly. Adults new to the faith were taught to read and write, and a school system was introduced which in concept and operation was startlingly revolutionary. The innovator of the system may well have been Peter Riedemann, the sixteenth-century leader, who insisted that the communities maintain their own schools, since, in his words, the "worldly" schools "teach but the wisdom, art, and practises of the world, and are silent about things divine."

Riedemann then outlined the components of the Hutterian system: "As soon as the mother hath weaned the child she giveth it to the school. Here there are sisters, appointed by the church to care for them, who have been recognized to be competent and diligent therein. . . . With them children remain until their fifth or sixth year, that is, until they are able to learn to read and write." [1] This kindergarten school was to be followed by a regular school for the children between the ages of six and twelve, or older. Here again the emphasis was to be placed on religious instruction.

From this school the boys and girls were to be apprenticed to the various trades and households. Special classes in catechism and Bible knowledge were to be continued for them preparatory to their joining the Church, which was not before they reached the age of about twenty.

The Ideals of Walpot

Riedemann set the objectives and pattern for community education, but it remained for a teacher, Peter Walpot, to translate these into reality. On November 15, 1568, before a gathering of all the Hutterian community schoolmasters, Walpot outlined the standards that should mark community schools.[2] His remarkable address reveals that these standards were far in advance of their time. Since Walpot was at this time the *Vorsteher*, or leader, of all Hutterian households, it is clear that he spoke with authority.

Perhaps the most interesting section of Walpot's address is the part dealing with hygiene and health practiced in school, this at a time when preventive health measures were almost unknown. "In regard to the children who are not well," said Walpot, "or where there is uncertainty, the bed clothing and night shirts of such should not be mixed with the clothing of the children or washed together with it. It should be kept by itself. Likewise in the food and drink one cannot take too much care, for there is very much danger among so many children."

In the Hutterian School Regulations of 1578 these ideas of Walpot crystallized into definite instructions. The teachers were advised not to use excessive punishment, "seeing that the Lord does not deal with us elder ones always according to our deserts, but according to grace." Furthermore, the schoolmasters were told not to occupy "the time of the children with long preaching and with much reading of many quotations, because the children can understand and grasp but little." The teachers were to "show sympathy to the little folk who have just started attending school and should not undertake at once to break the self-will, lest injury come therefrom." Another rule required children who were brought to school, presumably by outsiders, "to be carefully examined" for contagious diseases. Infected children "should be separated from the rest in sleeping and drinking, and especially in washing."

These policies spread the fame of Hutterian schools. Rudolf Wolkan, the Viennese historian, writes: "So superior were the schools of the Brethren in those days that, despite of their hated religion, people of other faiths sent their children to Hutterian schools by preference." [3]

Though it is evident from the emphasis which the early Hutterian leaders placed on education that they realized its value, it is also clear that the emphasis was confined to elementary education. Higher education was rejected. Possibly the leaders of the community felt that it was dangerous to expose its young members to the temptations of the cities in which the institutions of higher learning were located. Or again they may have felt that higher education in itself would have injected a discordant note into the egalitarian community life.

This distrustful attitude toward higher education has remained a salient characteristic of Hutterian education to this day. Colony education, as distinguished from the public schools, is generally limited to kindergarten, German school, Sunday school, and an informal apprenticeship with the various community enterprises. Of these institutions as they function at the colonies today the kindergarten shows by far the strongest and most attractive features.

The Kindergarten

The kindergarten is known by the Hutterians as the *kleine Schul'* (small school). It operates from early spring to late autumn for preschool children between the ages of two and a half and five or six. The school is headed by a supervisor variously known as the *Schulmutter* (school mother), *Kinderweib* (woman in charge of the children), *Schulangela* (school guardian), or simply *Angela*. She is generally a middle-aged woman when she takes up her duties, and occupies the position for life. Since she, like all other women, has some household work at home, the colony usually provides her with an alternate. At the large New Rosedale colony the supervisor is the wife of the farm foreman and the alternate is the wife of the minister. At the Crystal Spring colony the supervisor is the mother of the minister, and also the grandmother of a goodly number of her charges. The supervisors and alternates have the help of two or three assistants, girls of eighteen to twenty. These girls take turns between kindergarten work and other colony duties.

Each kindergarten has a special schoolhouse. Quite often it is the most attractive building in the colony. As a rule it is the only building that is fenced in. There is a yard with a sandbox, swings, and other playground equipment. The kindergarten at New Rosedale colony, which may be regarded as typical, has three rooms: a vestibule with washing facilities, a classroom with long miniature tables and benches, and a bedroom.

The children come to school a little after eight o'clock in the morning, and spend some time at play. They are then washed and combed by the school mother or her assistants. Meanwhile one of the assistants has brought breakfast over from the community kitchen, which is usually only a few yards away. Boys and girls then seat themselves in long rows on the benches, fold their hands, close their eyes, and together with the teachers recite a long prayer. Breakfast consists of cereals or porridge or boiled eggs, milk, toast, butter, and honey. The children are well trained, the smaller ones getting help from the assistants whenever necessary. Another prayer of thanks closes the meal. So ingrained becomes this habit that regardless of the age of the Hutterian or the place where he eats, in a restaurant in Winnipeg or in a café in Headingly or Portage la Prairie, he bows his head twice, once before and once after each meal, for grace and thanksgiving.

After breakfast the very informal instruction begins. There is some singing, the teacher tells a Bible story and teaches the children a song or prayer. Repeatedly instruction is interrupted by active games. At around ten o'clock the children have a snack. There may be cookies, fruit, and occasionally warm soup. Then there are more lessons. Shortly before 11:30 the children wash and then have their main meal. After dinner all children again file past the washbasin and then go to sleep for the *Mittags-schläfchen*.

Even the three-year-olds toddle to the bedroom without any coaxing. The bedroom generally has two rows of low bunks running the full length of the room. It may also have one or two beds for the teachers. The children stretch out in neat rows, without any partitions between them; some of the bigger boys may prefer to take a pillow and sleep on the floor. My observation was that in at most fifteen minutes all children were asleep. As soon as a child wakes up, he leaves quietly to play outside so as not to disturb those still sleeping. By three o'clock they are all ready for another snack.

Then there are more lessons, more singing, more Bible stories. Between games and lessons some children may decide to spend a little time at home. There are no strict rules against this. If a child should absent himself too often, colony disapproval, working through the adults and the children, would effect a change in behavior. Shortly after five o'clock supper is served and the children all leave for home. They continue to play their games, on the grounds of the kindergarten or of the colony, but they are now the responsibility of their own mothers.

At nine o'clock the school mother sends one of the girls to ring the big bell in the dining hall tower. This is the signal for mothers to call the children in and send them to bed. They have another apple or cookie and wind their way upstairs. Indeed, some sleepyheads may have escaped the turmoil of the day even before this. While visiting at one home I saw a four-year-old boy come to his father and beg him, "I am sleepy; will you spank me and send me to bed?" The father complied with a gentle slap to the back and the boy went to bed.

Hutterians are bilingual even before they learn English, which is their third language. Small children speak only a Tirolese dialect used by the Hutterians among themselves. While kindergarten is conducted in this vernacular, children become familiar with standard German by learning songs, Bible verses, and Bible stories. At some colonies English is introduced at the senior kindergarten stage. Here children sing "Heavenly Sunshine" as lustily as *Wenn die Schule geschlossen*.

Two or three colonies in Manitoba have no kindergarten because there is a temporary housing shortage there and the school is used for a family dwelling. However, if a colony should make no serious attempt to provide a *kleine Schul'* its prestige among the other colonies would suffer considerably.

At three Hutterian public schools the children in grades three to five were asked, at my request, to write compositions on their kindergarten days. The following two papers were among those submitted to the teachers:

My Kindergarten Days

In the morning at eight o'clock I went to kindergarten. We had breakfast and always said our prayers. Then we went out to play. Grandmother gave us candy and we went on the swings and ate candy. When we had finished our candy we went to play in the sandbox. We often played house in which we had nice dishes. For the night we put our toys into the school. Grandmother sat on a bench with her knitting and we sat all around her. She told us about Jesus. When she had finished we went to play again in our playhouse. Sometimes the older children came and helped us dry the dishes. In the afternoon we slept for two hours.

Kindergarten

Kindergarten is the first school little children attend. It is very interesting. Some of the children don't like to go every day, but they can't do anything about it. They just have to go when the season begins.

The first day is usually a Monday in May. Every morning the children arrange the tables and learn a lot of prayers and German songs by memory. Afterwards they play in the yard. Very often the children play school.

After dinner the children run around until after the dishes are washed. Then they scrub their hands and faces and go for a nap. That's what some of them hate most about kindergarten. After they have slept they run and play outside. Later they come in again and the teachers teach them manners, songs, and prayers. In the afternoon at five o'clock they have their supper and run home. The teacher and her helpers stay and clean the school so that it will be neat and tidy for the next day.

The transfer of the kindergarten pupil to the German school takes place simultaneously with his enrollment as a beginner in public school. The public school and the German school are housed in the same building.

The German School

Hutterians know this school as the *grosse Schul'* (big school), and use the term German school only when they have occasion to refer to it in English. This school is attended by children of public school age. The instruction takes place before nine in the morning and after three thirty in the afternoon, that is, before and after public instruction.

The function of the German school, like that of the kindergarten, was outlined by Riedemann. Children are to be "entrusted to the schoolmaster who teacheth them" and "instructeth them more and more in the knowledge of God, that they learn to know God and his will and strive to keep the same. He observeth the following order with them: when they all come together in the morning to school he teacheth them to thank the Lord together, and to pray to Him. Then he preacheth to them as children for the space of half an hour, telling them how they ought to obey, be subject to and honour their parents, teachers and those set over them, and illustrateth from the Old and New Testaments both the promise to godly and the punishment of disobedient and obstinate children." [4]

The German teachers are usually mature men who are respected by their pupils and take a genuine interest in them. Few of the present German teachers have any pedagogical training, but they tend to be fathers of large families and thus bring into the classroom some elementary knowledge of pedagogy. Some of them regularly attend public school teachers' conventions.

Beginning pupils at the German school have a *Fibel*, a German primer. Texts for the other classes are the New and the Old Testament, and the catechism. A number of the schools also have some German readers. All schools teach German spelling and a little Hutterian history. Pupils spend much of their time in the memorization of hymns and the learning of prayers and Bible verses. Corporal punishment is administered "when necessary"; but the teacher avoids the exhibition of ill-temper, sarcasm, and angry words.[5]

The educational standards of the German school are low. This is realized at some colonies and is a cause of concern. It has been suggested that the American and Canadian public schools destroyed the Hutterian educational system and that all that has been salvaged of the Hutterian heritage is the kindergarten.[6]

The Sunday School

Children over nine or ten years of age and young people are required to attend Sunday school until they join the Church. The German teacher and sometimes the minister provide instruction. In many colonies the class is held in the afternoon and the morning's service is carefully explained. Detailed instruction in church doctrine is also part of the program of studies. This school terminates with an intensive study of the catechism in which only the candidates for baptism take part. When a candidate feels he understands the teachings of the Church and is ready to accept the obligations of a church member, and when the ministers and the colony in turn feel that the candidate is ready, the rite of baptism making him a full-fledged member of the community of believers is administered.

The Church at all times has given its schools excellent support. The church regulations advise parents that education leads to maturity and *Gemeinsinn* (community spirit) and direct parents to send their children to school at the proper age and support the teachers.[7] They counsel parents not to spoil their children in the hope that school will discipline them. Nor should parents provide their children with too many presents. Not only is this a wasteful practice, according to the regulations, but it is also the cause of envy and quarrels among the children. The schools have sometimes been praised by outsiders for the fact that the children were "in the hands of the same educators from morning till night, so that the activities of the whole day were intelligently correlated." [8]

A discussion of secular and higher education is contained in the next chapter.

Apprenticeship

At the age of fifteen, when most of the Hutterian children leave the public school, they also leave German school. During the entire period from the time they started public school until they leave it, the children have been treated as a special colony group. They sleep at home, but eat in their own dining room under the supervision of the German teacher. At fifteen they are given special instruction by this teacher preparatory to their transfer to the adult group. Henceforth they eat with the adults and begin to assume the responsibilities of adults.

The boys, now young men, are apprenticed to different enterprises. Each boy spends some time working in a department until he is familiar with its operations, and then transfers to another enterprise. The arrangement is quite informal, and the young man may be working under the supervision of his own father. There is no definite period of time set for his training in any of the enterprises. If there is a labor shortage in one department, he may be required to remain for a longer period of time. In any case, within a few years he will have thoroughly familiarized himself with the routine work of a number of enterprises, and before long, if he shows special aptitude, he may be asked to head one of the departments.

The girls' training during this time is even more informal. They help at home with the children, do laundry work, help in the kitchen, work in the garden, and spend the winter knitting and sewing. Those who show special ability may be assigned to assist the kindergarten teacher in looking after the *kleine Schul'*.

Hutterian education is a pervasive influence, in a large measure responsible for molding the young people into dedicated, community-minded people, willing to work and assume responsibilities which carry with them no special rewards or privileges. In the kindergarten the emphasis is on socializing the child and teaching him to subordinate his own wishes to the interests of the whole group. In the German and Sunday schools the emphasis shifts to formal religious instruction, with the objective of indoctrinating the young with the traditional Hutterian beliefs.

Parental control over children is very strong in Hutterian society. In return there is a strong identification on the part of the children with their parents. Moreover, the social education of the young Hutterian child begins at a very early age. He is usually a member of a large family, and throughout his childhood he is surrounded by playmates and companions of his own age. This horizontal association, characteristic of communal living, is supplemented as a control factor by parental authority, for even in the informal associations there is usually the guiding hand of an adult. One result of this system is that the conflict of generations, with children rebelling against their parents, is almost completely absent from Hutterian society.

X

THE HUTTERIANS AND THE PUBLIC SCHOOL

THE PUBLIC SCHOOL is the outside agency that has penetrated Hutterian society most powerfully. One of its ultimate objectives is to integrate or assimilate the Hutterians into the larger Canadian population stream. Its overt objective is to educate young Hutterians, but it also has the covert objective of influencing them to turn away from what are regarded by outsiders as outmoded ways and institutions. The public school as an agent of social disorganization poses a sustained threat to Hutterian survival. The teacher may embody the challenge of the larger culture most clearly outside the classroom, as this incident, related by a teacher, shows:

Possibly the greatest worldly temptation this writer brought to the Brethren was his television set. Many had never seen television before, but all except the most pious elders had made a visit to the writer's teacherage to view it before the year was over. Several married men admitted they had come to watch television in spite of their wives' objections and threats that they were going to tell the preacher. A noticeable decrease in the number of visits to the teacherage was observed toward the end of the year and the writer assumed that Hutterian beliefs and indoctrination held firm and won the battle over "the devil's own instrument of temptation." [1]

But though television may be an evil outside influence, the values of public school instruction are a more fundamental menace to the colonies' way of life. From the Hutterian point of view the public school is *weltlich* (worldly) in its orientation. It sets up materialistic objectives; one of its major goals is to prepare pupils and students for the struggle of life in which they must succeed. Furthermore, the atmosphere in the "worldly" public school is deliberately exploratory. Intellectual curiosity and an examination of the existing order and values are accepted by the world as positive attributes of a good school. All this is in sharp contrast to Hutterian doctrine and to the aim of Hutterian education. The schools, according to the Hutterians, should be oriented away from worldliness and the material objectives that come only too naturally to man. They should exist to acquaint the child with the eternal truths, God's imperatives, and a speculative approach to them is morally wrong.

Although Hutterians feel that the public school will adversely affect the future of their community, consistent with their doctrine of nonresistance they have at no time challenged the position of the imposed institution. They did introduce religious instruction, conducted by their own colony teachers, before and after regular school hours. It is the Hutterian view that this instruction with its exclusive emphasis on religion partly offsets the "negative, one-sided" influence of the public school.

The Organization of the Public Schools

The school question plagued Manitoba for many years (see Chapter 3). By the time the Hutterians came to the province in 1918 it was almost settled. The Hutterians realized that they would be required to comply with existing school laws, and were prepared to do so. When they moved to Manitoba the provincial government immediately took steps to see that public schools were formed in their colonies. This was chiefly the work of Dr. Robert Fletcher, who was deputy minister of education for Manitoba from 1906 to 1938. Dr. Fletcher took an active interest in the Hutterians.

The Hutterians settled in areas where the existing schools were too small to accommodate the increased number of children. Thereupon the Department of Education formed the Hutterian landholdings into school districts. Pending the provision of school buildings classes were held in Hutterian community buildings. Fully qualified English-speaking teachers were employed.[2]

This arrangement solved the problem which the compact communities posed to the public school districts in which they were located. If the Hutterian children had been required to attend existing schools the affected districts would have had to enlarge their schools and engage additional teachers. The taxpayers most likely would have protested, as they did in an analogous situation in Alberta. Pitt in his Alberta study reports that during the 1930's the Hutterian elders of one colony approached a district board "with the request that, since the colony paid all local school taxes assessed on its property within the district, the Hutterite children be admitted to the Daly Creek school." The board "was reluctant to grant" this request.[3] The Hutterians did not press for admission, and later changed their stand and continued to operate their own public school without provincial aid.

The Hutterians could not elect their own school board, for two reasons. According to the Manitoba School Act school trustees must be born or naturalized Canadians. The Hutterians were American citizens. Furthermore, elected school trustees must be registered and resident landowners. Because the Hutterians are not individually registered property owners they do not qualify for the office of school trustee.

Public school inspectors were assigned to inspect and report on the colony public schools in their districts in the same manner as on other schools. This system remained in operation for thirty years. The anti-Hutterian agitation after World War II included a demand that the public school intensify its integration work among the colony people. In 1947, the Select Special Committee of the Manitoba legislature recommended that "the function of the School Administrator, the School Inspector, and the Attendance Officer be vested in a single official who should have jurisdiction over the Hutterite colonies."[4] Acting on this recommendation the Department of Education appointed B. Grafton to the position, who worked in close cooperation with the chief inspector of schools, C. K. Rogers. Both men were known throughout Manitoba as educators and administrators, and were also greatly respected by the Hutterians. The relationship between the colonies and the officials of the Department of Education has been consistently excellent for the past forty years.

All colony schools employ qualified teachers, who are engaged by the official administrator. The colonies whose landholdings are coterminous with the school district operate and finance their own public schools in the same manner as other school districts. In four colonies the community landholdings are included in previously organized school districts. These districts are reluctant to relinquish taxable land, and the Hutterians are equally unwilling to send their children to schools attended by non-Hutterian children. One reason is that the colony would have no control over the introduction of audiovisual aids, which are not approved by the community. Under these circumstances the four Hutterian colonies choose to continue to pay school taxes to the municipality, but independently finance another school in the colony. Technically these are private schools, but the Hutterians make no attempt to interfere in their regular school program. They are for practical purposes public schools which get no municipal or provincial aid.

Annual meetings are held in all colonies, and, according to Mr. Grafton, are well attended. The official trustee or administrator is present and available for advice. His recommendations are usually endorsed. Thus the Hutterian public schools operate more efficiently in many ways than some rural schools in Manitoba. There is no warm sentiment among the Hutterians for these schools, for reasons already indicated, but they accept them. With the passing of time a kind of symbiosis has developed, and the colony cooperates with the government administrators in charge of these schools. In most cases the officials of the Department of Education have resisted the temptation to use the schools deliberately for disruption of colony life. Instead they maintain that the primary objective of the public school is to raise the existing standards in all grades and extend general interest in education beyond the grade school level. It is on this basis that the Hutterians tolerate and even support the public school.

In Alberta and Saskatchewan the colony public schools occupy a status similar to that which they have in Manitoba.[5] There too the colonies insist on having the public schools within their own communities. The administration, however, is in the hands of the larger area school boards. The curriculums are those prescribed in the respective provinces, and certified teachers are employed as instructors.

The relation of the Hutterians to the public schools in the United States does not differ markedly from that existing in Canada. A South Dakota experiment in educational coexistence, however, ended in failure, as a 1961 Associated Press report illustrates.

Doland, S.D. (AP) — Students from the Clark and Hillside Hutterite colonies won't be attending the Doland public school much longer.

A decision to pull the 52 children from grades one through eight out of the 477-student school system here was reached at a recent meeting of the South Dakota Hutterite Council.

"One of the main reasons is that we're losing our whole religious training because the children have to ride the school bus," commented Rev. Fred Waldner, president of the Clark colony near Raymond.

Waldner explained that it took more than an hour each way on the bus which cut into the time allotted for religious training at the Clark and Hillside colonies, both of which made history when they enrolled colony students in the school here August 28.

It marked the first time Hutterite children had attended a public school in the 400 years [sic] the sect has been active in the United States.

Although Rev. Waldner said the main reason for the decision was loss of religious training time, he did mention "other reasons." He said most Hutterite parents were satisfied with the schooling received at Doland "but the parents of the little ones are not completely satisfied."

Rev. Waldner explained that only [sic] about six of the first graders could speak only German. "Their teacher couldn't speak German so the learning process was very slow," he said.

Supt. Donald Peckham of the Doland school system was disappointed over the decision. He said the Hutterite children — girls dressed in ankle-length skirts and boys in black trousers — got along well with the teachers and other students.

"They were a bright-eyed bunch of youngsters and I know they are going to be disappointed to go back to the colony school," he said.[6]

The Curriculum and Teachers

The public schools in the Hutterian communities in Manitoba follow the program of studies prescribed for the province, as has been noted. I visited a number of schools on different occasions and the routine at the colony public schools was the same as in any rural school. Colony schools are also inspected regularly.

A survey which I made in the school years 1956–1957 and 1957–1958 revealed that almost half of the colony teachers were of Anglo-Saxon stock. An almost equal number were of German, mostly Mennonite, origin, and the rest were of Ukrainian, French, and Scandinavian descent. About a third of the teachers employed were male. As in other rural schools in the province a very large proportion of the colony public school teachers had only permit qualifications.

These teachers attend the annual fall conventions, for which two or three inspectorates are generally combined. It is a common practice at Manitoba conventions for teachers to subdivide into smaller groups. Generally the teachers in Hutterian schools meet in one special session during which common problems are discussed. The teachers often develop a strong attachment to the Hutterian children and even to the colonies. Pitt also reports that in Alberta the teachers at Hutterian schools "speak well of the children's cleanliness and manners, of their neatly kept, warm school buildings, and of the fine spirit of co-operation shown the teachers by the Hutterian Elders." [7] A similar note was struck by C. K. Rogers, the chief inspector of schools for Manitoba, in an address to a Winnipeg club in 1955. [8]

I attended two special convention sessions in Manitoba and met almost all the teachers employed at Hutterian schools. The consensus was, "We like it there." A number of the teachers have remained at the same school for many years. Miss W. Fitzmaurice has taught at the Milltown colony school for twenty-nine years. In her report to the convention Miss Fitzmaurice said that several French-Canadian families send their children to the Hutterian school, and everybody "gets along fine."

Almost without exception the teachers take an active interest in the colony. Often they attend weddings and funerals. If they are sufficiently conversant with German they sometimes attend church services. A few comments selected from teachers' reports which I received illustrate their relationship with the colony people. Mrs. Florence Dundas, teacher at the Oak Bluff colony, who lives only a short distance away from the colony, wrote: "When I have occasion to stay over night I am always invited to spend the evening at different homes and am made very welcome." "One day in summer half of the colony women brought a couple of bags of beans down and helped me can them," reported Mrs. Tolton of Crystal Spring colony. "The girls come down occasionally and help me with the housecleaning." Miss Viola Dufresne of Lakeside colony wrote: "I see a great deal of the people. They are all so friendly." When interviewed, another young teacher, A. Wiebe, at the Blumengart colony, said: "I eat at the community dining hall and the colony does not want to accept payment for room and board." Harvey Doell, at the Waldheim colony, provided the following information: "I am paying $20 a month. This covers rent for a three room teacherage, oil for heating, electricity, and board."

When I arrived at Rosedale colony at lunchtime I visited the two young teachers living at the teacherage. They did their own light housekeeping, but the colony girls had laid out a complete meal, including roast chicken, potatoes, and gravy. The two young female teachers said that this was done almost every day of the week.

Though the teacher remains an "outsider," the community's feeling is never hostile toward him. Generally it is the German teacher who provides the initial liaison between the public school teacher and the community.

Should the inexperienced teacher encounter discipline problems a report to the German teacher, who is greatly respected by the children, is usually enough to check any misbehavior. "The attitude towards education depends a great deal on the German teacher," wrote Mrs. Tolton. "If he takes an interest in the children's schoolwork they are more inclined to be ambitious."

The influence of the colony atmosphere is inescapable for the teachers exposed to it. A male teacher maintained he felt "wicked" when he smoked at the colony. A young female teacher said that whenever she used cosmetics and jewelry too generously she felt "positively sinful" in company with Hutterians. Other teachers, usually very young men and women, were less sensitive to the colony mores and said they sometimes offered cigarettes to older boys or invited young people for special radio or television programs. When a good-looking teacher was teased by a colleague who said that she was seeing too much of the Hutterian boys the teacher turned defensively to me and said: "Those boys are more gentlemanly than our boys. I wouldn't be ashamed being seen with them anywhere in the city. Except for their clothes they are nice, and no different from other people." The Hutterians themselves would hardly be pleased to hear that they were "no different from other people."

A very detailed and lively account of her experiences as a teacher of Hutterian children was given by Miss Joan Sigurdson, now living in Winnipeg. Miss Sigurdson taught at a public school when the Hutterians moved into the district. They did not have a school of their own, and she consented to take care of the additional enrollment of Hutterian children. She briefed her pupils, and when the colony children arrived school routine continued without interruption. There were a number of surprises in store for the Hutterian pupils. "I recall the look on the faces of the very young ones," reported Miss Sigurdson, "when I brought a radio into the school. They seemed much like what I imagine the Indians must have looked like when they inspected their first cannon."

Miss Sigurdson coaxed the Hutterian children to participate in the Christmas concert, for "many of them had lovely voices for choir work." She took the colony children to a field day which "they enjoyed to the hilt, a number of them taking ribbons for events." Sometimes, Miss Sigurdson said, she felt "much like someone sitting on a land mine," and the Hutterian parents, too, may have had some reason to feel like Indians inspecting their first cannon.

On the whole the public school teachers respect colony ways. The community-teacher relationship is good. The public school teachers in Hutterian colonies are in every respect indistinguishable from a cross section of rural Manitoba schoolteachers.

The School Buildings

Most of the Hutterian school plants are satisfactory. All schools have electricity, and many of them have indoor toilets, running water, and oil heat. Usually the German teacher supervises the heating, and teachers stated that the schools were comfortably warm all winter. All schools have some playground equipment. Many have teeters, swings, sandboxes, and even merry-go-rounds. These are all supplied by the colony enterprises, the blacksmith shop and the carpentry department. Bats and balls are standard school equipment. All textbooks and school supplies are provided by the colony.

The colony schools lack teaching aids like projectors, television sets, radios, phonographs, and pianos. The Hutterians disapprove of them on religious grounds. Since they are not compulsory and many rural schools in the province do not have them, the official administrator has not forced them on colony schools.

Many colonies have teacherages, but I found some of them barely satisfactory. In a questionnaire filled out by the teachers, most of them were classified from fair to good. When I discussed the subject with one married teacher the latter's rejoinder was that in most rural school districts in Manitoba no teacherages were provided, and married teachers were not engaged or were required to live in barely habitable quarters. In comparison, the colony teacherages, usually complete with heating facilities and electricity, were good. The single teachers are usually supplied with a few pieces of furniture by the colony. A typical colony teacherage for the public school teacher has a bed, mattress, dresser, table, chairs, washstand, washbasin, and pitcher for water. Since most non-Hutterian school districts in rural Manitoba have no teacherages, and those that exist are bare of all furniture and usually lack even a heater, teachers appreciate the extras they receive at the colony teacherages.

Most colonies have cement sidewalks leading from the homes and the community hall area to the school. In addition colony girls sweep and clean the school, and colony men start the fire in the morning. These are chores which in many rural schools of the province are left to the teacher.

On a trip which I made to ten colonies just before the opening of school in the fall of 1957 I found without exception that colony girls had carefully scrubbed the floors and desks. The blackboards were clean and the libraries were in good order. Where there were teacherages these too had been washed and cleaned.

A senior official of the Department of Education claimed that if any rural municipality in Manitoba cared to make a random selection of its schools and to compare twenty-five of them with the twenty-five Hutterian schools, the latter would "come out on top." To check this statement I visited a number of rural non-Hutterian schools along the old Number One highway from Headingly to Portage la Prairie. In comparison with these schools the colony public school plants were in a better state and were better equipped.

The Hutterian Schoolchild

The colony child is as a rule friendly, cooperative, uninhibited, and obedient, but is always ready for a little diversion. The teachers also find that most pupils lack aggressive initiative and the desire to excel. They rate the teacher's and parents' approval very high. The remarkable thing is that though the colony child is exposed for eight or more years to the influence of the public school, daily meets an "outsider" in the person of the teacher, and in his lessons in history, geography, and literature is introduced to other peoples and other ways, he emerges in the end a thorough Hutterian, convinced that community life as lived in the colony is the best way of life.

One teacher, new to the profession and to the colony ways, told her class about life in the outside world. She painted it in glowing colors, and the children were intensely interested and listened eagerly. When she had finished the teacher asked the senior pupils to write a composition on the topic "The Outside World." The best essay, written by a girl in grade seven, read as follows:

The outside world is very different from our world. The people do different things which we are not allowed to do on the colony. They go to dances, which are evil. They paint their finger-nails and lips, and put on funny-looking eyebrows. They smoke, which is just a waste of money and does them no good.

They go to shows in which pictures show a lot about fighting and family quarrels. The families stay up till twelve o'clock at night, which tires the children and can lead to no good. Some parents teach their children only good manners and forget about religion, which is very necessary.

People in the outside world drink and quarrel. Some read bad magazines. Some even steal, rob and kill, as if they didn't have anything better to do. In the summer they spend their time at the beaches instead of doing something useful. People outside do not live in community as we do. They live and work only for themselves.

This essay is typical of those that were handed in. To explore the colony child's attitudes and interests further, I conducted a project in cooperation with a number of teachers to assess the loyalty to and identification with the colony of Hutterian pupils. Children who had spent seven or eight years at the public school were given a choice of essay topics. Out of twenty pupils only two showed an interest in the world beyond the colony.

The most popular topic selected was "Our Family." In their essays the children revealed a great attachment to their brothers, sisters, and parents, and other relatives who may live in several colonies. Another favorite topic, especially among the boys, was "Our Colony." The children were well informed on the life of the colony and expressed what they knew fairly clearly. There usually emerged a complete survey in which the pupils stated the colony population, the number of families and family dwellings, the size of barns, the number of farm animals and the size of poultry flocks, and the different kinds of machinery used by the community. Beyond that the boys showed a great familiarity with every colony enterprise. They knew the number of eggs gathered every day, the price of the land, the yield per acre of different farm crops, and other relevant information. The girls were equally familiar with the work of their mothers and older sisters. "In winter my sisters often sew all day long," wrote one girl. "Rebecca can sew as many as eleven men's shirts a day and they look just as nice as those you can buy at the store."

Some pupils wrote on the topic "An Interesting Trip," but even a tour through some Winnipeg feed mill or department store soon developed into a description of the feeding of poults at the colony, or the purchase of material "from which mother makes the clothes for our family." In two compositions on "My Most Exciting Experience" the experiences turned out to be a mishap with a truck and an incident in which an older brother brought home and tamed a squirrel.

A number of girls selected the subject "Sunday at the Colony." The theme in the essays submitted was "It is wonderful that God takes care of us." There was a moralizing undercurrent: "In church we pray on bended knees like all Christians should." Small bits of information were introduced in passing which showed that important colony events are remembered and discussed: "Our younger preacher held the service. He was made preacher on February 15th, 1956."

The one subject selected that indicated an interest beyond the colony was "What I Would Like to Be When I Grow Up." One boy wanted to be a trapper, and another a bush pilot. The rest began their essays, "When I grow up I want to be a chicken-man like my father," or "I want to be a cat-man [caterpillar operator] when I grow up."

One teacher, Miss Mary Nikkel, of Sunnyside colony, summarized the essays written by her pupils as follows: "The general attitude expressed in them was a desire to remain on the colony. The girls wanted to keep a clean house and do the work in the kitchen with the others. One of the boys said he wanted to be a pilot."

In most ways the Hutterian schoolchild is not very different from other schoolchildren. Among the things colony children like in school are reading storybooks, singing and drawing, parties and Christmas concerts, recess, "four o'clock," games, and "when our teacher says 'Put your books away.'" The same group stated their dislikes: too much work, short recess, children who laugh and talk in school, children who make the teacher angry, long school days, and short summer holidays. About as many school subjects were liked as were disliked.

At one colony a new teacher, after introducing herself to the pupils, told them that the outlandish ways of their parents were not in keeping with Canadian ways. She stressed to the children that it was permissible for them as Canadians to break some of the "silly" colony rules. The teacher was soon surrounded inside and outside the classroom by a passivity that made receptive teaching almost impossible. She did not change her conviction that the people should be integrated, but felt that her initial technique had been faulty. "As people and as parents the Hutterians are fine," she said, "but their odd customs and clothes have no place in Canada."

This attitude and the consequent relationship are not usual. The teacher comes to the colony as a total stranger, but is accepted as a friend. The children especially anticipate the coming of the new teacher with great eagerness. Nineteen-year-old Audrey Bennet, teaching at the Rosedale colony, thought she had never met nicer people. "I am invited to their houses," said Miss Bennet, "and I feel at home there. Mrs. Waldner, for instance, is like a second mother to me." Another young girl described her first Sunday at the colony: "The girls invited me to church. I had on a Dacron blouse, and they asked me whether I had a coat to wear over it. I felt that the only reason for this request was that the girls wanted their people and the minister to think well of me. When I joined in the singing they liked it." At Christmas the parents of this teacher, who resided in Winnipeg, had to come by car to get all the presents home. Though the number of Christmas presents may depend on the colony and the personality of the teacher, some of the teachers are amply "rewarded." One married teacher received for Christmas a home-woven laundry basket, pillowcases, knitted socks, colony-made wine, sausages, a duck, towels, and many smaller gifts.

The Christmas concert, attended by parents and older brothers and sisters, has been discontinued by some colonies. The reason is that many teachers, unfamiliar with Hutterian tradition, prepared concerts typical of Manitoba rural schools. There were comical acts and dialogues, painted faces and padded Santas. Though the Hutterians enjoyed these programs, they felt that they were not in keeping with their tradition. Now the teachers, if they have concerts at all, have their programs on the last day of school. Only the schoolchildren, dressed in their Sunday clothes, attend. A teacher who has been at the colony for some time may take greater liberty, and this is permitted by the colony. Compositions written by John Dyck's pupils of Barickman colony refer to Christmas as the highlight of the year, with the parents in attendance for the concert.

Most Hutterian school districts allot about one dollar per pupil with which the teacher buys presents for the pupils at Christmas. The inexperienced teacher, or the teacher who delegates the work to the shopper of a department store, may present the children with jewelry, ties, and other articles appreciated by the children but not approved by the colony.

One teacher commented on the lack of a competitive spirit in his school. "The children are happy in whatever grade they are." Another teacher who had taught for many years in rural schools, and spent eight years teaching at one colony school before he retired from the profession, said, "School there is very much like elsewhere, except that their singing is livelier."

Attendance at colony schools is exceptionally good. Twenty colony teachers returned a questionnaire reporting attendance for the first half of the school year 1956–1957. The average attendance was 94.4 per cent. Since the schools are located in the colonies, transportation and bad weather are no problem. Some teachers reported that for months the attendance would be almost perfect. The Department of Education awards special certificates to schools with perfect monthly attendance. One young teacher was discouraged when month after month his school had almost perfect attendance, but always, quite by accident, some pupil would stay away from school to see a dentist or get some medical attention. The pupil would fully realize that his absence spoiled the record, and that the visit to the dentist could have been postponed. But the children could not see any reason why they should earn a certificate.

Writing about the education of Hutterian children in Alberta, Pitt maintains that it is "fairly good, in so far as it goes. The trouble, of course, is that it does not go nearly far enough." [9] This is equally true for Manitoba. As soon as the Hutterian schoolchild reaches the age when he may legally stop going to school, he does so. Only within the last few years have some students continued beyond grade eight. For the school year 1957–1958 about a third of the colony schools had grade nine or grade ten correspondence students. This does not compare unfavorably with many other rural schools in the province.

The school library is used extensively by some colonies. At one community a group of young married men spent the winter evenings studying mathematics, English, and other subjects, quite on their own. The colony asked one of these men, the hog-man, whether he would care to continue his education and perhaps eventually qualify as a public school teacher. Hesitatingly the man, who was in charge of one of the finest hog enterprises in the province, consented. His brother was elected the new hog-man, and the prospective teacher, aged thirty-three, married, and with a family of eight children, went to a private school in Winnipeg to complete his high school work. The former hog-man, Peter Maendel of the New Rosedale colony, has now graduated from Manitoba Teachers College and is teaching at a colony public school. When I asked him about his important decision, he carefully corrected me. "It was not my decision," he said. "It was made by the community."

To speak of this development as a trend is premature. It is important that secondary education is being discussed at the colonies. Senior Elder

Peter Hofer sees no objection to higher education except that it exposes young people during their formative years to temptations and worldly influences. Submerged indications, too blurred to assess with confidence, are that the next ten years may see a less rigid rejection of secondary education.

On the whole, the public school performs its purpose in providing elementary education in the English language to all Hutterian children. Sometimes small incidents at the colony, carelessly reported, may distort the outsider's view of the community people. During and immediately after World War II a rumor was circulated widely that Hutterians removed the picture of the king from school walls. This story was partly true. Schoolrooms are frequently used for church services. Since the Hutterians have an iconoclastic tradition, pictures were sometimes removed or hung face to the wall during the service.[10] As soon as the Hutterians found that this practice was considered disrespectful to the monarch it was abandoned. At colony schools the picture of the queen smiles benignly down on her Hutterian subjects, and they sing "God Save the Queen" and "O Canada" as lustily as other Canadian children.

In comparison with other rural schools colony schools operate satisfactorily. They are centrally administered by an experienced official. The school program is the same as for the rest of the province. The school plants, including supplies and equipment, are as good as or better than those generally found in the rural areas of Manitoba. The problem of getting qualified teachers is acute, as it is for all rural schools. Since the colony school is one of the very few contacts with the outside world available to the Hutterian child, perhaps even greater efforts could be made to engage qualified and capable teachers for the Hutterian school. However, the fact remains that Hutterians expressly suspect higher education as "nonconductive to the fear of God" (Friedmann), and discourage it. Edwin Pitt, in his Alberta survey, says, "The Hutterians remain opposed to higher education because they are still convinced that it makes for dissatisfaction with a simple, homely existence, and with manual toil."[11]

XI

SOME ASPECTS OF HUTTERIAN
COMMUNITY STABILITY

OBSERVERS have often been impressed with the stability as well as the vigorous growth of the Hutterian communities. Some of the indicators that are often used to measure community stability are the natural increase of the group, the physical and mental health of its members, the prevalence or absence of crime and delinquency, and the degree of acceptance or rejection of traditional institutions and mores. Using these indicators as a measure confirms the impression of the stability of the Hutterian communities.

Hutterian Multiplication

The Hutterians have been called the most prolific people in North America. Some Manitoba briefs demanding restrictive legislation against the Hutterians voiced the opinion that if left unchecked the group would soon populate most of rural Manitoba. C. F. Bentley, professor of soil science at the University of Alberta, projected the population increase of the Hutterians to the year 2302 and found that by that time they would number 20,594,432,000.[1] Though this alarming figure justly reflects a part of the current worldwide concern over the population explosion, nevertheless, because of the small size of the Hutterian communities, it poses no immediate problem. Even if the present rate of increase among the Hutterians continues and their population doubles every eighteen to twenty years, there would be fewer than 20,000 Hutterians in Manitoba by the year 2000. And while a proportional increase in the number of colonies would affect the rural pattern of settlement in the province, it would hardly dominate Manitoba's countryside.

The fact remains that the Hutterians' birth rate is hardly equalled in the Western world, and their low death rate is approached only by the most advanced countries, as the accompanying tabulation indicates.[2]

Population	Period	Birth Rate per 1000	Death Rate per 1000	Rate of Increase
Hutterians	1946–1950	45.9	4.4	41.5
Canada	1946–1951	27.4	9.3	18.1
United States	1949–1951	24.0	9.7	14.3
Mexico	1949–1951	44.9	17.0	27.9

In their study Eaton and Weil place the Hutterian infant mortality rate at 45 per thousand, and the total Hutterian death rate as "similar to that of the United States white population." [3] The Canadian infant mortality rate for the period between 1946 to 1950 ranges from 41 to 47 per thousand, and thus approximates the infant death rate cited by Eaton and Weil for the Hutterians.

While the actual death rate among Hutterians is low, the figure of 4.4 per thousand, provided by the *Population Bulletin*, at first inspection appears excessively low. The explanation lies in the high birth rate and the relative youthfulness of the colony population. The life expectancy of the Hutterian approximates that of the Canadian and American white population.

The Hutterians do not equal the high birth rate of the French-Canadians, who reached their peak in the period from 1681 to 1720.[4] Their birth rate stood at 53.7 per thousand. This high birth rate was offset by a high death rate of 21.5. The rate of natural increase was thus 32.2 per thousand, which is lower than that of the Hutterians.

The late marriages among the Hutterians reduce their birth rate considerably below its theoretically possible level. In Canada and the United States over 70 out of 1000 females in the 15 to 19 age group give birth to infants. Among the Hutterians only 12 out of 1000 females in this age group give birth to infants. Once married, Hutterian women continue to reproduce sometimes even beyond the age of forty-five. The Church does not sanction birth control, nor is it practiced. Women may sometimes sigh over their frequent pregnancies, but they concur with the general attitude of the colony, which is to let nature take its course.

The Hutterian population pattern is not characterized by cycles like those of most Western societies, where economic depressions, wars, or other factors influence population growth. Instead the Hutterian demographic trend may be described as stable but not stationary.

Hutterian Physical Health

The health of the members of the colony is the concern of the whole community. While the interest in health in individualistic society is largely in terms of monetary values, the cost of medical services, and the loss in earnings, this concern with the economic implications of poor health is secondary in a Hutterian colony. The sick and invalided and their families have no worries about the cost of medical care, the loss of wages through unemployment, or the economic future of the family in case of the death of a parent. Hutterians carry no life insurance[5] but the family provider's illness or death in no way affects the financial security of his family. The resultant absence of worry may partly explain the group's good mental health.

Hutterians are health-conscious. A group of small children who followed me at a tour of one colony were told by the kindergarten teacher to stay out of the pig barns. Turning to me the teacher explained, "There are flies there. Besides, there are the farm animals, any one of which could be a disease carrier. For this reason I do not permit the small children to play around the barn." At the same time it should be mentioned that most colony barns are kept remarkably free from flies and insects.[6]

Another example of Hutterian concern for their health was provided by a visit to Riverside colony in Manitoba. I asked an old Hutterian where I could find the minister. The man interrupted his work and, waving toward the kitchen, said: "He is with the nurses. *Mir sind zu fett* [We are too fat]." Later the minister explained to me that the community felt its diet was too rich, and he had invited a dietician from Brandon and a public health nurse to analyze the colony kitchen's menus for the week. A few days later I visited the same colony again and noticed that for the afternoon coffee break the kitchen tables had, beside the customary pastries and sandwiches, large bowls of oranges and apples. This conscious awareness of the importance of health to the community is pronounced in most colonies.

Hutterian attention to physical health becomes apparent when it is realized that the per capita outlay for medical purposes of Hutterian communities in Manitoba stood at well over thirty dollars in 1957. This covered hospitalization, medication, and the services of doctors, dentists, and opticians. The rise in cost of medical services to the colonies has been considerable. A colony with a population of 104 spent $3391.14 for medical services in 1955; in 1960 a colony with a population of 114 spent $5484.20. Colony members are free to select their doctors and hospitals. The first-mentioned colony employed the services of nineteen professional people residing in four towns and in the city of Winnipeg. Its patients used local and Winnipeg hospitals. One patient also used the services of the Mayo Clinic at Rochester, Minnesota.

Referring particularly to the women, Dr. Clark attributes "their abounding good health" to "being out of doors so much." [7] Another reason may be the regular rhythm of Hutterian routine. The old axiom "Early to bed, early to rise" is followed literally. All older children and adults rise at about the same time, between five and six in summer and six and seven o'clock in winter. Bedtime varies with different families, but is rarely after eleven o'clock. There are no radio and television programs to influence sleeping routine.

Meals are served very punctually, and the emphasis is on home-raised and home-grown produce (see Chapter VII). Patients and invalids eat in their homes. Colony women, usually under the supervision of the colony midwife or the head cook, attend to their needs. Medical doctors who were interviewed spoke highly of the work of the midwives. They generally have no professional training, but have learned their skill from their predecessors. On the whole, however, the colonies increasingly rely on the medical services of professional people outside the colonies.

To the observer who spends some time at a colony the mangled fingers, gashes, and cuts sustained by children and adults alike seem to occur with unusual frequency. Advanced mechanization from kitchen to livestock barns and the proximity of playgrounds to workshops and heavy machinery may make the Hutterians more prone to accidents than their farm neighbors. This at least was my impression; figures to substantiate or invalidate this observation were not available.

Hutterian endogamy over several centuries has resulted in considerable inbreeding. Family records in almost all cases can be traced for well over two hundred years, and they show that the Hutterians at no time permitted the marriage of individuals related more closely than the degrees permitted by Canadian law today. There is also evidence that the Hutterian leaders have always been aware of the problem of inbreeding and have consulted medical authorities on this matter. According to one Manitoba doctor the dangers of inbreeding, always more acute in weak than in healthy stock, are not present today among the Hutterians. The group is sufficiently large to permit mate selection with the greatest assurance of safety.

Though no intensive study of the physical health of the Hutterians has been made to date, the almost complete absence of polio and some other diseases has attracted the attention of medical and biological researchers.[8] On the whole the relatively good health enjoyed by the members of the colonies may be the result of a number of factors: they are of healthy peasant stock, have adequate access to medical services, lead regulated lives, believe in plain fare, and consciously practice temperance in all things.

Hutterian Mental Health

The Hutterians lay no claim to immunity from mental illness. However, an Alberta study drew attention to the mental health of the Hutterians, and a Manitoba report stated that the Hutterians do not "contribute to the overcrowding of our mental hospitals since the mental security derived from their system results in a complete absence of mental illness."[9] When it came to the attention of the National Institute of Mental Health of the United States Public Health Service that Hutterians enjoyed a reputation for good mental health, that body undertook to send a team of American and Canadian scientists, under Dr. Joseph W. Eaton, to investigate this aspect of community life.[10]

Their study concluded that the Hutterian "lifetime risk of all types of mental disorders is as low or lower than that of any contemporary Euro-American group." Moreover, the report said, while the Hutterian way provided no "antidote for severe mental disorders," it did provide "an atmosphere within which emotionally disturbed persons were encouraged to get well or to function in a socially accepted manner within the limits imposed by their illness."[11]

Dr. Eaton's team consulted fifty-five Canadian and American medical men who had Hutterian patients. Their clinical judgments were that, compared to their other, non-Hutterian patients, the Hutterians had "less" of the following symptoms: stuttering, nail-biting, chronic headaches, night-walking, cancer, chronic constipation, spastic colitis, chronic digestive disturbances, kidney malfunctions, hypertensive complications in pregnancy, complaints of menstrual disorders, female frigidity, aggressiveness in personal relationships, worry about illness, feelings of personal inadequacy, chronic nightmares, amnesia, drug addiction, extreme alcoholism, nervous tics, fainting, hysterical seizures, asthma, food allergies, hay fever, suicides (including attempts), complaints of poor appetite, urinary tract infections, syphilis, male impotence, and fear of death.

Between the Hutterians and their other patients the same doctors found "little or no difference" in these symptoms: hypochondriac complaints, arteriosclerosis, chronic bedwetting, and eczema. Also, the average life expectancy was approximately the same.

Finally in a third category the doctors reported that Hutterians had "more" than other patients of: obesity, fats in their diet, and capacity to endure pain. The overall conclusion was that the general physical and mental health of the Hutterians was better than that of their other patients.[12]

The investigators found that heterosexual relationships were extremely "sound" among the colony people, and that cases of homosexuality were unknown. Furthermore, that illegitimacy was almost unknown among them and that Hutterian marriages were characterized by a "remarkable stability." They report only one divorce and two separations for all communities in Canada and the United States, presumably extending over their entire period on this continent. On the whole they were impressed with "the balance, poise and maturity" of the Hutterian people.

Even before the group made its survey two American sociologists, Dr. Bertha Clark and Dr. Lee Emerson Deets, had conducted individual research among the Hutterians and had noted the absence of murder, arson, burglary, forgery, and other forms of crime.[13] The solicitor of the Hutterian communities, E. A. Fletcher, Q.C., of Winnipeg, who has been their legal adviser since shortly after they came to Canada in 1918, stated that no Hutterian had ever been charged with a major offense. Interviews I had with representatives of the Canadian Mounted Police and the Winnipeg City Police corroborated this. Said one constable: "Once or twice when a young Hutterian delinquent was hauled up for a misdemeanor we found it best to turn him over to their own elders. They know how to handle such cases better than anyone else."

In one such instance where four young Hutterians on a rabbit hunt did some damage to a neighbor's farm they were taken into custody by the police. The press report on the incident follows:

An elderly spokesman for the colony told the court the four had never been in any trouble before. Apparently it just seemed a good idea at the time.

"You are not youngsters," Magistrate Potter told the accused, "You are old enough to have brains to know that you are doing wrong. If it was not this time of year I would keep you in jail for a week." The magistrate then asked the colony spokesman what punishment would be meted out to the men by the Hutterites. The spokesman said: "In the case of the younger ones they are given a licking, but these will face punishment in the church. They will be punished for what they did."

The spokesman said the damages and fines and costs would be looked after by the colony.[14]

Perhaps the most serious offense with which Hutterians have been charged is that of smuggling. Hutterians commute freely between the United States and Canada, exchanging truckloads of feed for truckloads of watermelons, and engage in other forms of intercolony barter. As a rule these exchanges and the importation of purchased articles are reported at the border. However, there have been exceptions. In 1957 two Hutterian communities were charged with a breach of the Customs Act and fines were imposed. The crown counsel said that the colony leaders had given the police every cooperation in their investigations.[15]

In discussing law violations under the heading of mental health it is not necessarily suggested that law infringement and crime always can be traced back to mental abnormality. But unquestionably tension, mental illness, and the social disintegration of a culture or society provide a favorable climate for misdemeanor, vice, and crime. The well-integrated Hutterian society, economic security, and life led in a familiar and accepted pattern are all factors that contribute to a lessening of individual and group tension and conflict. The result is a society practically void of crime in every form.

Misdemeanor and Punishment

The Hutterians make no claim that their colonies are communities of saints. Though the everyday life is usually harmonious enough, there are problems which periodically confront the community. These may range from minor misdemeanors to serious violations of congregation-community regulations. The possession of a musical instrument, a radio, or cigarettes, drunkenness or vanity in clothes, dishonesty, and disobedience would alike set into motion the colony's disciplinary machinery. Transgressions are usually soon discovered. The intimacy of communal life, the almost complete lack of privacy in a community where all work is generally done in groups, leisure time is spent and enjoyed at the colony under the eyes of companions, and any member may go into any colony home without even the formality of knocking at the door, makes everyone his brother's keeper.

Social control, the approval or the disapproval of the group, is the great regulator of colony behavior. But more tangible disciplinary measures may be applied. The milder forms range from physical punishment of children to admonitions from the ministers or members of the colony council. A more serious misdemeanor by a baptized member may require the delinquent to appear before the congregation at the end of the church service to voice contrition. In very serious cases the congregation may resort to the *Meidung* (avoidance, or shunning), which is the extreme form of punishment.

Boys and men are more often involved in misdemeanors and infractions than girls and women. Woman's work is usually done in larger groups and the social control may be correspondingly stronger. It would also appear that an admonition by the minister is more effective with women than with men. As a rule if a girl is found using cosmetics or is guilty of frivolous behavior, the disapproval of the group or a lecture by the minister will bring about immediate conformity, if not repentance. Even the most daring girls, however good looking and intelligent, are generally careful to remain within the rules set by the community, and see to it that their sleeves are not too short and their kerchiefs not too colorful. With the women gossip or petty jealousy may sometimes disturb the harmony of the community, and in such cases a visit from the minister suffices to achieve contrition.

Boys are more ready than girls to violate community rules. Smoking and the possession of a radio concealed in a room are perhaps the most common delinquencies.[16] Usually the boys who break some regulation are not baptized and are thus officially not members of the Church. If the guilt is established the first offense may be dismissed with a lecture. If it is repeated the community council may ask the parent to administer corporal punishment. If the violation is continued and the parental punishment is deemed unsatisfactory the council may ask the German teacher as the custodian of the community youth to punish the delinquent.

Edna Staebler recorded the following story after a visit to an Alberta colony:

"I hat once a phonograph, just a liddle box it wass with Golden Slibbers and Beautiful Brown Eyes and all dem nize records," a raffish man told us. "I played it to myself in my room and one time I took it oud in the fields and played it for a couple of girls but my mother told the preajer on me and he made me sell it."

"Did he punish you?" Nadene asked.

"Yo, but he never punishes us bad; he just tells everybody in church what all sins we done and that shames us so we don't try it again for maybe a week anyways."

"It lasts longer than that," a sixteen-year-old said ruefully, and everyone laughed.[17]

The very informal modes of punishment for deviant behavior are stages of physical and spiritual isolation, depending on the seriousness of the violation. To the outsider they would appear almost ludicrously ineffectual. But the offender's conditioned sensitivity to group disapproval and sincere awareness of guilt make communal life extremely unpleasant for him until he shows remorse. These stages of *Meidung*, the deliberate avoidance of the culprit, the Hutterians aptly term *den Frieden nehmen* (taking away the peace). Taking away the delinquent's peace of mind until he shows contrition or makes amends is the purpose of shunning.

In serious transgressions the offender may be forbidden to communicate with other members of the colony, including even his own wife. There may be physical isolation, in which he is assigned a special room for the night. This does not mean solitary confinement, for the offender is expected to continue with his regular duties. But he will be required to take his meals alone in the community dining room. Since by his offense the delinquent has excluded himself from the spiritual community of the Brotherhood, he is also isolated from the physical community. If he attends a church service he is seated at the back, separated from the others. When he is thus constantly surrounded by a disapproving, but not hostile, group, shunning as a punishment takes effect and becomes more and more oppressive with time. The delinquent's peace is not restored until he is prepared to ask God and the congregation for forgiveness. This he does before the assembled congregation.

Once the community readmits the offender the other members are forbidden to refer to the offense. But the offender's name and the violation are entered in the church record book. On the whole the community's patience with offending members is most remarkable. It is literally based on Jesus's answer to Peter when the latter asked whether forgiving a brother seven times was sufficient, and Jesus told him, not seven times "but until seventy times seven" (Matthew 18:22).

One typical colony near Winnipeg had the names of four offenders in its annals in the first eight years of its existence. None of the offenses appeared very serious to the outsider; they concerned such matters as the purchase of a colorful parka and the use of tobacco, both interdicted by colony rules.

No member of the community, whether baptized or not, is punished by exclusion from the colony unless his behavior is such that exclusion appears to be the only solution. Only one case of this nature is on record for the province of Manitoba, and it goes back over thirty years. The head of a Hutterian family joined the Jehovah's Witnesses. He was not physically excluded from the Brotherhood but was asked not to proselytize for a belief that was contrary to Hutterian doctrine. When the member persisted in using the community as his mission field he was asked to leave. The man left and his family decided to leave with him. However, there does not appear to have been ill-feeling on either side.

If a person occupies an important position in the colony and it becomes known that he has committed a misdemeanor, he relinquishes the post. The term "deposed" is used by outsiders, but the actual process is more subtle. The communal training is such that the delinquent, once it becomes known that he has violated a regulation, does not wait for a formal censure but of his own volition retires from the position of trust, thus in effect admitting his guilt. In the fall of 1957 a colony steward was guilty of a fraudulent act: he took community funds for personal use without accounting for them. Before long this was discovered, he resigned, and Hutterian justice took its course. I discussed the matter at the time with members of various communities. At the home community as well as at other communities one could feel the concern and sympathy toward the offender who had been weighed and found wanting. In effect this very sympathy contributes to the guilt feeling of the delinquent. From the outset there appeared to be a general acceptance of his eventual rehabilitation. After some years the man again came to occupy a position of trust.

As has been said there are no cases on record where Hutterians were involved in murder, arson, robbery, or other major offenses. There has been one case of suicide in Hutterian history since they came to this continent over ninety years ago. It occurred in one of the colonies in Manitoba and its apparent cause was extreme alcoholism.

There are no alcoholics in the colonies now. The Hutterian position on alcohol is that taken in moderation it is harmless. At the colony home-made or purchased wine may be served on Sundays or festive occasions. H. Goerz, who spent many years as a public school teacher at Hutterian colonies, maintains that drunkenness there is "very rare indeed." When I asked the waiter at the Elie hotel (one-third of the Manitoba colonies are around Elie) about Hutterian drinking habits he said that the men returning from Winnipeg sometimes "drop in for a glass of beer." They "drink it quietly and leave." In his experience none of them had ever "taken too much."

A widespread opinion held by outsiders is that Hutterians are given to theft, that they will steal from the colony to sell for private gain, or steal from neighbors or from counters in department stores. It is generally assumed that it must be a simple matter for the hog-man or the poultry-man to steal several pigs or crates of eggs, sell them, and pocket the money. Though the colony has no formal system of checks to guard its interests, it takes for granted the honesty of its members. The community setting is essentially an extended family setting. In any case the life, work, and possessions of any member are an open book to the entire colony.[18] Furthermore, it is very rare for a person to leave the colony by himself. He is usually accompanied by his family, or, on a business trip, by one or two helpers. The poultry-man or the hog-man does not necessarily take the products of his own enterprise to market. In short, it would require a series of risky machinations for anyone to commit fraud. This and the general dedication of the member to his congregation make theft from the colony a rarity. That it does occur is evidenced by the case of the "deposed" colony manager already mentioned.

According to Eaton the opinion that Hutterians do not respect private property of others is based on rumors. He suggests that these rumors reflect the outsiders' feelings "about the unusual features of the Hutterite way of life." When these rumors were traced to their source they "turned out to have no validity." [19] In several instances I traced rumors about Hutterian dishonesty and my findings were a corroboration of Eaton's thesis.

A doctor's receptionist claimed that in the office she had seen two Hutterian women looking over their stolen goods, some pillowcases. When the receptionist was asked how she knew the articles were stolen her explanation was that "everybody knows these women carry no money, and I wouldn't put it past them that if they saw something they liked they'd put their hands on it."

H. G. Payment, the secretary-treasurer of the municipality of Cartier for almost as long as the Hutterians have lived in it, said that in earlier years people would accuse the Hutterians every time an article disappeared, but this had changed. There are ten Hutterian communities in the municipality and Mr. Payment could not recall a single instance in which a charge of pilfering or theft could be substantiated.

It is not suggested that all Hutterians have a clear record of honesty. But the evidence is undeniable that they as a group are at least no more guilty of this form of delinquency than their neighbors.

Leaving the community for the outside world is, in the Hutterian view, an offense. While some colonies have not lost a single member of the community, there are some where a number have left the colony sanctuary. At one colony four young men left in one year. In most cases those who leave are young unmarried men who have not yet joined the Church. Statistics on this subject are misleading, for almost all of those who leave eventually return. Women very rarely leave the community for life outside it. In two or three cases they left the colony only to follow their husbands; in as many cases they refused to do even this.

Many of the boys between the ages of seventeen and twenty who leave do so with the understanding, but not with the colony's approval, that they will return after one or two years. Others, again, stay away much longer. At one colony the German teacher was away for twenty-three years, operated his own business, then returned and settled down apparently quite contented. It is significant that he did not marry until he returned to the colony. Another member of the same community spent fourteen years as a sailor on the Great Lakes before he came back. Once the member returns, shows penitence, and accepts punishment, the episode is forgotten. One man who spent many years away from the colony was recently ordained colony minister.

During the anti-Hutterian agitation in Manitoba in 1947 (see Chapter IV) those people who favored restriction of Hutterian communities also favored legislation "whereby any man, woman, or child" who left the colony would get his "equitable share of the colony assets." [20] The Hutterians opposed the move, maintaining that it would disrupt their colonies. There were also practical grounds for objections, as has been pointed out. Courts would find it difficult to apportion "equitable shares" to members who repeatedly left and returned to their colonies. For many years, despite the agitation, no Manitoba Hutterian who had left his colony demanded in court or outside of court a part of the colony assets, nor did any of them support the demands for legislation that would permit them a share in colony assets. In the spring of 1965 one such case developed; according to a press report "a statement of claim" was filed against the Interlake colony near Teulon, Manitoba.[21] This case had not been decided at the time this book went to press.

The men who leave the colony usually find no difficulty in making their way. Since they have spent some time as apprentices at various colony enterprises they are familiar with carpentry, work at machine shops and garages, or any type of farm work. They generally qualify for good jobs but not white-collar positions, for which they lack the requisite formal education. One Hutterian teen-ager left a colony shortly before World War II and found employment at a garage where his workmanship and skill soon became an asset to the garage.[22] With the outbreak of the war he joined a tank unit and went overseas. After the war he returned to work for a well-known service garage in Winnipeg, where he occupied a position of responsibility. Then one day he packed his belongings, returned to the colony, joined the Church, and married.

Another young man, Sam Kleinsasser, ran away from a Manitoba colony twice before the age of eighteen, but was taken back each time by his parents. As soon as he came of age he left again and joined the army. After the war he married a non-Hutterian girl and is now comfortably settled in one of the better residential areas of Winnipeg. He owns a good home, attractively furnished and complete with a television set. The man, his wife, and their three children are indistinguishable from other families in the neighborhood. The wife had not known her husband's background before they were married. The family visits the husband's former colony several times a year, and is in turn visited by his relatives. Though the wife finds life very different in the colony and took exception to their clothes and language, which she does not speak, her attitude toward the colony people is anything but hostile.

The husband, who has been away from the colony for eighteen years, is not prepared to exclude the possibility of going back but admits that now that he has a family it is unlikely. Still, the family ties are strong. Joey, the oldest Kleinsasser boy, was an incubator baby and required much attention at birth. His grandmother at the colony took him to her home, and here he remained until he developed into a healthy baby. Again before the third child arrived the Kleinsassers took the two older children to their grandmother at the colony.[28]

Invariably former colony members show marked tolerance and often actual loyalty toward the Hutterian communities and their institutions. "I am not a good enough Christian to live in community, and don't feel at ease outside of it," was the way one man who left the colony explained it. "Perhaps the whole fault lies with us," said a twenty-six-year-old former colony — but not church — member, "for the colony religion is good. When I visit the colony I attend church service. When I left the colony I told the boys I would be back in two years. That was six years ago, and now I don't know when I'll go back." He does know, however, that regardless of where he is or how long he stays away, his parents, his brothers and sisters, his childhood companions will all be there at their familiar tasks. "Colony people don't know how well off they are," said Mr. Kleinsasser reflectively. A nostalgic longing, it would seem, draws many of the deserters irresistibly back to their colonies.

At the same time every colony discourages its members and young people from leaving the colony sanctuary for the temptations of the world. It was also my impression that those who had left and returned were regarded with an ever so slight but lingering suspicion.

On the whole, deviant behavior, including colony desertion, is rare. It is not a serious factor contributing to colony disintegration. Hutterians themselves talk freely about the inroads "the world" is making on their way of life. Young men would just as soon have station wagons as the cumbersome buses used for transportation, and sometimes young girls chafe about regulations that require them not to mark their shawls with artistically embroidered names. But to the outsider these and other inroads of "the world" appear trivial.

The popular notion that the ministers form a hierarchy and wield despotic power over the "colony inmates" is not consistent with the facts. On the whole the Hutterians, old and young, men and women, are sincerely dedicated to the ideal of the Christian brotherhood, which to them is expressed in their *Gemeinschaft*, or community. This devotion to a common ideal is the strongest cohesive force and provides the basis for communal stability.

Intercolony Organization

For many years the three major branches of Hutterianism in North America — the *Lehrerleut'* and *Dariusleut'* in Alberta, Saskatchewan, and Montana, and the *Schmiedeleut'* of Manitoba and South Dakota — had no formal ties with each other, but the restrictive legislation of Alberta and the Manitoba Hutterian inquiry achieved indirectly a consolidation of these congregations. In 1950 a unified association was formed which for legal reasons included only the Canadian colonies. The association was incorporated the following year under the name of the Hutterian Brethren Church.[24] The executive of the association meets once a year. The function of the association is largely to represent the Hutterian Church whenever matters of common concern, like the introduction of restrictive legislation in a province, present a common danger. The association has no powers in matters affecting the internal organization of the three component groups.

Each of the three groups has its own organization headed by a bishop known as *Ältester* or *Vorsteher*. The *Vorsteher* of the *Schmiedeleut'* which includes all colonies in Manitoba and South Dakota, is Reverend Peter Hofer, of the James Valley community, at Starbuck in Manitoba. Indeed, since the Hutterians came to Manitoba the *Schmiedeleut'* leader has always been a resident of this province. Peter Hofer's predecessors were Paul Gross, Iberville colony, *Vorsteher* from 1917 to 1931; Joseph Kleinsasser, Milltown colony, 1931–1947; Joseph Waldner, at first of Poplar Point colony and, after it branched out, of Springfield colony, 1947–1951. Hofer, a conservative even by Hutterian standards, was sixty-five years old when he was elected to his present position in 1951.

Since Mr. Hofer heads the Manitoba Hutterians and his work and background in some measure reflect Hutterian ways and ideals, a short biographical sketch may be in place.

Peter Hofer, who was born in South Dakota in 1885, became a German and public school teacher at one of the colonies there. A transcript of his college grades indicates that young Hofer was an able and diligent student.[25] Later he confined his work to the German school. His present home at the James Valley colony in no way differs structurally from the other colony homes. In the living room, which he also uses as a study, are a filing cabinet, a typewriter, and a duplicator. As the senior leader he has assistants, ministers from other colonies who periodically come to help him with his work. Mr. Hofer spends much of his time in reading. His library contains among other books different translations of the Bible, Biblical reference books, and German and English encyclopedias. He is particularly interested in history. In his conversation he shows a keen interest in national and international developments.

The informal atmosphere that characterizes colony life extends to the *Vorsteher*'s home. During my visit our conversation was repeatedly interrupted. Among the callers who came and joined in the discussion was Jacob Hofer, twin brother to Peter, who was the colony shoemaker, beekeeper, and bookbinder. A boy came in with the day's mail, which consisted of letters, periodicals, and newspapers, among them *Time* magazine and the *Winnipeg Free Press*. Mr. Hofer gave the impression that he was quite familiar with developments in the outside world, but he also gave the impression of carrying a deep conviction that the Hutterian way was the nearest way there was to the realization of Christian living.

Each year all the ministers and stewards of the *Schmiedeleut'* meet at a colony designated by the *Vorsteher* to discuss mutual problems. At the conference held at the Waldheim colony on February 9, 1960, a number of new regulations were added to help guide colony behavior. It was decided that Hutterians should avoid beer parlors, and should not order more than one glass of beer with a meal in a restaurant. The conference also went on record as opposing the purchase of clothing like parkas that violated the uniformity of colony garb. It outlined the quota of clothes to be allotted to men and boys, women and girls. Finally the conference discussed the material needs of three South Dakotan colonies, and the assistance that should be given to them. An account of the annual conference proceedings is mimeographed by the *Vorsteher*'s office and distributed among the colonies.

One of the most positive features of community solidarity is its mutual aid system. Colonies may secure interest-free repayable loans from other colonies. Moreover, if one colony should meet with disaster, crop failure, flood, or fire damage, intercolony aid, in both produce and cash, is given freely. The needy community draws up a list of its minimum requirements and the other colonies contribute feed grain, garden products, and money until the needs have been filled. There have been a few cases where colonies established themselves on rented land but dissolved and returned to their home colonies when economic conditions made retrenchment necessary. In these cases special assistance was rendered to the affected colonists.

Mutual aid may also take the form of a labor pool. When a new colony is formed or when a colony is engaged in a building program, neighboring colonies may release their carpenters to help in the erection of buildings. At times Manitoba Hutterians have helped fellow-colonists with their harvesting in South Dakota, and South Dakotans have come to help with the harvest or with the haying at a Manitoba colony. All this mutual aid is of an informal nature, a result of oral rather than written agreements.

The main source of strength of the Hutterian communities is the loyalty and devotion of its members to the community ideal. The high birth rate and a low mortality rate and the relatively good health of the members contribute to the phenomenal growth of the communities. Important, also, is the effectiveness as a control factor of the social-religious mores to which the Hutterians as a group and as individuals adhere with remarkable tenacity. While religion dominates the thinking of the colony members, they are not unaware of the economic well-being of the Brotherhood. Indeed, in Hutterian thinking industrious work and spiritual life cannot be divorced. Moreover, the economic stability of the colonies is assured not only by the willingness of individual members to work for the community and by the discipline exercised within the colony, but also by an informal intercolony aid organization.

He only says, "Good fences make good neighbors." ROBERT FROST

Part Three

THE HUTTERIANS AND THE OUTSIDE WORLD

XII

KINDRED SOCIETIES, CONVERTS,
AND NEIGHBORS

THE HUTTERIAN IDEAL is "the hidden man" of "meek and quiet spirit" (I Peter 3:4). Hutterians deliberately avoid drawing attention to themselves. There are no Hutterian rallies, large conventions, or missionary campaigns. But the Hutterians are not hostile to outsiders. At the Riverside colony, in Manitoba, I met John Yates, a Quaker from England who lives and works with the colony people without having joined their Church. At the Sturgeon Creek colony I met two young German immigrants who were seriously considering joining the group. Johann Brueckner, from Burgenland, Austria, and Reinhold Konrad, from Belgrade, Yugoslavia, felt that they had had enough of life's excitement and were now considering exchanging it for the peace of community life. Thus it is evident that the Hutterians do not lack a certain attraction to some outsiders. But until the rapid expansion of their colonies the Hutterians as a whole passed almost unnoticed. Major encyclopedias, while dealing fully with smaller and less important groups, failed to mention them. Calverton in his history of communal societies in the United States omitted the Hutterians entirely. It is evident that he had not even heard of them, for in referring to American communal societies in his preface he states, "Many endured a long time; none survive today." [1]

The relationship of the Hutterians with the outside world falls into several categories. There is the relationship with kindred groups, that with the converts, and that with outsiders either on a social or business basis.

171

The Amana and the Harmony Society

Long before the Hutterians came to North America the United States was familiar with numerous communal societies. Historically the Hutterians had nothing in common with them, but they established contact with two groups, the Amana and the Harmony societies, both of which had scriptural bases rather than the secular idealism of some other communes. The Hutterian chronicle reports under the entry date of 1878 that the Dakota Brethren received some assistance from the Amana Society of Iowa, and that the relations between the two groups were "most cordial." The friendly relations were strengthened by mutual visits, but after a while the contacts ceased. In Hutterian eyes the Amana people became too worldly.

The Amana Society, founded in New York State in 1842 by Christian Metz, a German immigrant, also practiced community of goods. To isolate the group Metz moved it to Iowa, where it occupied 26,000 acres. It became very wealthy. Succeeding generations, however, grew lax in the faith of the founders and the Amana communities began to disintegrate and lose membership. By 1931 the society faced bankruptcy, but reorganized into a cooperative corporation. Community ownership was replaced by a complex system of stockholding. Since then the original $50 stock has risen to the value of $3600 a share. Today the Amana Society has a membership of about 1400. Its people continue to live in their villages near Cedar Rapids, in Iowa, but the piety and the ideals of the founders are gone.[2]

The relationship between Hutterians and the Amana Society never reached the intimacy that was achieved between them and the Harmony Society. This group, also known as the Rappists, was founded by George Rapp, another German religious idealist who came to the United States in 1803. The following year Rapp established the communal colony of Harmony in Indiana, which was sold ten years later to Scottish Robert Owen, who conducted his own experiment in socialism there.[3] Rapp thereupon moved his group to Pennsylvania, where he founded the communal colony of Economy.

In 1875, when the Hutterians had just settled in the Dakota Territory, the Harmony people came to their assistance and granted them a loan.[4] In succeeding years the Rappists, who had educated people, including lawyers, in their midst, gave assistance and provided legal counsel in land deals. In 1878 the Bon Homme colony branched out to establish another colony. The Harmonists owned land which they were prepared to grant to the Bon Homme people on most generous terms. The Hutterians at Bon Homme agreed; they dissolved their newly founded colony, and its members transferred to Pennsylvania to found the colony of Tidioute, in Warren County. However, the Bon Homme colony, contrary to the stipulation of the agreement, did not dissolve its own community and transfer east. In 1884, after a two-year stay at Tidioute, the already transferred Hutterians returned to Dakota.

The reasons for the move back are nebulous. I discussed the subject with several colony people in Manitoba, including Mrs. Barbara Waldner of Rosedale, whose parents had lived in Pennsylvania for some time, but the information I could get was vague. Zieglschmid suggests that the hilly, wooded land may have appeared uninviting to the Hutterians, who were accustomed to the steppes of Russia and the prairies of Dakota.[5] Another reason may have been the discovery of oil in the region. Perhaps the Hutterians sensed that the area had an industrial future, and that this would threaten their secluded way of life. Then too the Harmony Society had always depended very much on the personality of its leaders, and some of them may have appeared too visionary and impractical to the Hutterians.

The relationship with the Harmonists remained friendly even after the severance of their economic ties, but it faded with time. The Harmonists, who had introduced celibacy at one stage in their history, dissolved in 1903, dividing the colony assets among the few remaining members.

It would appear that the experience with the Amana and the Harmony societies had little lasting significance to the Hutterians, except that it demonstrated that under certain conditions the Hutterians are prepared to merge their interests with those of kindred groups.

The Society of Brothers

A not unimportant phase in the Hutterian history was their relationship with the group known as the Society of Brothers. The society at present has *Bruderhof* communities on three continents, but none in Canada. The temporary fusion of the two spiritually kindred groups took place in Canada and was to have a special significance to the Manitoba colonies.

The Society of Brothers had its origin in Germany after World War I. Its founder and early leader was Dr. Eberhard Arnold (1883–1935). According to one writer Arnold was the type of man who, had he been a

Catholic, and had he lived a few centuries earlier, would have been declared a saint.[6] Arnold, who had been the secretary of the German Christian Student Union, founded an informal communal colony at Sanerz, in southern Germany. In 1928 he learned that descendants of the early Moravian Anabaptists had preserved the ideal of community living and were now in Canada and the United States.

Arnold began a correspondence with the congregations in Canada, and in 1930–1931 he visited all the communities in North America. The Hutterians were impressed with Arnold's Christian humility and his zeal for communal life. When he finally asked whether his group would be accepted in the Brotherhood, membership was readily granted. Eberhard Arnold himself, in December 1930, "was confirmed in the service of the Word with laying on of hands by the elders Christian Waldner, Elias Walter, Johannes Kleinsasser, and Johannes Entz"[7] at the Stand-Off colony, in Alberta.

Arnold's association with the Hutterians was at least partly motivated by the hope of improving, with their assistance, the economic position of the German *Bruderhof*. This was also understood by the Hutterians, who were particularly interested in Arnold's experience as a publisher and his willingness to have his colony publish the old Hutterian writings. In any case, on Arnold's return from North America the German community entered upon intense activity. The members engaged in missionary work, in agriculture, and in the publishing business. In addition they expanded their boarding school. But the financial position of the community remained desperate, and Arnold again and again appealed for assistance. "We require $25,000, and $15,000 of it very urgently," he wrote in 1932.[8] At the same time his group expanded and established the Almbruderhof in Liechtenstein. In 1935 Arnold died and his people, known by the Hutterians as *Arnoldleut'*, were leaderless.

Meanwhile Hitler had risen to power and it soon became evident that the totalitarian *Volksgemeinschaft* state had little sympathy for the *Gütergemeinschaft* of the Brethren. The introduction of compulsory military service in 1935 aggravated the problems of the *Arnoldleut'*, who were opposed to military service. In 1937 the authorities dissolved the community on the apparently valid legal charge of bankruptcy.[9] Two Hutterians who came from North America, David Hofer of James Valley colony in Manitoba and Michael Waldner of Bon Homme colony in South Dakota, could do nothing to avert the dissolution.

But a year earlier and with the help of some English friends the *Arnold-leut'* had established the Cotswold *Bruderhof* in England. The members from the German and Liechtenstein communities now transferred to England.

Then came World War II and the friendly English atmosphere turned frigid to a group which was largely German and objected to military service. The group now planned to emigrate. Canada was considered, but the Canadian government turned them down. There was a slight stir on their behalf in the Canadian press.[10] However, the group could not wait and appealed to Paraguay, which, always willing to accept immigrants, readily gave them permission to settle there. In 1940 about 350 people, divided into six groups, made the long voyage across the submarine-infested Atlantic. A small group remained in England to complete the disposal of the communal property. Before this process was finished the group gained a number of converts and with the consent of the Paraguay members they began a new colony in England, the Wheathill *Bruderhof*, a community which is engaged largely in publishing.

In Paraguay the Brethren settled on an 8000-hectare tract (almost 20,000 acres) of land in Primavera, on which they established three communities: Loma-Hoby, Ibaté, and Isla Margarita. These engage in agriculture, ranching, and industry. There are flour and saw mills, woodworking shops, brick-burning and sugar-processing plants, and potteries. The group has a large contingent of German and British intellectuals, and the communities have excellent libraries, hospitals, and schools.[11] Some Spaniards joined the Brethren, and instruction and conversation in the communities is trilingual. The group also maintains two outposts, one at Asunción and one at Montevideo, Uruguay.

When rumors reached the North American Hutterians that the South American Brethren encouraged folk dancing and amateur theater groups and tolerated smoking and movies, they were disturbed. The Paraguayan group thereupon sent two men, Bruce Sumner and Allan Stevenson, known to the North American Hutterians as *Brucevetter* and *Allanvetter*, to Canada and the United States to dispel the fears, to ask for increased material aid, and to invite the Hutterians to send a delegation to Paraguay. Sumner and Stevenson traveled from colony to colony and partly succeeded in allaying the misgivings. The two men, educated in England but dressed in the plain garb of the Hutterians, impressed the congregations, and also the Winnipeg Grain Exchange when they visited it.[12]

In response to the appeal for help the Hutterians collected tons of clothing, tools, machinery, and hardware which were sent to Paraguay. The invitation to send delegates to Paraguay was also accepted. At a meeting held at the Huron colony in Manitoba the Hutterians decided to send two delegates, and these were elected at a subsequent meeting held at Sturgeon Creek colony. The two men were Samuel Kleinsasser of Manitoba and Johann Wipf of South Dakota.

Kleinsasser and Wipf made the trip to Paraguay in 1950 and were warmly received there.[13] They soon perceived, however, that the rumors circulated at home were well founded. There followed a frank exchange of views in which neither side was willing to change its stand. The Hutterian delegates charged the Paraguayan Brethren with "worldliness"; the Brethren maintained that the Hutterians had lost their missionary zeal and were not a living witness. Kleinsasser and Wipf returned home and reported their findings. There now followed letters and admonitions, but since these were ignored by the Paraguayans it is likely that the two groups would have drifted apart without serious consequences for either side. But a changed situation projected practical implications.

The Paraguayans, who had accused the Hutterians of lack of missionary zeal, became increasingly aware that their extreme isolation in the South American interior limited their own missionary work. They asked the North American congregations to admit a limited number of the Paraguayan Brethren who would join them and also act as missionaries in the surrounding area. This request was turned down, and some Hutterians openly expressed the opinion that it was a stratagem to take over the Canadian and American colonies. The Forest River colony, however, dissociated itself from the decision and prepared to accept a group of Paraguayan Brethren.

Forest River colony, near Inkster, is the only Hutterian *Bruderhof* in North Dakota. It branched out from the Manitoba New Rosedale colony in 1952. When Forest River took the important step of inviting some Paraguayan Brethren to join them its own community-congregation was not unanimously in favor of it. To proceed deliberately on a course that did not have the unanimous consent of all the members was a violation of Hutterian tradition. The initiators maintained that the congregation was ready for new ideas and that the members who objected to the course would soon change their views. Instead the senior leader, Andreas Hofer, and about half the community returned to Manitoba.

The remaining group, which included the second minister, extended a warm welcome to the Paraguayan Brethren, among them young Eberhard Arnold, son of the founder of the group. Jointly the Brethren of diverse backgrounds and training attempted to manage the farm enterprises. The Hutterians admired the learning of the new Brethren. The newly organized school began at the nursery stage, which led to the toddler class, which in turn went on to the preschool kindergarten. But the Hutterians also discovered that the new members, untrained and unaccustomed to seasonal farm tempo, insisted on short workdays. They preferred to spend the pleasant twilight hours in reading, writing, and painting, instead of "sweating it out" on a tractor or a combine.

The cold, bleak Dakota winters kept the Brethren at home and the visitors away. Another group from Paraguay had settled at Rifton, in New York, where it had opened a toy factory. The Society Brethren, discouraged by unaccustomed manual labor and monotonously long winters, left North Dakota and persuaded several members of the Hutterians of Forest River, among them the minister and his family, to join them. They bought an eighty-room luxury hotel near Farmington in Pennsylvania, and named it the Oak Lake *Bruderhof*. The hotel was transformed into a community dormitory and a toy factory.

After the break the Paraguayans took the name of the Society of Brothers. Its present membership stands at about 1500, made up of some twenty nationalities. Besides the communities in South America it has at present three in the United States, two in England, and one in Germany. The colonies in the United States and Germany specialize in the manufacture of toys. When I visited the Sinntalhof at Bad Brückenau in southern Germany in 1959, I found that its manager was an Englishman, Peter Rutherford. A former atheist, Rutherford, who is married and has a family, was attracted to communal life and decided to join the Brethren. The woman in charge of designing and coloring the toys, Margaret Böning, was a friend of the artist Käthe Kollwitz.[14] The sales director of the community was Hermann Arnold, a nephew of the founder. Arnold had joined Neuhof community in the early 1930's, gone to Liechtenstein in 1935, and from there moved to the colony in England in 1940. The following seventeen years he spent in Paraguay, and the next two in the United States, after which he was back once more in Germany. This gives an indication of the national and cultural differences within the group and also of the mobility of its members.

Meanwhile the remaining families at the Forest River colony in North Dakota were completely bewildered. Forsaken by their new friends, they had also been rejected by the Hutterian congregations. At a meeting held at James Valley colony in Manitoba in 1955 the *Schmiedeleut'* congregations decided to place Forest River colony, which had gone its own way without considering the will of the majority and showed no penitence, under the *Meidung.*[15] This ban lasted until late 1963, when the group sought readmission and its members were again received into the congregation.

It is too early to assess the influence of the short common journey of the Hutterian Brethren and the Society of Brothers. The literary productivity of the society is astounding. In addition they republish old Hutterian writings, and this literature is read by the Hutterians. Otherwise Hutterian ways appear unchanged from the encounter.

Julius Kubassek

Julius Kubassek was a Hungarian Catholic who came to Canada from Budapest after World War I. As a laborer in British Columbia's lumber camps he devoted much of his time to reading the Bible. He became convinced that community life was the substance of Christ's teachings. When he wanted to organize a community he was told that a group of people in Alberta practiced communal living. Kubassek left for Alberta and joined a Hutterian congregation where he stayed for about a year.

Kubassek did not care for grain farming, in which he had little training. In 1940, together with a few Brethren, he moved to a farm near Bright, in Ontario. The Alberta and Manitoba congregations provided some financial assistance and Julius Kubassek's new community was a success. In 1958 the colony, known as the Community Farm of the Brethren, had 1500 acres of farmland, but concentrated on the raising of geese. It has the largest goose flock in Canada, and the second largest in North America. A magazine account reports that the Community Farm of the Brethren has succeeded in breeding what is called a bacon type of goose. These geese, the account continues, "have very little excess fat, and are extremely full breasted, meaty birds." [16] The article speaks in laudatory terms of all the community's farm enterprises. Though the Community Farm of the Brethren developed beyond expectations, it was disturbed by internal unrest. Two Brethren were summarily excluded from the congregation, and this brought the problem to the surface.

The two Brethren went to the Hutterians in the West and were admitted to their communities. When the Hutterian elders asked the Ontario leader to explain his conduct he ignored the request. It would appear that Julius Kubassek was not overly concerned in preserving the link with the Hutterian brotherhood. The Hutterian communities function on firmly democratic lines. Each leader, duly elected, is first and foremost a servant of the community. An authoritarian and dynamic personality, determined on bending the colony's will to his own, would jar Hutterian sensitivity and disrupt institutionalized routine. Only years of conditioning in community living subordinate the personality to submit under all conditions to the common will. Kubassek not only lacked this background, but was a man of singular determination and authority. "He may be a good man," said *Dornvetter*, a former member of Kubassek's group, "but his is not the Hutterian way. It is Julius's way."

The Ontario leader continued to ignore the conciliatory moves of the Hutterian Brethren, until these terminated all connections. Some more members drifted from the Ontario community to the West, but Kubassek, who had a large family, and seven other families, largely new converts, remained aloof. The Community Farm of the Brethren, with a population of fifty-two, continues to operate as a successful enterprise. Kubassek died in 1963.

Hutterian Converts

The Hutterians do not promote active missionary work, but the communities are open to anyone. There are only about twelve Hutterians in Manitoba who joined as converts and were not born into colony life. An aged couple who arrived penniless in Canada live in one colony and enjoy all the privileges of members from birth. There are also some intelligent young men who joined because they were imbued with genuine idealism. Occasionally, a fervent outsider roams through the communities lecturing the young folk on their sinful ways, only to leave again in pursuit of new fields. One of them, John Gabor, was last heard of from Virginia, where he was working among Negroes. The younger people may resent these intrusions, but the older Hutterians take them stoically: "it does no harm."

If a convert asks to be accepted into the Brotherhood, the Hutterian elders advise him to weigh his step carefully. He is asked to wait a year or longer, to live in community, and to study Hutterian doctrine. During this period any property or assets the convert may have remain his own. If at the end of the trial period the convert insists that his decision to stay is final, and the congregation agrees that he qualifies for membership, he is accepted into the Church. He then transfers all his private property to the community. Whether he was a pauper or a rich man when he joined, if he decides to leave the community he forfeits all claim to the community's assets. This principle is now being disputed in the courts of Manitoba (see Chapter XI).

During his trial period the novice performs his assigned duties and is treated in effect like a full-fledged member, except that he has no voice in the administration of the community. Should a novice decide to remain at the colony indefinitely without joining the Church, most congregations would not object, provided he led a life in keeping with Hutterian regulations.

Perhaps one of the staunchest Hutterians is Christian Dorn, known in the communities as *der Dornvetter*. Dorn brought considerable assets with him when he joined an Alberta congregation. He later transferred to the Kubassek group to help launch its colony. Disappointed in Kubassek's leadership, Dorn returned west and joined a Manitoba community. His oldest son, who married a Hutterian woman, is now one of the colony's carpenters. Dorn's two younger sons joined the community later. A widower, *Dornvetter* is tireless in his praise of communal living.

In 1957, a family consisting of parents and eight young children joined a Manitoba community. The members of the family were permitted to use their own clothes, presumably until these were worn out. The man grew a heavy beard and his wife could be seen working in the kitchen. The oldest child, an intelligent boy of fourteen, thoroughly enjoyed the responsibilities which Hutterian men are accustomed to delegate to boys. In the fall of the same year the husband decided that community life was too demanding for one not born into it. Some members of the family, especially the oldest boy, appeared to regret the decision to leave the colony. The trial period was terminated by mutual consent without ill-feeling.

The fact that only a few converts join the communities is one of the sources of strength of the Brotherhood. The new converts at no time form a group strong enough to challenge the traditional pattern of the community. Instead the individuals are assimilated, enter the kinship group by marriage, sometimes occupy positions of responsibility, and identify themselves fully with the group.

The Hutterians and Their Neighbors

The relationship between Hutterian communities and their neighbors varies from colony to colony. The anti-Hutterian petitions and resolutions were not so much actions directed against existing communities as an expression of concern over their expansion. Even agitators for restrictive legislation are often on friendly terms with their immediate Hutterian neighbors. Many colonies have excellent relations with the surrounding farmers, while others live in an atmosphere of practical coexistence; no colony is surrounded by hostility.

Many farmers and business people visit the colonies, often accompanied by their families. Though the Hutterians are very hospitable they do not often visit neighboring farmers. One reason for this is that these people have radios or television sets in their homes which carry programs considered immoral or at least frivolous by the Hutterians. If a well-known and respected person in the district dies, the Hutterians may be seen at the funeral. In an emergency, an accident or mishap, they will offer their assistance. Beyond that they generally remain on the *Bruderhof*. Their faith and attitude, language, garb, and appearance isolate them as effectively as if walls surrounded their communities.

The Hutterians remain aloof from most neighborhood undertakings. They are rarely seen at political meetings, fairs, field and sports days, dances and weddings, and similar occasions. But in times of crisis they cooperate with their neighbors. When the Assiniboine River overflows its banks and the farmers rally to man the dikes, the Hutterians can be counted upon to contribute more than their share. During a recent flood the army was ordered to assist in the diking. The soldiers were impressed with the efficiency of the Hutterians. One army officer recalled an emergency which demanded that a man take some sandbags into shoulder-deep, cold, and treacherous water. Without hesitation a colony manager jumped into the water and performed the task.

On another occasion an officer in charge of diking placed a telephone call to a neighboring town and demanded additional help. Jokingly he added, "Send out ten men or five Hutterites." One farmer pointed out that the Hutterians never hesitated to help diking along the northern banks of the river, though their own lands all lay south of the Assiniboine, and reinforcing the dikes on the northern banks correspondingly increased the flood threat along the southern banks.

Important data on public attitudes toward the Hutterian Brethren were gathered by the Canadian Mental Health Association in its Saskatchewan survey. To the question "What sort of people do you think the Hutterites are?" the following responses were given: friendly; moral, decent; work well together, cooperative; look different, dress, beards, etc.; won't mix, take part in community affairs; good businessmen and farmers; they buy goods in the community; they don't spend much money in town.[17] Before this question there was one asking the person being interviewed to state specifically what he did not like about the district. Significantly, not one response included the Hutterians. Only when the question was narrowed down to "Have there been any recent happenings around Maple Creek district that will be problems for the community as a whole, do you think?" did 11 per cent name the Hutterians.[18]

Sometimes outsiders take offense where none is intended because they are unfamiliar with Hutterian ways and manners. In their own colonies the Hutterians move within a close kinship group, and the language used is straightforward and direct. Quite uninhibitedly a Hutterian will give expression to his opinions even to a stranger, be the opinions complimentary or otherwise. Our sophisticated society is not accustomed to this.

Furthermore, the very appearance of the Hutterian marks him as a member of a religious group. People will use a correspondingly severe measuring stick on him, as if each and every Hutterian were a man of the cloth. When a colony uses its snowplow to clear its own roads a neighbor may say, "If they were real Christians they would clear the half mile to my farm." I heard this remark from a farmer who would never expect this service from any of his other neighbors. In another district the neighbors stated that colony equipment did clear some municipal roads in winter and did grade them in summer without either the farmers or the municipality paying the Hutterians for the service.

Usually people who have had few contacts with the Hutterians have the strongest prejudices against them. Two educated professional men whom I interviewed in Winnipeg spoke of the Hutterians as "the beards" or "the hook-and-eye boys." (Hutterian men grow beards after marriage; Hutterians use hooks and eyes instead of buttons on their clothing.) One of these men had visited a colony and generalized, "In their homes a dipper may be used alternatively for filling the kerosene lamp and serving wine to guests." The conversation then turned to Hutterian morality. "It stands to reason," was the comment of the other, who had never visited a colony, "that a group that refuses to mix with other people must lack ethical standards."

It seems quite possible that the nonconforming ways of the Hutterians are in some cases themselves sufficient to disturb, irritate, and arouse the prejudice of otherwise rational and generous people.

Most people who know the Hutterians, of course, are free from this prejudice, which is the result of ignorance. A member of the Winnipeg police force said in an interview that he had become acquainted with the colony people when his father had shared a ward with a Hutterian in one of the Winnipeg hospitals. Since both families had visited the respective patients, they had got to know each other, and this had developed into a genuine friendship. Over a period of years now they had visited the colony, and the colony people had visited them. He summed up his impressions in these words: "They are fine people and good Christians. We could learn much from them." A similar opinion was expressed by the late Dr. Robert Fletcher, for many years deputy minister of education for Manitoba. In a letter to me he described the Hutterians as "industrious people and communists in the real sense of the word, like the early Christians."

There is other evidence that the Hutterians, despite their policy of withdrawing from the world, can be good and generous neighbors. During my stay at the New Rosedale colony, near Portage la Prairie, I saw reservation Indians and their families repeatedly come to the community kitchen and get full meals, as well as bread to take home. In the same colony I also noticed a child in non-Hutterian clothes playing in the kindergarten. The kindergarten teacher explained that Eliza was the youngest of five children of a neighboring farmer. The man was poor and his wife had left him. Every week the colony boys took some girls to the farmer's home where they did the housecleaning. With the farmer's consent they sometimes took the smaller children to the colony, and little Eliza spent most of her time there. This kind of work is done not with a missionary zeal but with the awareness that man is surrounded by duties and obligations to his fellowman, and these he must discharge.

The Hutterian attitude to outsiders may be summed up in this way: (1) the Hutterians are not averse to entering into binding relationships with kindred groups as long as these relationships do not mean a compromise with their beliefs and traditions; (2) the Hutterians accept converts willingly, but the finality of the break with the outside world and the austerity of community life have restricted the number of converts; (3) the colony-neighborhood relationship is on the whole characterized by a mutually friendly atmosphere.

Altogether the colonies and the Hutterians as individuals have succeeded to a remarkable degree in confining their social commitments and economic activities in the world about them to a bare minimum. Avoidance of the world, a basic tenet of their belief, has remained an effective barrier to integration with the larger surrounding community.

CONCLUSION

THE HUTTERIAN COLONIES in Manitoba, as well as those in other parts of Canada and the United States, today show remarkable stability, cohesion, and vitality. No disintegration of their way of life is apparent. Severe restrictive legislation would drive out the communities, but not change them. In the absence of such legislation, the Hutterian colonies will remain a noticeable ingredient of ethnic diversity in the provinces they live in. A summary statement of some of the Hutterian institutions, practices, and beliefs that we have examined offers support for this general conclusion, and may also indicate areas in which change can be accommodated by the Hutterians, as well as those in which it cannot.

The Church

In doctrine and in organization the Hutterian Church has not changed. Its articles of faith have been rigidly maintained, and young Hutterians are dedicated and loyal to the beliefs enunciated by their ancestors four hundred years ago. They unreservedly subscribe to such teachings as adult baptism, communal living, and refusal to bear arms and to take the oath. Even those who have left the colonies, when interviewed, indicated no basic disagreement with these doctrines.

The organization of the Church has remained intact. The rural *Bruderhof* community, which the Hutterians consider the Church, provides the isolated habitat, the sanctuary where the members of the Brotherhood find safety and shelter from what they consider the temptations of the outside world. The ministers are still elected for life. They have neither asked for nor received concessions that would set them apart, but their leadership in spiritual matters is endorsed without reservation. Disagreement on policy among individuals is common, and ministers will engage in discussions as freely as any member of the community. Ministers sometimes disagree among themselves. Thus at a joint meeting of Hutterians and civic leaders which was also attended by a reporter some of the Hutterian ministers disagreed sharply with their chief elder, Rev. Peter Hofer.[1] Such disagreements on policy are not uncommon, but they do not extend to church organization, that is, the colony, and to doctrine. These are universally accepted among the Hutterians.

The Colony

The Hutterian colony of today is perhaps as close to the ideal outlined by Huter and Ehrenpreis as it has ever been in the past. For Huter the colonies were to provide the economic basis for a Christian brotherhood, and to this Ehrenpreis added the requisite of a Christlike gentleness as the lubricant for intercolony relationship. This ideal is very solidly in operation on the Canadian and American prairies as the colonies themselves, their friends, their opponents, and scholars who have studied them testify. The opponents of the Hutterian colonies rarely criticize the Hutterians or the colonies; on the contrary, they praise them. The basis for their criticism is that the Hutterian way of life adversely affects the economic and social rhythm of the surrounding individualistic society.

To the Hutterians the colony, which provides them with complete security from the cradle to the grave, is an essential expression of their creed. Colony life is a matter of dogma to them; moreover, it is a belief buttressed by reason. A few years ago some members of the Manitoba government unofficially attempted to persuade the Hutterians to change their ways in order to appease their opponents. When Gerald Wright interviewed a young Hutterian, Sam Kleinsasser, on this point, the latter replied, "We considered their suggestions carefully. . . . We asked ourselves whether they [that is, the outside world] really had anything better to offer us. We felt that they hadn't, so we decided to hang on to what we have."[2] Kleinsasser, who was under thirty years of age at the time, is intelligent and well read, and very successfully manages his colony's hog enterprise. He may be regarded as typical of the young generation of Hutterians. Knowing him and his colony, one may dismiss his statement, "We considered their suggestions carefully," as the rhetoric of courtesy.

There have been other communal groups on this continent, and some of them, like the Amanas of Iowa, have lasted for many generations. Invariably a noticeable breakdown of "religion" preceded general colony disintegration. A sympathetic observer of the Amanas wrote, "Without its spiritual significance the communism of Amana was as empty as a chrysalis from which the butterfly had flown." [3] This breakdown in doctrine and in faith in their system is not measurably apparent among the younger generation of Hutterians.

The School

The Hutterian school is designed to indoctrinate the children in the traditional beliefs of the colony people. This function it achieves effectively. The public schools, on the other hand, are charged with the secular education of their pupils. These schools, in Manitoba as elsewhere, operate under the supervision of government officials. Hutterians have always distrusted secular education, especially higher education, because they fear that it may draw their children away from the colonies.

This distrust is augmented when some government officials and other people openly state that the public school is an instrument to wean the young generation from the colony. "They see education as a tool," writes Douglas Sanders, "by which the close-knit colony structure can be broken up." [4] As a result of these attitudes the public school has not only failed to effect a change in the Hutterian way of life, but has also failed to convince the Hutterians that these schools are the best medium for secular education. When the matter of Hutterian education came up for debate recently in the Manitoba legislature, Arthur Wright, a member of the New Democracy Party, said that he admired and respected the Hutterians, "but I'm disappointed in their attitude toward education." Joining him was former provincial premier Douglas Campbell, who stated that "most people had thought that the Hutterites would develop closer links with the community through education. This has not been the case." [5]

The Hutterians thus have successfully resisted the attempt to use the public school for the purpose of colony disintegration. It is increasingly realized, especially by school officials in Manitoba, that the public school should have only the function of bringing secular education to the colonies.

The standard of education among young Hutterians is unsatisfactory. This is realized to some extent by older colony people. They feel that, in order to keep abreast of new developments in agricultural technology and farm animal feeding and housing, the Hutterians must depend increasingly on books, periodicals, and other sources of information, rather than on traditional ways and costly trial and error. There apparently is no great colony demand for higher education, but there is recognition of a need for more practical education beyond the public school.

In any case, it appears premature to assess the full impact of the public school. So far it has failed as an agency for change. However, a public school dedicated to the sole purpose of education, without overt or hidden side objectives, would meet a great colony need.

Kinship, Customs, Language

Family and kinship ties are very strong among the Hutterians. Sociologists maintain that kinship ties weaken as the group increases numerically. Today it is still possible for the chief elder, Peter Hofer, to send mimeographed letters to the congregations in Manitoba and refer to *Samuelvetter* of Elmspring colony, *Johannvetter* of Spink colony, or *Jakobvetter* of Bon Homme colony, all in South Dakota,[6] and know that all his readers will know exactly whom he means, without using their surnames. At the rate of growth of Hutterian membership this will be impossible two or three generations hence. Numerical increase will inevitably lead to a loosening of kinship feeling, and this in turn will affect the cohesion of the group. Group identification and solidarity may have reached its optimum.

Customs such as the beards worn by the men after they marry, or the garb, serve to set the members of the group apart. The Hutterian who leaves the colony on a business trip to the city or the nearest town does not feel uncomfortable or timid because he is different in his ways and appearance. Rather he feels like an ambassador of a nation who is fully aware he is away from home, but is more concerned with what people at home think of him than with what the people think whom he is dealing with at the moment.

Except in isolated instances, and then among the young, there is no objection among the Hutterians to the clothes they are required to wear. Slight departures in dress from old ways are sometimes approved by the annual conference of Hutterian leaders, others are condemned. Thus the introduction of parkas was disapproved by the annual meeting in 1951, and again in 1959. If an increasing number of Hutterians insist on wearing parkas, the leaders at some future time may agree that parkas are here to stay, provided they are black or of a suitably dark color. In these matters the Hutterian system is flexible.

All Hutterians speak German. Not only is that language a link between the present and the past, it also sets them apart from their neighbors. Since the public school does not teach German as a subject, and the colony school uses it only as a vehicle for religious instruction, formal German is steadily losing ground. All Hutterians of school age and older read and write German, but the younger generation is more at ease writing in English than in German. Since the language must be considered as a factor strengthening the cohesion of the group, the decline of formal German among the Hutterians contributes to community disintegration. At least in part this is the work of the public school, for it replaced the old Hutterian day school, which taught the fundamentals of German.

The failure of the Hutterians to emerge from their self-imposed cultural and physical isolation was and is disapproved by the larger society in Manitoba, as in North America as a whole. It is the general opinion that a nation must of necessity achieve a high degree of homogeneity. In Canada and the United States there are strong elements which insist on the cultural assimilation and uniformity of all citizens. These groups feel that the Hutterians, who have democratic institutions in their own colonies but voluntarily forfeit many of the rights and responsibilities of citizenship, impede the national destinies of their countries. That the Hutterians make little claim on the public purse does not ameliorate the case against them. On the contrary, it more firmly marks their special status. But in the complex Hutterian pattern religious and cultural values are so interwoven that the group feels that an infraction of any one of the traditional rules and practices, or the displacement of any of the old values, is a threat to the survival of its way of life.

Within recent years voices have been raised in Canada and in the United States against excessive cultural leveling. "Perhaps it is only necessary that cultural assimilation be achieved on a certain level," suggests one sociologist, "and that below that level, assimilation need not take place. It may even enrich the variety of social experience of all to have diversity throughout these levels." [7] Indeed, the Hutterian communities provide a natural setting for the study of human relationships and behavior that no artificial control group could offer. An example of the value of such a group was provided by the Hutterian mental health study directed by Professor Eaton. Another example is the human genetics study undertaken by Western Reserve University under the direction of Professor Arthur G. Steinberg. Currently the United States Office of Health, Education, and Welfare is engaged in a research project initiated by Professor John A. Hostetler.

Meanwhile the Hutterians will carry on in their old ways. Whatever contribution they have to offer to society in the form of scientific knowledge will have to be pried from them. They themselves are satisfied to work, but not to work too hard; to extend their hospitality to friends and strangers, but never to press it on them; to be "in this world, but not of this world."

APPENDIX

CONSTITUTION OF THE HUTTERIAN
BRETHREN CHURCH

Name

1. The name shall be the HUTTERIAN BRETHREN CHURCH.

Objects and Powers

2. The objects and powers for which the said Church is formed are:

(a) To obtain for its members and their dependent minors, as also for the novices, children and persons in need under its care, without distinction of race, class, social standing, nationality, religion, age or sex, spiritual, cultural, educational and economic assistance based upon the life and mission of Jesus Christ and the Apostles, in the spirit and way of the first Christian community in Jerusalem and of the community re-established by Jacob Hutter in 1533 at the time of the origin of the "Baptisers' movement" in such a way that the members achieve one entire spiritual unit in complete community of goods (whether production or consumption) in perfect purity in mutual relationships, absolute truthfulness and a real attitude of peace, confessing and testifying by work and by deed that Love, Justice, Truth and Peace is God's will for all men on earth. All the members, and especially the Elders, are responsible for carrying out the objects of the Church by following exactly the spontaneous direction of the Holy Spirit and by mutual stimulation and education.

(b) Complete dedication in the work for the aims and objects of the Church is expected from all members thereof. The capital and sur-

SOURCE: *Constitution of the Hutterian Brethren Church and Rules as to Community of Property* [1950], pages 4–10.

plus produce and surplus funds of each individual congregation or community of the Church is to be used by such community for social work to which the Church is constantly dedicated, helping poor, weak and sickly persons who need, ask for and accept this help, especially children, and for the purchase of lands, stock and equipment for the use of such congregation or community in order that the members thereof may maintain themselves and acquire funds for the purposes of carrying out the aims of the Church.

(c) Each congregation or community of the said Church is empowered:

i. To engage in, and carry on farming, stock-raising, milling, and all branches of these industries; and to manufacture and deal with the products and by-products of these industries;

ii. To carry on any other business (whether manufacturing or otherwise) which may seem to said congregation or community of said Church capable of being conveniently carried on in connection with its business or calculated directly or indirectly to enhance the property or rights of the congregation or community;

iii. To acquire or undertake the whole or any part of the business property and liabilities of any person or company carrying on any business which said congregation or community of said Church is authorized to carry on, or possessed of property suitable for the purposes of the congregation or community of said Church;

iv. To apply for, purchase or otherwise acquire any patents, licenses, concessions and the like, conferring any exclusive or non-exclusive or limited right to use, or any secret or other information as to any invention which may seem capable of being used for any of the purposes of the congregation or community of the said Church, or the acquisition of which may seem calculated directly or indirectly to benefit the congregation or community of the said Church, and to use, exercise and develop or grant licenses in respect of, or otherwise turn to account the property, rights or information so acquired:

v. To do all or any of the above things as principal, agents, contractors, or otherwise and either alone or in conjunction with others;

vi. To do such other things as are incidental to or conducive to the attainment of the above objects.

(d) Each congregation or community of the said Church in furtherance of the religious objects of the Church and for its own benefit may purchase, acquire, take, have, hold, exchange, receive, possess, inherit; retain and enjoy, property, real or personal, corporeal or in-corporeal, whatsoever, and for any or every estate or interest therein whatsoever given, granted, devised or bequeathed to it or appropri-ated, purchased or acquired by it in any manner or way whatsoever and may also sell, convey, exchange, alienate, mortgage, lease, de-mise or otherwise dispose of any such real or personal property.

(e) Each congregation or community of the said Church shall have power to borrow money, to issue bonds, debentures, or other securi-ties; to pledge or sell such bonds, debentures or securities for such sum and at such price as may be deemed expedient or be necessary; to charge, hypothecate, mortgage or pledge any or all of its real or personal property, rights and powers, undertakings, franchises, in-cluding book debts to secure any bonds, debentures or other securities or any liability of the said congregation or community.

(f) Each congregation or community of the said Church at a meet-ing at which not less than four-fifths of the male members thereof are present shall have full power to make, establish, and sanction, amend, repeal or abrogate all such rules, regulations, and by-laws as they judge necessary for its good administration and government, providing the same be not contrary to law or to these Articles.

Organization

3. The Church shall be comprised of all of the congregations or com-munities hereinbefore named and such other congregations and com-munities wheresoever existing that shall be chosen and elected to membership in accordance with the terms of these Articles and any amendments thereof.

4. The Head Office of the said Church shall be at the Town of Wilson Siding, in the Province of Alberta.

5. The said Church shall be divided into three Conferences, namely

(a) Darius-Leut Group of Hutterian congregations or communi-ties in the Province of Alberta;

(b) The Lehrer-Leut Group of Hutterian congregations or com-munities in the Province of Alberta;

(c) The Schmied-Leut Group of Hutterian congregations or com-munities in the Province of Manitoba.

Board of Managers

6. The Church dogma and Church discipline and the affairs, powers, privileges and all matters affecting and pertaining to Hutterian Breth-ren generally, shall be administered, managed, exercised, transacted, conducted and controlled by a Board of nine managers, three of whom shall be appointed by each of the said Conferences, provided, how-ever, that except as to matters of a purely administrative nature, no

resolution or decision of the said Board shall be binding or effective until approved, ratified and confirmed by each of the said Conferences.

7. The said managers shall elect from among their numbers:

    (a) A President who shall be known as the Senior Elder;

    (b) A Vice-President who shall be known as the Assistant Senior Elder;

    (c) A Secretary-Treasurer who shall be known as the Secretary-Treasurer.

8. The name and residences of the Managers who are to serve as Managers of the Church until the election of such Managers and Officers are: [The names change from year to year].

9. The managers of the said Church shall hold office for the term of three years or until their successors are elected or appointed.

10. Any of the said managers may be expelled or removed by a vote of a majority of the members of such Board of Managers, or by the conference by which he was elected or appointed.

11. Vacancies caused by death, removal, expulsion or otherwise shall be filled by the Conference by which the said manager was elected.

12. Whenever a vacancy occurs in the office of Senior Elder, Assistant Senior Elder or Secretary the Board of Managers may from their own number fill such vacancy at any annual, general or special meeting of the Managers, and such officer appointed to fill the vacancy shall hold office for the remainder of the term of such office which became vacant or until a successor has been elected.

13. No officer or manager of the said Church shall receive or be entitled to any reward or compensation of any amount or character whatsoever for any time, labor or service that he may give or render to the Church.

14. At any meeting of Managers each member present in person or represented by proxy shall have one vote and all questions arising at such meetings shall be decided by a majority vote, and the Senior Elder or the person acting in his stead shall have a casting vote, or if it is the wish of such meeting a question may be settled by lot rather than by the Senior Elder's casting vote.

15. At any meeting of the Board of Managers five members of the Board shall constitute a quorum.

16. An Annual Meeting of the Board of Managers shall be held on the second Tuesday in June at 2:00 o'clock in the afternoon.

17. Any meeting of the Managers may be held at any place by order of the Senior Elder.

18. Special Meetings of the Managers may be called at any time by order of the Senior Elder by two of the Managers by notice in writing sent by mail at least seven clear days before the day fixed for the holding of such meeting.

Organization of Conferences

19. There shall be three Conferences, namely, the Darius-Leut Conference, with head office at Wilson Siding, Alberta; the Lehrer-Leut Conference with head office at Rockport Colony, Magrath, Alberta; and the Schmied-Leut Conference with head office at Poplar Point Colony in the Postal District of Poplar Point, in Manitoba. [Subsequently changed to James Valley colony, Starbuck, Manitoba.]

20. The affairs, powers and privileges of each of the said Conferences shall be administered, managed, exercised, transacted, conducted and controlled by a Board consisting of two delegates from each of the congregations or communities comprising the Conferences.

21. The said Board shall be known as the Conference Board and it shall have a Chairman, a Vice-Chairman and a Secretary, all of whom shall be elected by the members of the Conference Board and shall hold office for a period of two years.

22. The names and residences of the Conference Board who are to serve as representatives of the respective Conferences until the election or appointment of such Board members and officers are: [There follows a list of the members for the *Dariusleut'*, the *Lehrerleut'*, and the *Schmiedeleut'*].

23. The Conference Board shall exercise control over the Church dogma and Church discipline within their respective Conferences, and shall have charge of all matters pertaining to the Hutterian Brethren generally within their respective Conferences, and shall have power to take such action as they deem meet in respect to matters affecting or pertaining to the Hutterian Brethren within their respective Conferences.

24. Any member of the said Conference Board may be expelled or removed by a vote of the majority of the members of such Boards.

25. Vacancies caused by death, removal, expulsion or otherwise shall be filled by the congregation or community by which the Board member was appointed.

26. Whenever a vacancy occurs in the office of Chairman, Vice-Chairman or Secretary the Conference Board may from their own number fill such vacancy at any annual, general or special meeting of the Board, and any such officer appointed to fill the vacancy shall hold office for the remainder of the term of such office which became vacant or until a successor has been elected.

27. No member of the Conference Board shall receive or be entitled to any reward or compensation of any amount or character whatsoever for any time, labor or service which he may give or render to the Conference.

28. At any meeting of the Conference Board each member present in person or represented by proxy shall have one vote and all questions arising at such meeting shall be decided by majority vote, and the

Chairman or the person acting in his stead shall have a casting vote, or if it is the wish of such meeting, a question may be settled by lot rather than by the Chairman's casting vote.

29. At any meeting of the Conference Board two-thirds of the total number of Board members shall constitute a quorum.

30. An Annual Meeting of each Conference Board shall be held at such time and at such place as the Chairman shall appoint.

31. Special Meetings of the Conference Board may be called at any time by order of the Chairman or by five of the members of the Conference Board, by notice in writing, sent by mail at least four clear days before the day fixed for the holding of such meeting, and such meeting may be held at any place indicated in the said notice.

32. At the Annual Meeting in 1951 and every third year thereafter the Conference Board will elect from among themselves three members of the Board of Managers of the Church.

Organization of Congregations

33. The property, affairs and concerns of each congregation or community of the Church shall be managed and the business of the said congregation or community shall be carried on in accordance with such by-laws, rules and regulations as may be made and enacted as provided in Article 2(f) hereof.

34. No congregation or community of said Church shall be liable for the debts, liabilities, or any financial obligation whatsoever of any other congregation or community of said Church.

Membership

35. Each congregation or community shall be comprised of all persons who have been elected to membership in that congregation or community upon their request and who have become members and communicants of the Hutterian Brethren Church in the manner set forth in the book written by Peter Riedemann hereinbefore referred to, and who have been chosen and elected to membership upon a majority vote of all the male members of that congregation or community at any annual, general or special meeting thereof.

Holding of Property

36. No individual member of a congregation or community shall have any assignable or transferable interest in any of its property, real or personal.

37. All property, real and personal, of a congregation or community, from whomsoever, whensoever, and howsoever it may have been obtained, shall forever be owned, used, occupied, controlled and possessed by the congregation or community for the common use, inter-

est, and benefit of each and all members thereof, for the purposes of the said congregation or community.

38. All the property, both real and personal, that each and every member of a congregation or community has, or may have, own, possess or may be entitled to at the time he or she joins such congregation or community, or becomes a member thereof, and all the property, both real and personal, that each and every member of the congregation or community may have, obtain, inherit, possess or be entitled to, after he or she becomes a member of a congregation or community, shall be and become the property of the congregation or community to be owned, used, occupied and possessed by the congregation or community for the common use, interest and benefit of each and all of the members thereof.

39. None of the property, either real or personal, of a congregation or community shall ever be taken, held, owned, removed or withdrawn from the congregation or community in accordance with its by-laws, rules and regulations and the provisions of these Articles, and if any member of a congregation or community shall be expelled therefrom, or cease to be a member thereof, he or she shall not have, take, withdraw from, grant, sell, transfer or convey, or be entitled to any of the property of the congregation or community or any interest therein; and if any member of the congregation or community shall die, be expelled therefrom, or cease to be a member thereof, his or her personal representatives, heirs at law, legatees or devisees or creditors or any other person shall not be entitled to, or have any of the property of the congregation or community, or interest therein, whether or not he or she owned, possessed or had any interest in or to any of the property of the congregation or community at the time he or she became a member thereof, or at any time before or thereafter, or had given, granted, conveyed or transferred any property or property interest to the congregation or community at any time.

Rights and Duties of Members

40. Each and every member of a congregation or community shall give and devote all his or her time, labor, services, earnings and energies to that congregation or community, and the purposes for which it is formed, freely, voluntarily, and without compensation or reward of any kind whatsoever, other than herein expressed.

41. The members of a congregation or community shall be entitled to and have their husbands, wives and children, who are not members thereof, reside with them, and be supported, maintained, instructed and educated by that congregation or community, according to the rules, regulations and requirements of that congregation or community, during the time and so long as they obey, abide by and conform to the rules,

regulations, instructions and requirements of that congregation or community.

42. Whenever a member of the congregation or community shall die, then his or her husband, wife and children, who are not members thereof, shall have the right to remain with, and be supported, instructed and educated by that congregation or community, during the time, and as long as they give and devote all of their time, labor, services, earnings and energies to the congregation or community, and the purposes thereof, and obey and conform to the rules, regulations and requirements of the congregation or community, the same as if the said member had lived.

43. The husbands, wives and children of each and all the members of a congregation or community, who are not members thereof, shall give and devote all their time, labor, services, earnings, and energies to that congregation or community and purposes for which it is formed, freely, voluntarily and without compensation of any kind whatsoever other than as herein provided, and obey and conform to all the rules, regulations and requirements of the congregation or community, while they remain in or with the congregation or community.

44. No congregation or community shall be dissolved without the consent of all of its members.

45. The act of becoming a member of a congregation or community shall be considered as a Grant, Release, Transfer, Assignment, and Conveyance to that congregation or community of all property, whether real or personal, owned by any person at the time of his or her becoming a member of the congregation or community, or acquired or inherited at any time subsequent thereto; such property to be owned, occupied, possessed and used by the congregation or community for the common use of all its members.

Expulsion of Members

46. Any member of a congregation or community may be expelled or dismissed therefrom at any annual or general meeting of that congregation or community upon a majority vote of all the members thereof, or upon the request of such member, or by his or her having left or abandoned the congregation or community, or having refused to obey the rules and regulations and the officers of the congregation or community, or having refused to give and devote all his or her time, labor, services, earnings and energies to the congregation or community and the purposes thereof, or to do and perform the work, labor, acts and things required of him or her by the congregation or community or to attend and engage in the regular meetings, worship and service of the members of the congregation or community.

Officers Given Certain Powers

47. The officers of a congregation or community upon first having obtained the consent of the majority of the male members of that congregation or community may from time to time if they see fit so to do contract for, buy, sell, assign, transfer, encumber, guarantee, hypothecate, mortgage, pledge, charge, lease and dispose of any or all of the real or personal property or assets of that congregation or community for any purpose whatsoever; and also as security for any moneys borrowed or any part thereof may give to any money lender, mortgagee, bank, person, firm or corporation all or any bonds, debentures, warehouse receipts, bills of lading, negotiable instruments and all such other securities and documents necessary or required by or on behalf of such money lender, mortgagee, bank, person, firm or corporation, and may also give to any bank securities as required under the Bank Act as security for any moneys borrowed from time to time from the bank.

Admission of Further Congregations

48. The Board of Managers may by a majority vote admit to membership in the Church and may join to one of the existing conferences or otherwise as they deem meet any congregation or community which makes application to join the Church and which complies with and conforms to the religious doctrine and faith of the Hutterian Brethren Church.

Amendments

49. These Articles of Association may be repealed or amended or new Articles may be adopted from time to time at any annual, general or special meeting of the Board of Managers or at any other meeting of the member Conferences called for that purpose by the Board of Managers.

WE, the undersigned, being the proper officers in that behalf of the said congregations or communities, having severally read over and had explained to us the foregoing Articles of Association, and understanding the same and having been so authorized by the congregations or communities to which we respectively belong, DO HEREBY SEVERALLY AGREE to adopt and abide by the said Articles of Association. IN WITNESS WHEREOF the several congregations herein named have executed these Articles by the hands of their proper officers in that behalf.

DATED THIS FIRST DAY OF AUGUST, A.D. 1950.

[There then follow the signatures of the managers, in each case the minister and the colony manager of the community, of the *Dariusleut'* group, the *Lehrerleut'* group, and the *Schmiedeleut'* group.]

A HUTTERIAN GIRL TELLS HER STORY

by Ruth Baer

WAS THAT REALLY the second bell I heard? It must have been, for the house is very quiet. This means that everyone has gone to breakfast. I must have failed to hear the 6:45 bell, and the second bell at 7 means that everybody should be in the dining hall, or at least on the way there.

I simply do not understand how I could have fallen asleep again after Mother had called me. I only hope that I get to the dining hall in time so that I do not have to kneel all by myself for prayer. Well, this morning I'll just put my cap and shawl on without combing my hair. Nobody can tell. I'll just wind it up a little tighter.

Now I had better run. The children's dining room is only a few hundred feet from my home, so I might just make it. As I run past the adult dining room I hear the "Amen." The adults have finished saying grace and I can hear the clatter of cutlery and plates as they begin to eat.

"Oh, well, the children's prayer is much longer, so they won't be finished yet," I console myself. Yes, they are still kneeling. I see them all leaning heavily with their elbows on the bench, reciting their prayer aloud and in unison as fast as possible. I had better kneel down quickly before they are finished. Some of the others must have been late too, for they are kneeling right at the door, and I have to kneel half out of the doorway.

NOTE. This story was written by Ruth Baer, aged twenty. The parents of Ruth Baer joined a Manitoba Hutterian colony when she was a small child. Years later, when Miss Baer was sixteen years old, the Baer family, together with the children, left the colony and returned to "individualistic" society. They are at present farming in Minnesota. Miss Baer is a student at Moorhead State College, majoring in history.

A few more mumbled sentences and the morning prayer is finished. There is a lot of noise and shuffling as the benches are pulled out, and finally everybody is seated. Now we say grace, but this is short. The boys who sit across from us on the other side of the dining room, at a long table, usually have their knives or spoons in their folded hands ready to start eating as soon as they hear the "Amen."

One of the girls is really late this morning. She kneels down at her place at the table and in a few minutes she is finished. "That was a quick prayer," says her neighbor. "I bet you didn't say all of it." How long we kneel when we are late usually depends on how long we judge it takes to say the prayer. Sometimes we don't kneel long enough and the German teacher, who is always standing in the room checking our manners and watching us so that we eat quietly, will have us kneel a little longer.

The most embarrassing thing for me is to ask for something extra at the table. If we need more bread someone will hold up the empty plate and sing out the word b-r-e-a-d. The *Essenschul' Angela* (woman supervisor), a very understanding, motherly type of person, will wait on us. When she thinks that everybody has had enough, she will let us know, and that is it.

Soon everyone is finished, and we say another prayer. We are lucky today. The *Schullehrer* (German teacher) has left early. There is a big scramble as everyone heads for the door and out. That is, all except the eight oldest girls who stay and clean up.

Once they are outside we, who have to clean up, have lots of time. We just sit around and talk. We have a new song to learn for German school and only a few of the girls know the tune. They sing it and the rest of us sing along until we know the song.

Time goes so fast. There are only a few minutes left before the bell will ring for German school and I still have not cleaned the house at home. This week it is mother's turn to do the cooking so she will not have time to do the cleaning. My younger sister, Miriam, takes care of the children next door. The mother there has a new baby and she needs someone to take care of her two-year-old twins. Sometimes I wish I could work for someone else. It gets to be rather tiresome to take care of my own brothers and work in our own home. But because I am the oldest I have to help at home and be almost a second mother to my younger brothers.

There goes the bell for German school. In the morning German school is fun. We sing and recite the poems and songs that were assigned to us the day before. There are forty children in the school and it lasts only an hour. After that English school begins. The teacher does not have time to listen to everyone recite. Usually the older ones are last and most of the time we wait until 4 o'clock in the afternoon when we have another hour of German school. So if we did not have time to memorize or study our lessons we can find some time during the day to study them.

The lessons are short and most of the children learn them. There is no excuse for not knowing an assigned lesson. At the end of the hour all those who did not know their lesson go up to the teacher's desk and he opens his desk drawer and brings out his black leather strap. They all know that this is the punishment for not learning a lesson, so they walk bravely to the desk and hold out their hands. One little boy comes back with a grimace for a smile. "It didn't hurt," he says as he rubs his hands on the seat of his pants.

While the teacher has the strap out, there are a few more things to be straightened out. Last night there were two aisles of the schoolroom that had not been swept. The evening service was held in the same room so it really was not nice to see two aisles still covered with sawdust that had been spread to keep down the dust while sweeping. It was the responsibility of the eight oldest girls to clean the school. We had had an argument about which row each had to sweep, and in anger two of the girls left and did not do their rows. Of course we felt slightly guilty at leaving the work undone and realized that the minister would see it. But we did not want to give in, and now had to bear the consequences.

All eight of us go to the front of the room and line up. We are embarrassed to have to be punished in front of the whole class. All the boys, especially those of our age, between twelve and fifteen, will make fun of us afterwards. We can see them snicker already. We get the strap, but that does not hurt nearly as much as our wounded pride. In this instance, as well as in many other instances, we learn to feel a sense of responsibility toward the members of our group. We also learn that each of us has to do her share.

On the whole we all are very attached to each other. When the English teacher, for instance, has someone stay in school during the noon hour as a punishment, one of us will run to the kitchen and get something to eat for the one who has to stay. We usually have a way of sneaking the food in to her through the window.

We always felt good when we were all together. We never felt embarrassed or out of place when we would go to town, even though our dresses were so different. We would make fun of the short dresses and short hair worn by the other girls and women, and it really shocked us to see a woman in slacks or in jeans. At the age of twelve or thirteen the girls considered themselves young women and they would not be seen with a dress that did not come down to their ankles. This prevented us from doing things like climbing trees, but we would still play softball with the boys during recess when the English teacher would be our supervisor. To us children there were only two nationalities, German and English. Everyone in the community was German, and everyone outside was English. Our teacher was an outsider, so she was labeled as English regardless of her background.

Our favorite game or pastime was playing house. We would build little shacks in the woods with straw bales. The shacks were large enough to hold comfortably three or four girls. During the summer we almost lived in these playhouses. If mothers found that dishes, curtains, pillows, or other household articles had disappeared from the homes they would usually know where to look for them — in the playhouse. Each group wanted to have the nicest house, and anything we could find around the home that would make our house more attractive we would drag to the playhouse. For each house there was one girl who had the authority to add new members to the group, and another girl who could send those away who quarreled.

In the winter we spent most of our time at home either learning how to sew or knit, or else taking care of children. What we looked forward to most was our fifteenth birthday when we would be considered adults. The girls from fifteen to twenty-five generally worked together as a group, and they had lots of fun. We envied the girl who was next in line to graduate from the children's dining room to the adult dining room. This was quite a solemn occasion. The boy or girl would stand up after his last meal in the children's dining room and announce that he was fifteen years old. The *Schullehrer* would then proceed to give him a lecture on the responsibilities of an adult. He would even give final instructions in table manners.

For us to become fifteen meant freedom, no more German school, and no more supervision by the *Schullehrer*. But we would still have to go to Sunday school. Even in school we would think of the time when we would turn fifteen. We were thinking of the girls plastering and painting a new house, getting it ready for a family to move in, or doing some other task. Then we heard the bell, the community bell, and we knew that it must be for the women telling them to get ready to start work on plucking the chickens that had been ordered by some hotel in town, and again we wished we could be with them.

Sunday was the day we looked forward to most, especially if our mothers had made for us a new dress which we wanted to show off. The teenage girls usually stayed at home during church service to take care of the children under five years of age. If a girl had a new dress she would generally find someone to stay with the children for her so that she could go.

There was something very special about Sundays. The whole atmosphere was quiet and peaceful. The girls of every family had spent Saturday cleaning, waxing, and polishing the whole house. All the little girls of ten years and under had had their hair washed and braided in tight little French braids. These would last them till the following Saturday.

About half an hour before it was time for church all the families were gathered in their homes, generally around the table close to some window from which they could see the minister's house. As soon as the minister stepped out of his house he would announce in a loud voice *"Zum Gebet"* ("to prayers"), and right away all the other doors would open and the people would pour out. First the fathers and mothers of each family and behind them all their children of various ages and sizes would come out and walk to the church building. All the men and boys wore black hats and homemade suits, and the women wore different shades of blue, green, brown, or black.

Once in the church building the women and girls went to one side of the room and the men and boys to the other. Everyone had his own place. The older people would sit farthest back and the younger ones closer to the front under the watchful eyes of the minister. The steward, the farm manager, and most certainly our *Schullehrer* sat on the front bench next to the minister, facing everyone else. Sometimes, if there was not enough room on the benches or school desks, the little girls would sit up in front on the other side of the minister, facing the congregation. There they were sure to be quiet.

Some of the songs we sang had over a hundred verses. We would sing a few verses and leave the rest for the services during the week and the following Sundays. There was no music. The minister would read the first line or phrase and the oldest woman would lead in singing it. The minister would repeat the second line and so on. Sometimes the song would be started too high, and another woman would start singing it lower, and everyone followed her. Sometimes someone would feel it was now too low, and start the next line a little higher. This was done until the right pitch had been found. We would sing about six verses.

After the singing everyone rose and the minister said a short prayer. After that came the long service, which lasted for about two hours, but it seemed even longer than that. You had to look attentive for there was the *Schullehrer* who could see everything that was going on. The bench was hard and seemed to grow harder with the passing of time. Some of the younger children were lucky for they could sit in the school desks, they could lean on them, could even fall asleep, could perhaps play with a pencil or something that had been left in the desk. But we older ones had to pay attention and could not let our minds wander, at least not until we had heard one or two of the scripture verses in the sermon. We would have to repeat a verse from the sermon in Sunday School in the afternoon.

The whole sermon was read in a monotonous voice. The minister seemed to use three different tones of voice, and if you listened carefully you could tell how soon he would finish. Then there came what seemed the longest part of the service, when everybody knelt for prayer. You had your back to the bench and could not lean on it, and many times it seemed as if the prayer would never end. But end it did, and after one more song everyone would file out of church and go to the dining room.

LIST OF HUTTERIAN COLONIES

Name of Colony	Minister	Address	Year Founded	Population
	Lehrerleut' Colonies			
	ALBERTA, CANADA			
1. Rockport	John Hofer	Magrath	1918	70
2. Old Elmspring	Andreas Wurtz	Magrath	1918	119
3. New Elmspring	John Entz	Magrath	1918	100
4. Milford	John Wipf	Raymond	1918	122
5. Big Bend	John Waldner	Cardston	1920	120
6. Miami	George Waldner	New Dayton	1924	78
7. Elmspring	Michael Maendel	Warner	1929	78
8. Hutterville	John Waldner	Magrath	1932	142
9. New Rockport	John Wipf	New Dayton	1932	131
10. O.K.	Jacob Waldner	Raymond	1934	95
11. Rocklake	John Gross	Wrentham	1935	128
12. Sunnysite	Michael Hofer	Warner	1935	84
13. Macmillan	Jacob Wipf	Cayley	1937	110
14. Crystal Spring	John Entz	Magrath	1937	124
15. Newdale	Andreas Dekker	Queenstown	1950	108
16. Acadia	Peter Entz	Oyen	1952	133
17. New Milford	John Hofer	Winnifred	1953	155
18. Rosedale	Michael Hofer	Etzikom	1953	129
19. Springside	Joseph Waldner	Duchess	1955	136
20. Handhills	Sam Kleinsasser	Hanna	1956	111
21. Newell	Joseph Kleinsasser	Bassano	1962	98
22. Bow City	Jacob Hofer	Bow City	1964	83
	SASKATCHEWAN, CANADA			
1. Bench	Jacob Wipf	Shaunavon	1953	118
2. Cypress	Jacob Entz	Maple Creek	1953	70
3. Slade	Andreas Wipf	Tompkins	1954	100
4. Glidden	Peter Hofer	Glidden	1963	83
5. Waldeck	George Waldner	Waldeck	1963	92
6. Main Centre	David Hofer	Main Centre	1963	80

Name of Colony	Minister	Address	Year Founded	Popu-lation
	MONTANA, U.S.A.			
1. Birch Creek	Jacob Waldner	Valier	1947	79
2. Millfort	Joseph Kleinsasser	Augusta	1948	97
3. New Rockport	Peter Hofer	Choteau	1948	131
4. Miami	Issak Wurtz	Pendroy	1948	80
5. Rockport	John Kleinsasser	Pendroy	1948	78
6. Miller Ranch	David Hofer	Choteau	1949	98
7. Glacier	Joseph Waldner	Cut Bank	1951	132
8. Hillside	Andreas Wurtz	Sweet Grass	1951	91
9. Martindale	John Wipf	Martindale	1959	93
10. Springdale....	Peter Wipf	White Sulphur	1959	97
11. Sage Creek	Paul Wipf	Chester	1961	106
12. Duncan Ranch	John Entz	Twodot	1963	81
13. Rimrock	Peter Hofer	Sunburst	1963	82
14. Hilldale	Joseph Waldner	Havre	1963	103

Dariusleut' Colonies

ALBERTA, CANADA

1. Stand-Off	Jacob Walter	Fort Macleod	1918	118
2. West Raley	Christian Walter	Cardston	1918	98
3. Wilson Siding	John Wurtz	Lethbridge	1918	50
4. Springvale	Michael Wurz	Rockyford	1918	65
5. Rosebud	George Hofer	Rockyford	1918	119
6. East Cardston	Paul Hofer	Cardston	1918	70
7. Stahlville	David Waldner	Rockyford	1919	85
8. New York	Jacob Hofer	Maybutt	1924	130
9. Ewelme	Darius Walter	Fort Macleod	1925	105
10. New Rosebud	Paul Stahl	Beiseker	1926	61
11. Pincher Creek	Darius Gross	Pincher Creek	1926	71
12. Granum	Peter Tschetter	Granum	1930	82
13. Wolf Creek	Peter Hofer	Stirling	1930	67
14. Riverside	Joseph Tschetter	Fort Macleod	1933	64
15. Lakeside	Joseph Wipf	Cranford	1935	90
16. Sandhill	John Wurz	Beiseker	1936	98
17. Cayley	Paul Walter	Cayley	1937	67
18. Thompson	Joseph Walter	Glenwood	1939	60
19. Fairview	Christian Tschetter	Crossfield	1944	130
20. Pine Hill	Peter Hofer	Ponoka	1948	96
21. Tschetter	Jacob Stahl	Irricana	1948	120
22. Camrose	Elias Hofer	Camrose	1949	90
23. Ferrybank	Michael Wipf	Ponoka	1949	103
24. Holt (Irma)	Michael Tschetter	Irma	1949	70
25. Red Willow	Jacob Stahl	Red Willow	1949	120
26. Pibrock	Elias Tschetter	Pibrock	1953	120
27. Scottford	John Hofer	Ft. Saskatchewan	1953	115
28. Spring Creek	John Hofer	Walsh	1956	97
29. Sunshine	Christian Walter	Hussar	1956	40
30. Veteran	Michael Stahl	Veteran	1956	97
31. B.O.	Paul Tschetter	Marwayne	1957	70
32. Huxley	Paul Stahl	Huxley	1958	104

Name of Colony	Minister	Address	Year Founded	Popu- lation
33. Box Elder	David Hofer	Walsh	1960	95
34. Minburn	Peter Tschetter	Minburn	1960	50
35. Ribstone	Paul Walter	Edgarton	1960	90
36. Spring Point	Martin Walter	Brockett	1960	95

SASKATCHEWAN, CANADA

1. Riverview	Darius Tschetter	Sutherland	1955	71
2. Leask	Frank Wollman	Leask	1956	89
3. Estuary	Peter Tschetter	Estuary	1958	80
4. New Wolf Creek...	Jacob Hofer	Maple Creek	1958	92
5. West Bench	Darius Walter	Ravenscrag	1960	60
6. Hillsvale	Joseph Wurtz	Ballwinton	1961	64
7. Simmie	Jacob Hofer	Simmie	1964	*

MONTANA, U.S.A.

1. King Ranch	Elias Walter	Lewistown	1935	50
2. Ayers	John Stahl	Lewistown	1945	55
3. Spring Creek	Paul Walter	Lewistown	1945	51
4. Deerfield	Paul Stahl	Denvers	1947	52
5. Turner	John Hofer	Turner	1957	75
6. Wolf Creek	Joseph Hofer	Harlem	1960	55
7. Wilson Range	Elias Walter	Stanford	1963	75

WASHINGTON, U.S.A.

1. Asponola	Paul Gross	Asponola	1960	45

Schmiedeleut' Colonies

MANITOBA, CANADA

1. Bon Homme	Joseph Waldner	Elie	1918	109
2. Huron	Joseph Glanzer	Elie	1918	79
3. Milltown	Michael Waldner	Benard	1918	116
4. Maxwell	Michael Waldner	Headingly	1918	110
5. (Old) Rosedale	Jacob Hofer	Elie	1918	140
6. James Valley	Peter Hofer	Starbuck	1918	130
7. Iberville	Andreas Gross	Headingly	1919	81
8. Barickman	David Waldner	Headingly	1920	148
9. Blumengart	Jacob Waldner	Plum Coulee	1922	70
10. Riverside	John Hofer	Arden	1933	106
11. Elm River	Jacob Waldner	Newton	1934	75
12. Waldheim	Michael Waldner	Elie	1934	130
13. Poplar Point	Fred Waldner	Poplar Point	1938	92
14. Sturgeon Creek	Elie Maendel	Headingly	1939	119
15. Sunnyside	Joseph Kleinsasser	Newton	1942	67
16. New Rosedale	Andreas Hofer	Portage la Prairie	1944	88
17. Riverdale	David Waldner	Gladstone	1945	86
18. Lakeside	George Wipf	Headingly	1946	74
19. Rock Lake	Fred Gross	Grosse Isle	1947	83
20. Springfield	Samuel Waldner	Anola	1950	172
21. Oak Bluff	David Hofer	Morris	1952	102

* Population included with parent colony.

Name of Colony	Minister	Address	Year Founded	Population
22. Bloomfield	John Hofer	Westbourne	1954	102
23. Greenwald	Jacob Hofer	Dencross	1955	104
24. Crystal Spring	Jacob Kleinsasser	Ste. Agathe	1956	130
25. Spring Valley	Jacob Waldner	Glen Souris	1956	108
26. Rose Valley	David Waldner	Graysville	1957	100
27. Hillside	John Hofer	Justice	1958	125
28. Grant	Jacob Waldner	Elie	1958	110
29. Bright Stone	George Waldner	Lac du Bonnet	1959	76
30. Fairholm	Jacob Maendel	Portage la Prairie	1959	120
31. Deerborne	David Wurz	Alexander	1959	73
32. Clearwater	John Waldner	Balmoral	1960	98
33. Pembina	David Hofer	Darlingford	1961	62
34. Homewood	Samuel Wipf	Sanford	1961	84
35. Interlake	Zacharias Hofer	Teulon	1961	80
36. Whiteshell	Peter Gross	River Hills	1961	71
37. Rainbow	Jacob Hofer	Isle De Chene	1964	73
38. Parkview	Jacob Waldner	Riding Mountain	1964	82
39. Spring Hill	Michael Maendel	Neepawa	1964	67

SOUTH DAKOTA, U.S.A.

1. Bon Homme	Jacob Waldner	Tabor	1874	108
2. Rockport	Daniel Wipf	Alexandria	1934	140
3. New Elmspring ...	Sam Wollman	Ethan	1936	125
4. Jamesville	David Glanzer	Utica	1937	95
5. Tschetter	David Dekker	Olivet	1942	104
6. Huron	Jacob Wollman	Huron	1944	95
7. Rosedale	Joseph Waldner	Mitchell	1945	147
8. Spink	John Wipf	Frankfort	1945	76
9. Gracevale	Samuel Hofer	Winfred	1948	75
10. Glendale	John Waldner	Frankfort	1949	162
11. Millerdale	John Waldner	Miller	1949	86
12. Maxwell	Joseph Hofer	Scotland	1949	68
13. Pearl Creek	Michael Waldner	Iroquois	1949	186
14. Platte	Joseph Waldner	Academy	1949	76
15. Riverside	John Waldner	Huron	1949	101
16. Blumengart	Jacob Hofer	Wecota	1952	102
17. Clark	Fred Waldner	Raymond	1955	88
18. Plainview	Joseph Wipf	Ipswich	1958	97
19. Hillside	Michael Waldner	Dolland	1960	76
20. Spring Creek	Jacob Wipf	Forbes	1961	74
21. Wolf Creek	Paul Dekker	Olivet	1964	91
22. Spring Valley	John Wurtz	Wessington Spring	1964	73

NORTH DAKOTA, U.S.A.

1. Forest River	Andrew Hofer	Inkster	1950	51

MINNESOTA, U.S.A.

1. Big Stone	Samuel Hofer	Graceville	1958	108

NOTE: This list was prepared with the assistance of Peter Entz, Waldeck colony, and Jacob Kleinsasser, Crystal Spring colony.

NOTES AND INDEX

NOTES

Chapter I. The Origin and Background of the
Hutterian Brotherhood, pages 9–19

1. Some useful readings on early Anabaptist history are: Roland H. Bainton, "The Left-Wing of the Reformation," *Journal of Religion*, 21:124–134 (1941); H. S. Bender, *Conrad Grebel, 1498–1526, Founder of the Swiss Brethren* (Goshen, Ind., 1950); H. Böhmer, *Urkunden zur Geschichte des Bauernkrieges und der Wiedertäufer* (Bonn, 1910); Gustav Bossart, *Quellen zur Geschichte der Wiedertäufer* (Leipzig, 1930); C. A. Cornelius, *Geschichte des Münsterischen Aufruhrs* (Leipzig, 1860); H. Fast, *Der linke Flügel der Reformation* (Bremen, 1962); Robert Friedmann, *Hutterite Studies* (Goshen, Ind., 1961); Beatrice Jenny, *Das Schleitheimer Täuferbekenntnis, 1527* (Thayngen, 1931); Ludwig Keller, *Ein Apostel der Wiedertäufer* (Leipzig, 1882); George H. Williams (editor), *Spiritual and Anabaptist Writers: Documents Illustrative of the Radical Reformation*, XXV (London, 1957).

2. Bender, *Conrad Grebel*, 98.

3. Jenny, *Das Schleitheimer Täuferbekenntnis*. The translation here is from John C. Wenger, "The Schleitheim Confession of Faith," *Mennonite Quarterly Review*, 19:244–253 (1945).

4. See Harold J. Grimm, *The Reformation Era* (New York, 1954), 265–271; Hajo Holborn, *A History of Modern Germany: The Reformation* (New York, 1959), 174–181.

5. Johann Loserth, *Doctor Balthaser Hubmaier und die Anfänge der Wiedertaufe in Mähren* (Brünn, 1893).

6. Holborn, *A History of Modern Germany: The Reformation*, 179.

7. The first German university was founded in Prague in 1348.

8. An unimaginative account of the family history is provided by Jakob Falke, *Geschichte des fürstlichen Hauses Liechtenstein* (3 vols.; Vienna, 1868, 1877, 1882).

9. Josef Beck, *Die Geschichts-Bücher der Wiedertäufer in Oesterreich-Ungarn* (Vienna, 1883), 48. This work is volume 43 of *Fontes Rerum Austriacarum, II. Abtheilung: Diplomataria et Acta*, published by the Kaiserliche Akademie der Wissenschaften.

10. Hubmaier's position was outlined in one of his brochures published in Friedberg in 1527.

11. Beck, *Geschichts-Bücher*, 57.

12. A. J. F. Zieglschmid (editor), *Die älteste Chronik der Hutterischen Brüder* (Philadelphia, 1943), 87.

13. Johann Loserth, *Der Communismus der mährischen Wiedertäufer* (Vienna, 1894), 142. It may be added as a postscript that modern history associates Nikolsburg and Austerlitz with important events of its own. In 1805, after his victory at Austerlitz, Napoleon wrote to his brother Joseph, in Paris, "Tonight I will sleep in a bed in the beautiful von Kaunitz castle at Austerlitz, and I changed shirts, which I had not done for the past eight days." And in 1866 William I and Bismarck stayed at the castle at Nikolsburg. It was here that William had "to bite into the sour apple," when Bismarck and the crown prince persuaded him not to occupy Vienna after the Prussian victory over the Austrians.

14. Hans Fischer, *Jakob Huter: Leben, Frömmigkeit, Briefe* (Newton, Kans., 1956). This was a doctoral dissertation at the University of Vienna.

15. Zieglschmid, *Die älteste Chronik*, 89.

16. *Mennonitisches Lexikon* (Frankfurt a.M., 1937), II, 503; G. Mecenseffy, *Geschichte des Protestantismus in Österreich* (Graz and Köln, 1956); Paul Dedic, *Der Protestantismus im Zeitalter der Reformation und Gegenreformation* (Leipzig, 1930).

17. Zieglschmid, *Die älteste Chronik*, 157–158.

18. Peter Riedemann, *Rechenschaft unsrer Religion*. An edition was printed in Berne, Ind., in 1902. English translation (from a copy in the British Museum of the original German 1565 edition) by K. E. Hasenberg, *Confession of Faith* (London, 1950).

19. Franz Heimann, "The Hutterian Doctrine of Church and Common Life: A Study of Peter Riedemann's *Confession of Faith* of 1540," *Mennonite Quarterly Review*, 26:22–47, 142–160 (1952). A translation of an unpublished dissertation, "Die Lehre von Kirche und Gemeinschaft der Hutterischen Täufergemeinde," University of Vienna, 1927.

20. Riedemann, *Confession of Faith*, 88. See Lydia Müller, *Kommunismus der mährischen Wiedertäufer* (Leipzig, 1927).

21. Karl Kautsky, *Die Vorläufer des neueren Sozialismus*, I (Stuttgart, 1895), Ch. 9: "Die Wiedertäufer in Mähren," 351–372. An English translation of this book, by J. L. and E. G. Mulliken, has been published under the title *Communism in Central Europe in the Time of the Reformation* (New York, 1959).

22. *Mennonite Encyclopedia*, II (Scottdale, Pa., 1956), 859.

23. Frantisek Hrubý, *Die Wiedertäufer in Mähren* (Leipzig, 1935).

24. A. J. F. Zieglschmid (editor), *Das Klein-Geschichtsbuch der Hutterischen Brüder* (Philadelphia, 1947), 96–97.

25. Letter of Albrecht von Boskowitz to a Hutterian minister, dated Pürschitz, 1569, reprinted in Hrubý, *Die Wiedertäufer in Mähren*, 122.

26. K. Cernohorský, *Počatcky habánskych fajance* (Opava-Troppau, 1931). Illustrations in *Mennonite Life*, 9:34–41 (1954).

27. Hrubý, *Die Wiedertäufer in Mähren*, 46–47. The Zierotins were strong supporters of the Hutterians in the Moravian *Landtag* (assembly); in return they expected special loyalty and service from the Hutterians.

28. *Mennonitisches Lexikon*, II, 679–682.

29. Robert Friedmann, "Adventures of an Anabaptist in Turkey," *Mennonite Quarterly Review*, 24:12–24 (1950).

30. Hrubý, *Die Wiedertäufer in Mähren*, 95.

Chapter II. Hutterian Migrations, pages 20–37

1. Zieglschmid, *Die älteste Chronik*, 264–265. Sabatisch was also known as Freischütz, and in Slovakian as Sobotiste.

2. "Dise Herren ware fro vnd sahens gern das man also arbaitet / reüttet / hawet vnd bawet." *Ibid.*, 320.

3. Also known as Gross-Schützen, in Slovakian as Velké Lewáre, in Hungarian as Nagy-Léward.

4. In Rumanian: Sibiu. From the thirteenth to the eighteenth century Hermannstadt was the capital of Transylvania (Siebenbürgen), and largely German.

5. Quoted in *Mennonitisches Lexikon*, I, 48.

6. Zieglschmid, *Das Klein-Geschichtsbuch*, 155.

7. *Ibid.*, 156–158.

8. *Ibid.*, 168–172.

9. Grimmelshausen's book, originally called *Der Abenteuerliche Simplicissimus*, appeared in 1669 and has been reprinted and translated numerous times. In the translation cited here the quoted passage appears on pp. 309–310.

10. The Hutterian leaders of the first century were all born in Germany. Thus, Jacob Huter, who died in 1536, came from Tirol; Hans Amon (leader from 1536 to 1542) came from Bavaria; the joint leaders Leonhard Lantzenstil (1542–1565) and Peter Riedemann (1542–1556) from Bavaria and Silesia respectively; Peter Walbot-Scherer (1565–1578) from Tirol; Hans Krail (1578–1583) from Tirol; Claus Braidl (1583–1611) from Hesse; Sebastian Dietrich (1611–1619) from Württemberg; Ulrich Laussling (1619–1621) from Switzerland; and Valtin Winter (1621–1631) from Württemberg.

11. Andreas Ehrenpreis, *Ein Sendbrief* (1652; reprinted in Scottdale, Pa., 1920). In August 1957 I conducted a survey at several Hutterian communities in Manitoba. Among the questions directed separately and individually to a number of family heads one required the listing of the authors on their bookshelves at home. Half of them began their list with Ehrenpreis.

12. *Ibid.*, 42–44.

13. *Ibid.*, 107.

14. The *Gemeindeordnungen* are reprinted in Zieglschmid, *Das Klein-Geschichtsbuch*, 519–565.

15. *Ibid.*, 519.

16. Beck, *Geschichts-Bücher*, 548–549.

17. *Ibid.*, 554. The government decree did not affect only the Hutterians. In 1685, for example, the authorities in Salzburg demanded of all Protestants conversion to the Roman Catholic faith. The alternative was exile within fourteen days and the leaving behind of the children in the custody of the Church. See Mecenseffy, *Geschichte des Protestantismus in Österreich*, 191–192.

18. Beck, *Geschichts-Bücher*, 573, also Mecenseffy, *Geschichte*, 202.

19. *Das Klein-Geschichtsbuch* speaks of the empress as an "arch-Catholic" and "a great lover of priests." See p. 231: "Nun, diese Maria Theresia war ein Erzkatholerin und ein grosse Liebhaberin der Pfaffen . . . und kunnte ihnen nit leichtlich etwas versagen."

20. Buda was formerly known as Ofen. It was joined with Pest in 1872 to form Budapest.

21. *Correctionshäuser.* In Austria proper these were known as "conversion homes" (*Conversionshäuser*). See Mecenseffy, *Geschichte*, 204, and Paul Dedic, *Der Geheimprotestantismus in Kärnten während der Regierung Karls VI* (Klagenfurt, 1940).

22. Beck, *Geschichts-Bücher*, 616.

23. A list of those who fled from Sabatisch and Lewär to Russia appears in *Das Klein-Geschichtsbuch*, 373–374.

24. See Robert Friedmann, *Die Habaner in der Slowakei* (Vienna, 1927).

25. David Hofer kept a diary, which is now in the possession of his son Joshua

Hofer, steward of the James Valley community, Manitoba, where I had the opportunity to read it.

26. The letter from Moore to William Caton is dated at Amsterdam, "in the Eleventh Month, 1663." It is reprinted in Joseph Besse, *A Collection of the Sufferings of the People Called Quakers* (London, 1752), 420–432. See also Carl Heath, *Social and Religious Heretics in Five Centuries* (London, 1936), 119.

27. See Ernst Nowotny, *Die Transmigration ober- und innerösterreichischer Protestanten nach Siebenbürgen im 18. Jahrhundert* (Jena, 1931).

28. *Das Klein-Geschichtsbuch*, 305.

29. The Herrnhuter, who derived their name from the estate of their beneficiary, Count von Zinzendorf, were not Hutterians. For a history of this group see Herwig Hafa, *Die Brüdergemeinde Sarepta* (Breslau, 1936).

30. *Polnoe Sobranie Sakonov Rossiyskoy Imperii* (The Complete Collection of Laws of the Russian Empire) (St. Petersburg, 1830), XVI, No. 11,880.

31. The agency was known as the *kontora opekunstva*; in German, *Vormundschaftskomitee*, and after 1818, *Fürsorgekomitee. Ibid.*, No. 11,881.

32. Count Peter Alexandrovich Rumiantsev (1725–1796) was the territorial commander in the Russo-Turkish war. In 1764 Rumiantsev had replaced the last Ukrainian hetman, Razumovsky, as governor of the Ukraine.

33. *Das Klein-Geschichtsbuch*, 324–325.

34. The privileges are listed in the *Sobranie Sakonov*, XXVI, No. 19,546.

35. Law of May 23, 1801. *Ibid.*, No. 19,492. (The time reckoning for the Russian period is according to the Julian calendar.)

36. *Das Klein-Geschichtsbuch*, 402.

37. The most important sources on the history of the Hutterians in Russia are *Das Klein-Geschichtsbuch* and Alexander Klaus, *Unsere Kolonien* (Odessa, 1887), 46–92. Klaus, a senior Russian government official, was not only personally acquainted with the Hutterians, but had the official government reports at his disposal. These reports, submitted by Kontenius, Bunin, Fadyeev, and Babievsky in their capacity as government councillors, inspectors, or legal advisers, form part of Klaus's work. The original Russian edition, *Nashi Kolonii*, was published in 1869.

38. Hafa, *Die Brüdergemeinde Sarepta*, 154.

39. It was introduced on January 1, 1874.

40. David M. Hofer, *Die Hungersnot in Russland* (Chicago, 1924), 129–137.

41. Senator Windom of Minnesota, on the Senate floor, quoted by C. H. Smith, *The Coming of the Russian Mennonites* (Berne, Ind., 1927), 84.

Chapter III. From the Steppes to the Prairies, pages 38–50

1. Immigration to the United States from Western European countries dropped in the 1870's. The following figures show the immigration for 1879, and in parentheses for 1873: from Great Britain, 22,150 (89,500); Ireland, 15,932 (77,344); Scandinavian countries, 12,254 (35,481); Germany, 29,313 (149,671). Immigration from Russia, including the Baltic states, and from Austria-Hungary, however, increased steadily. See U.S. Bureau of the Census, *Historical Statistics of the United States, 1789–1945* (Washington, D.C., 1949), 34.

2. In *Anhang*, Klaus, *Unsere Kolonien*.

3. Paul Tschetter's diary appears in *Das Klein-Geschichtsbuch*, 571–606. An English translation by J. M. Hofer, "The Diary of Paul Tschetter, 1873," appeared in the *Mennonite Quarterly Review*, 5:112–127, 198–220 (1931).

4. Cf. E. K. Francis, *In Search of Utopia* (Glencoe, Ill., 1955), 44–45. See also "Department of Agriculture Letters Sent" (John Lowe), Vol. 7, 1873, Public Archives of Canada, Ottawa; "Report of the Minister of Agriculture of the Dominion

of Canada for the Calendar Year 1873 on Mennonite Immigration" (Sessional Papers, 1874). These and other relevant documents are reprinted as "Sources on the Mennonite Immigration from Russia in the 1870's," Ernst Correll, editor, *Mennonite Quarterly Review*, 24:329–352 (1950).

5. Dated Washington, September 5, 1873. See also "Official Report of the Hon. William Seeger to the Hon. Horace Austin, Governor of Minnesota, on Russo-German Immigration, St. Paul, December 20, 1873." These documents are reprinted in Correll (see previous note).

6. Chief sources for this period: Zieglschmid, *Das Klein-Geschichtsbuch*; C. H. Smith, *The Coming of the Russian Mennonites* (Berne, Ind., 1927); Gertrude S. Young, "The Mennonites in South Dakota," in *South Dakota Historical Collections*, X (1920), 470–506, and Norman Thomas, "The Hutterian Brethren," *South Dakota Historical Collections*, XXV (1951), 265–299; D. E. Harder, "The Hutterian Church" (unpublished master's thesis, Bethel College, Kans., 1930); Tarrel Miller, "The Hutterites and Colony Life," a chapter from *The Dakotans*, reprinted in the *Freeman Courier*, Freeman, S.D., Nov. 28, 1963.

7. General Custer's band was annihilated by Indians in 1876. The Indian treaty which made settlement safe came after this.

8. Chaplain Guy P. Squire, "The Most Striking Result of the War," in *South Dakota Historical Collections*, XI (1922), 16.

9. More than half of all conscientious objectors were Mennonites and Hutterians. For an account of their experiences see J. S. Hartzler, *Mennonites in the World War* (Scottdale, Pa., 1922).

10. Smith quotes one Major W. G. Kellogg as describing some rural conscientious objectors who appeared before his board as "only half awake, with features that were heavy, dull and almost bovine." Smith, *op. cit.*, 289.

11. Thomas, "The Hutterian Brethren," 277; *Das Klein-Geschichtsbuch*, 486. The accounts that follow are also documented by these two sources.

12. Hartzler, *Mennonites in the World War*, 131–133, and Smith, *The Coming of the Russian Mennonites*, 276.

13. Young, *op. cit.*, 501.

14. Interview given by the secretary of the state council of defense to *The Republican*, Mitchell, S.D., September 26, 1919, and quoted by Young, *op. cit.*, 501–502.

15. A. M. Willms, "The Brethren Known as Hutterians," *Canadian Journal of Economics and Political Science*, 24:391–405 (1958). On p. 391 Willms quotes from Correspondence File 58764, Dept. of Citizenship and Immigration, letter from W. H. Rogers to Secretary, Dept. of Interior, July 6, 1898.

16. A copy of the petition and the reply are on file in the records of Mr. E. A. Fletcher, Q.C., Winnipeg, solicitor for the Hutterian Brethren in Canada.

17. Dept. of Citizenship and Immigration, file 58764, quoted by A. M. Willms, *op. cit.*, 392.

18. *Ibid.*, 393.

19. "Hutterites Defended," *Winnipeg Free Press*, August 12, 1919.

20. "Want Hutterites Now in Canada Deported. Great War Veterans Go Further Than to Prevent Any More Coming In," *Winnipeg Free Press*, April 9, 1919.

21. "Hutterites Appear Desirable Settlers," *Winnipeg Free Press*, August 21, 1919. However, the initial opposition of the war veterans to the Hutterians was sufficiently vocal to persuade the government to reverse its immigration policy with respect to them. In a letter dated September 15, 1919, and addressed to Joseph Kleinsasser, leader of the remaining Hutterians in South Dakota, J. A. Calder, minister of immigration and colonization, Ottawa, wrote: "I must advise you that after the most careful consideration of all the facts and circumstances, the government concluded that it would be inadvisable, owing to the general feel-

ing prevailing throughout Canada, to continue to permit certain persons to enter Canada because their custom, mode of life, habits, etc., were such as to prevent them becoming readily assimilated. These persons included Doukhobors, Mennonites, and Hutterites. We have had so much trouble in Canada in connection with school and other matters in the colonies and communities of these people that their neighbors and people generally insist that no more should be permitted to come." The letter is reprinted in *Das Klein-Geschichtsbuch*, 634–635.

This new policy barely affected the Hutterians. Except for one colony, they had by this time all transferred to Canada. The policy was shortly discarded by a new administration in Ottawa.

22. *Winnipeg Free Press*, December 15, 1922. The report had reference to the Hutterians who had bought the Mennonite village of Blumengart, near Plum Coulee, Manitoba. The Mennonites of Blumengart had moved to Mexico in protest against the replacement of their private school by a public school.

Chapter IV. Hutterian Expansion, a Cause of Controversy, pages 51–71

1. Edna Kells, "Hutterite Commune," *Maclean's Magazine*, March 15, 1937.

2. The telegrams and letters in connection with the Rockport colony that appear here are a selection of those contained in the Appendix attached to a "Brief submitted by L. S. Turcotte, Barrister of Lethbridge, Alberta, on behalf of the Hutterian Brethren living in the Province of Alberta to the Committee of the Legislative Assembly of the Province of Alberta sitting at the Court House, at Lethbridge, on February 10th, 1947." The Brief and Appendix appear in Zieglschmid, *Das Klein-Geschichtsbuch*, 638–649.

3. *Edmonton Journal*, March 17, 1942.

4. "The Communal Property Act being Chapter 52 of the Revised Statutes of Alberta, 1955, with amendments up to and including 1960," Department of Municipal Affairs, Edmonton, Alberta. See also "1962, Chapter 8, An Act to amend The Communal Property Act (Assented to April 5, 1962)"; "Report of the Hutterite Investigation Committee" (September 1959), Province of Alberta, Edmonton. The amendments of 1960 and 1962 removed the forty-mile restriction and replaced the director of communal property by a three-man board known as the Communal Property Control Board. South Dakota passed legislation patterned upon Alberta's Property Act. This was later declared unconstitutional by a federal judge, and the act was repealed. The government of Montana proposed restrictive legislation (a forty-mile limit and 6400 acres per colony), but it was rejected by the state legislature in 1961. There have been more recent signs of anti-Hutterian agitation in Montana (see article "Hutterite Farm Groups Facing Inquiry by Montana Legislature; Private Investigation Also Planned — Opponent of Sect Says Aim Is to Make Them 'Like Other People'" in the *New York Times*, June 2, 1963, p. 79) but no further action has been taken.

5. The Canadian Mental Health Association, "The Hutterites and Saskatchewan" (Regina, 1953, mimeographed).

6. Turcotte, "Brief." See note 2 above.

7. William Douglas Knill, "Hutterian Education: A Descriptive Study Based on the Hutterian Colonies within Warner County No. 5, Alberta, Canada" (unpublished master's thesis, Montana State University, 1958), 31–32.

8. "Looking for Lebensraum," *Time*, Canadian edition, February 5, 1965.

9. See Part 1 of a series of articles on the Hutterians by Jane Becker in the *St. Catherines Standard*, April 5, 1965.

10. "The Hutterite Issue in Manitoba," *Bulletin of the Manitoba Civil Liberties Association* (Winnipeg, 1947–1948).

11. "Report to the Honourable the Legislative Assembly of Manitoba of the Select Special Committee appointed to obtain information regarding colonies or societies of Hutterites or Hutterian Brethren and to report and make recommendations upon the same" (Provincial Library, Winnipeg, 1947, mimeographed, 33 pages).

12. *Ibid.*, 25.

13. "Meeting of Select Special Committee of Manitoba Legislature on Hutterite Legislation" (Provincial Library, Winnipeg, 1948, mimeographed, 96 pages).

14. *Ibid.*

15. *Ibid.*

16. "Municipalities Seek Clamp on Hutterites," and editorial, "Hutterite Rights," *Winnipeg Free Press*, November 25, 1954.

17. *Winnipeg Free Press*: "Hutterites under Attack," March 7, 1957; "New Shafts Fired at Hutterites," March 8, 1957.

18. "Hutterites, Opponents Choose Pact Rather Than Legislation," *Winnipeg Tribune*, April 29, 1957.

19. *Ibid.*

20. "Hutterites Agree to Curb Colonies," *Winnipeg Free Press*, April 27, 1957.

21. Editorial, "Voluntary Hutterite Curb," *Winnipeg Tribune*, April 29, 1957.

22. *Winnipeg Free Press*: "Petition Asks Control of Hutterite Expansion," August 16, 1957; "Government Refuses Bid to Curb Hutterites," August 19, 1957.

23. Bertha W. Clark, "The Huterian Communities," *Journal of Political Economy*, 32:357–374, 468–486 (1924). The variant spelling "Huterian" which Dr. Clark used has also been preferred by some other writers.

24. C. Frank Steele, "Canada's Hutterite Settlement," *Canadian Geographical Journal*, 22 (June 1941), 314.

25. News clippings from the *Winnipeg Free Press*, n.d.

26. *Winnipeg Free Press*, March 7, 1957.

27. *Ibid.*, March 8, 1957.

28. *Time,* Canadian edition, October 14, 1957.

29. *Calgary Herald*, October 13, 1956. Reprinted by permission.

30. *Winnipeg Free Press*, December 3 and 11, 1958.

31. *Winnipeg Free Press*, June 2, 1960.

32. *Winnipeg Free Press*, December 10, 1960.

33. *Winnipeg Free Press*, February 20, 1951.

34. *Winnipeg Tribune*, February 8, 1956.

35. *Winnipeg Free Press*, October 9, 1957.

36. *Winnipeg Tribune*, February 3, 1958.

37. *Winnipeg Free Press*, October 20, 1956. See also "The Promised Land," *Time*, Canadian edition, August 13, 1956; "Paying for the Mistakes of History," *Calgary Herald*, November 5, 1956; and Canadian Press reports in the *Winnipeg Free Press*: "Hutterite Expansion a Detriment," December 11, 1958; "He'd Make Hutterites Learn Birth Control," December 18, 1958; "Hutterite Colonies Rapped," December 10, 1960; "Halt Urged in Hutterite Expansion," December 12, 1960.

38. *Winnipeg Tribune*, May 7, 1947.

39. *Winnipeg Free Press*, June 2, 1960.

40. Peter Hofer, *The Hutterian Brethren and Their Beliefs* (James Valley Community, Starbuck, Manitoba, 1955).

41. *Winnipeg Free Press*, June 3, 1960.

42. The same process was operative in the United States, where farm consolidation in large areas threatened to create a "landless proletariat." See Lowry Nelson, *Rural Sociology* (New York, 1948).

43. *Canada Year Book* (Ottawa, 1954), 128. Cf. Canadian Press news release, "Farm Population Drops," *Winnipeg Free Press*, November 11, 1957.

44. "Exodus from the Farm," *Winnipeg Free Press*, November 23, 1957.

45. Dorothy Giffen, "The Hutterites and Civil Liberties," *Canadian Forum*, 27:55–57 (June 1947), 55.

46. *Ibid.*

47. Forrest E. LaViolette, *The Canadian Japanese and World War II* (Toronto, 1948). Preface by H. F. Angus, vii.

Chapter V. The Community-Congregation, pages 75–90

1. Bertha W. Clark, "The Huterian Communities," *Journal of Political Economy*, 32:357–374, 468–486 (1924); see p. 363.

2. Bert Kaplan and Thomas F. A. Plaut, *Personality in a Communal Society: An Analysis of the Mental Health of the Hutterites* (Lawrence, Kans., 1956), 12.

3. *Constitution of the Hutterian Brethren Church and Rules as to Community of Property* (E. A. Fletcher, Q.C., Winnipeg, for the Hutterian Brethren), 4. See Appendix to the present work.

4. Sources on Hutterian doctrine are: Peter Riedemann, *Confession of Faith*; Franz Heimann, "Die Lehre von Kirche und Gemeinschaft der Hutterischen Täufergemeinde" (unpublished doctoral dissertation, Vienna, 1927), English translation, "The Hutterian Doctrine of Church and Common Life: A Study of Peter Riedemann's *Confession of Faith* of 1540," *Mennonite Quarterly Review*, 26:22–47, 142–160 (1952); Robert Friedmann, "Peter Riedemann on Original Sin and the Way of Salvation," *Mennonite Quarterly Review*, 26:210–215 (1952).

5. Clark, "The Huterian Communities," 482.

6. Ulrich Stadler, "Cherished Instructions on Sin, Excommunication, and the Community of Goods" (*ca.* 1537), reprinted in George H. Williams (editor), *Spiritual and Anabaptist Writers: Documents Illustrative of the Radical Reformation*, XXV (London, 1957), 280.

7. Cf. Deuteronomy 19:15: "One witness shall not rise up against a man for any iniquity, or for any sin, in any sin that he sinneth: at the mouth of two witnesses, or at the mouth of three witnesses, shall the matter be established."

8. Joseph W. Eaton, *Exploring Tomorrow's Agriculture* (New York, 1943), 226.

9. Peter Hofer is the *Vorsteher* or *Ältester* (elder, or bishop) of the *Schmiedeleut'* colonies.

10. Tape-recorded interview at Crystal Spring colony, Ste. Agathe, Manitoba, August 4, 1957. There are minor variations in all customs. In the election of a minister the elder may take a number of blank slips of paper and mark one of them. Each qualified nominee then draws one slip out of a hat, and he who draws the marked slip becomes assistant minister.

11. Lee Emerson Deets, *The Hutterites: A Study in Social Cohesion* (Gettysburg, Pa., 1939), 63.

12. "*Der Gemein Ordnungen*," in *Das Klein-Geschichtsbuch*, 520. The *Gemeindeordnungen* from 1651 to 1873 occupy forty-six pages in the small chronicle (pp. 519–565). Dr. Robert Friedmann says of them: "In many regards these ordinances suggest the rules and regulations of mediaeval monasteries . . . the principle of merit is, however, completely absent. . . . The main tenor of all the *Ordnungen* is the battle against *Eigennutz* (selfishness, greed, profit-motive) and the admonition to live up to the requirements of a life in perfect community of goods." (*Mennonite Encyclopedia*, II, 454.)

13. The original title of the steward was *Diener der zeitlichen Notdurft* (minister for temporal needs). Mändel had been *Rentmeister* (steward) on the estate of the Lord of Liechtenstein (*Die älteste Chronik*, 87). The name of Mändel, or Maendel, is still very common among the Hutterians.

14. *Das Klein-Geschichtsbuch*, 533.

15. *Ibid.*, 536.

16. Dr. Johann Loserth of Graz University, in Austria, was a leading scholar of early Hutterian history.

17. *Weinzierl*: foreman of the vineyard.

18. *Constitution of the Hutterian Brethren Church*, 4. See Appendix.

19. *Ibid.*

20. Edna Kells, "Hutterite Commune," *Maclean's*, March 15, 1937.

21. Henrik Infield, *Cooperative Communities at Work* (New York, 1945), 35.

22. Clark, "The Huterian Communities," 364.

23. J. W. Eaton, *Exploring Tomorrow's Agriculture* (New York, 1943), 225.

24. Clark, "The Huterian Communities," 485.

Chapter VI. Colony Life, pages 91–105

1. Pitirim Sorokin, *Social and Cultural Dynamics* (Boston, 1957), 445.

2. Peter Riedemann, *Confession of Faith*, 97.

3. Robert C. Cook, "The North American Hutterites: A Study in Human Multiplication," *Population Bulletin*, 10:97–107 (December 1954), 98.

4. *Ibid.*, 103.

5. D. H. Epp, *Johann Cornies*, second edition (Rosthern, Saskatchewan, 1946), 98.

6. Tape-recorded interview at New Rosedale colony, July 28, 1957.

7. Edna Kells, "Hutterite Commune," *Maclean's*, March 15, 1937.

8. Edna Staebler, "The Lord Will Take Care of Us," *Maclean's*, March 15, 1952. Reprinted by permission of the author.

9. Deets, *The Hutterites*, 2.

10. Bloomfield colony church records as of November 25, 1957.

11. Joseph W. Eaton and Robert J. Weil, *Culture and Mental Disorders: A Comparative Study of the Hutterites and Other Populations* (Glencoe, Ill., 1955), 126–127.

12. This was part of a research project in which the public school teachers at Hutterian schools cooperated with me. In another project conducted in a metropolitan Winnipeg school the students named as their ideals characters from the comic page, the sporting world, the cinema, and history and fiction. Fewer than 2 per cent named their parents as an ideal. See Victor Peters, "Our Teeners and Their Answers," *Winnipeg Tribune*, March 5, 1955.

13. Cook, "The North American Hutterites," 100.

14. The inscriptions on tombstones generally appear in German. This one reads: *Es ist mir Leid um dich. Ich habe grosse Freude und Wonne an dir gehabt. Barbara.*

15. The 1924 study of Dr. Clark (*op cit.*, 480) includes the name of Janzen. This name died out among the Hutterians in 1927.

16. I attained a certain colony status when at some colonies Hutterians began to refer to me as *der Petersvetter*. The use of the surname in this case indicated a subtle distinction between an accepted outsider and a regular colony member.

17. Joseph Besse, *A Collection of the Sufferings of the People Called Quakers* (London, 1752), 421.

18. *Constitution of the Hutterian Brethren Church*, Article 41. See Appendix.

19. Staebler, *Maclean's*, March 15, 1952.

20. Clark, "The Huterian Communities," 374.

21. J. H. Hexter, *More's Utopia* (Princeton, 1952), 61.

Chapter VII. The Communal Economy and Colony Division, pages 106–119

1. Cf. Horace Miner, *St. Denis: A French Canadian Parish* (Chicago, 1939).

2. Quoted by Helen Waddell, *The Wandering Scholars*, Penguin edition, 182.

3. Dorothy Giffen, "The Hutterites and Civil Liberties," *Canadian Forum*, 27:55–57 (1947); see p. 57.

4. Riedemann, *Confession of Faith*, 126–128.

5. *Reports 1–12*, Royal Commission on Agriculture and Rural Life (Government of Saskatchewan, Regina, 1955).

6. *1956 Annual Report*, Manitoba Farm Accounting Clubs (University of Manitoba, 1957), Table III.

7. *Mechanization and Farm Cost, Report 2*, Royal Commission on Agriculture and Rural Life (Regina, 1955); "Exodus from the Farm," *Winnipeg Free Press*, November 23, 1957.

8. The staff of the Department of Agriculture of the University of Manitoba were most cooperative in supplying comparative data for this purpose. Interviews with numerous staff members assisted in giving me an overall picture of farm conditions in the province. Representatives of commercial industries dealing with the colonies also gave freely of their time, especially Mr. Norval Young of Feed-Right Mills, Winnipeg. The Hutterians in charge of colony enterprises were equally cooperative, and through Mr. E. A. Fletcher, Q.C., the colonies' solicitor, who is also in charge of their income tax returns, I had access to the financial files of all Manitoba colonies.

9. *1956 Annual Report*, Manitoba Farm Accounting Clubs (University of Manitoba, 1957).

10. O. Asklason, *Brookings Register* (Brookings, S.D., November 20, 1920), quoted by Young in *South Dakota Historical Collections*, X, 494.

11. Thomas, in *Historical Collections*, XXV, 283.

12. E. A. Fletcher, "The Hutterite Question," a four-page mimeographed report (Winnipeg, 1954).

13. Interview at Riverside colony, Arden, Manitoba, July 29, 1957.

14. In a colony division the population is generally almost equally divided, and the age composition remains relatively constant. For example, a few years after the Sturgeon Creek colony, at Headingly, founded the new colony of Crystal Spring, at Ste. Agathe, the former had 120 people, and the latter 94. Their age groupings were as follows:

Colony	20 Years and Under		21–39		40–59		60 and Over	
	M	F	M	F	M	F	M	F
Sturgeon Creek	33	36	8	12	4	4	3	2
Crystal Spring	27	31	17	13	0	1	3	2

Chapter VIII. The Cultural Heritage, pages 120–127

1. Josef Beck, *Die Geschichts-Bücher der Wiedertäufer in Oesterreich-Ungarn* (Vienna, 1883), Vol. 43 of *Fontes Rerum Austriacarum, II. Abtheilung: Diplomataria et Acta*.

2. Rudolf Wolkan (editor), *Geschichtsbuch der Hutterischen Brüder* (Vienna, Austria, and Standoff Colony, Macleod, Alberta, Canada, 1923).

3. A. J. F. Zieglschmid (editor), *Die älteste Chronik der Hutterischen Brüder* (Philadelphia, 1943).

4. A. J. F. Zieglschmid (editor), *Das Klein-Geschichtsbuch der Hutterischen Brüder* (Philadelphia, 1947).

5. Peter Riedemann, *Rechenschaft unsrer Religion, Lehre und Glaubens, von den Brüdern, die man die Hutterischen nennt* (latest edition: Berne, Ind., 1902).

6. Robert Friedmann, "Book Reviews," *Mennonite Quarterly Review*, 26:164–165 (1952).

7. Published in England by the Plough Publishing House, Bromdon, in 1957, with an introduction by Robert Friedmann.

8. *Die Lieder der Hutterischen Brüder* (Scottdale, Pa., 1914).

9. Cf. H. Goerz, "A Day with the Hutterites," *Mennonite Life*, 8:14–16 (1953). See also "A Hutterian Girl Tells Her Story," in the Appendix to the present work.

10. Loserth, in *Mennonite Encyclopedia*, I, 728. See also *Mennonite Life*, I, 2 (1946), and IX, 1 (1954).

11. Robert Friedmann, "Economic History of the Hutterian Brethren," in *Mennonite Encyclopedia*, II, 144.

12. Infield, *Cooperative Communities at Work*, 25.

Chapter IX. Hutterian Education, pages 128–136

1. Riedemann, *Confession of Faith*, 130–131.

2. Peter Walpot is sometimes called Scherer (clothes-cutter), for besides teaching he also followed his trade as a tailor. Walpot's address to the community teachers, together with the Hutterian School Discipline of 1578, which must be regarded as a corollary to the address, has repeatedly appeared in print. See Christian D'Elvert, *Geschichte der Studien-, Schul-, und Erziehungsanstalten in Mähren und österreich.-Schlesien, insbesonders der Olmützer Universität, in den neueren Zeiten*, Band 10, Heft 11 (Brünn, 1857), 465–480; *Mitteilungen der Gesellschaft für deutsche Erziehungs- und Schulgeschichte*, Jahrgang 11, Heft 2 (Berlin, 1901), 112–127; an English translation and introduction by H. S. Bender: "A Hutterite School Discipline of 1578 and Peter Scherer's Address of 1568 to the Schoolmasters," *Mennonite Quarterly Review*, 5:231–244 (1931). Passages quoted here are from this translation.

3. Quoted by Clark, "The Huterian Communities," 373.

4. Riedemann, *Confession of Faith*, 131.

5. Edwin L. Pitt, "The Hutterian Brethren in Alberta" (unpublished master's thesis, University of Alberta, 1949), 71.

6. Clark, "The Huterian Communities," 374.

7. See *Das Klein-Geschichtsbuch*, 517–565.

8. Clark, "The Huterian Brethren," 373.

Chapter X. The Hutterians and the Public School, pages 137–150

1. William Douglas Knill, "Hutterian Education: A Descriptive Study Based on the Hutterian Colonies within Warner County, Alberta, Canada No. 5," (unpublished master's thesis, Montana State University, 1958), 101.

2. The information on the early history of the public schools in Hutterian colonies is based on interviews which I had with Hutterians and school officials, and on correspondence with Dr. Robert Fletcher.

3. Edwin L. Pitt, "The Hutterian Brethren in Alberta" (master's thesis, University of Alberta, 1949), ii.

4. "Report to the Honourable the Legislative Assembly of Manitoba of the Select Committee . . .," 25.

5. Information on Hutterian education in Alberta and Saskatchewan is based on correspondence with H. C. Sweet, assistant chief superintendent of schools,

Edmonton, and R. J. Davidson, director of school administration, Regina. Two very important sources on Hutterian public schools in Alberta are the theses by Edwin L. Pitt and William Douglas Knill. Another unpublished thesis by Kenneth C. Thomas, completed in 1949, deals with the Hutterian schools in Alberta and Montana.

6. AP report in the *Fargo Forum and Moorhead News*, September 29, 1961.

7. Pitt, "The Hutterian Brethren in Alberta," 77.

8. "Hutterite Education Standard Praised by Chief Inspector," *Winnipeg Free Press*, March 4, 1955.

9. Pitt, "The Hutterian Brethren in Alberta," 77.

10. Cf. Exodus 20:4-5.

11. Pitt, "The Hutterian Brethren in Alberta," 74.

Chapter XI. Some Aspects of Hutterian Community Stability, pages 151–167

1. "He'd Make Hutterites Learn Birth Control," Canadian Press, Edmonton dateline, in *Winnipeg Free Press*, December 18, 1958.

2. Sources: Robert C. Cook, "The North American Hutterites," *Population Bulletin*, 10:97–107 (December 1954); *Canada Year Book 1954* (Ottawa); J. W. Eaton and A. J. Mayer, *Man's Capacity to Reproduce* (Glencoe, Ill., 1953).

3. Joseph W. Eaton and Robert J. Weil, *Culture and Mental Disorders: A Comparative Study of the Hutterites and Other Populations* (Glencoe, Ill., 1955), 25.

4. Jacques Henripin, *La Population Canadienne au Début de* xviiie *Siècle* (Paris, 1954), quoted by Cook, *Population Bulletin*.

5. Since compulsory medical health and hospitalization legislation has been introduced in the province of Manitoba, Hutterians, who pay premiums, also make use of its services.

6. A number of the members of the Manitoba Historical Society, who toured the Crystal Spring colony on September 23, 1961, commented on the absence of flies in the pig and dairy barns.

7. Clark, "The Huterian Brethren," 370.

8. Such a study, covering all Hutterian colonies and directed by Western Reserve University, is now in progress. This study also makes extensive use of Hutterian genealogy. Like the Eaton and Weil Hutterian mental health study, the Western Reserve University project receives solid Hutterian cooperation.

9. "Hutterite Study: Mental Health," *Winnipeg Free Press*, first of two articles (newspaper clipping, n.d.).

10. The team consisted of Dr. Joseph W. Eaton, sociologist then at Wayne University, Detroit, Dr. Robert J. Weil, psychiatrist then at Dalhousie University, and Dr. Bert Kaplan, psychologist then at Harvard.

11. Eaton and Weil, *Culture and Mental Disorders*, 210, 212. See also Bert Kaplan and Thomas F. A. Plaut, *Personality in a Communal Society* (Lawrence, Kans., 1956).

12. Eaton and Weil, *Culture and Mental Disorders*, 235–237.

13. Clark, "The Huterian Brethren," 482; Deets, *The Hutterites: A Study in Social Cohesion*, 2.

14. *Winnipeg Free Press*, December 30, 1955. Reprinted by permission.

15. *Winnipeg Free Press*, May 17 and July 5, 1957.

16. See Marcus Bach, *The Dream Gate* (New York, 1949). Professor Bach of the State University of Iowa, is the only author, so far as I know, who has made use of the Hutterian subject in the form of fiction. Whatever the literary qualities of the book may be, it does not succeed in capturing the atmosphere of the colony,

despite the author's obvious sympathy for his subject. The book was favorably reviewed by national periodicals and leading newspapers. Bach weaves into his story an episode about a forbidden musical instrument, the harmonica. The Canadian Broadcasting Corporation's televised production "The Devil's Instrument" was an adaptation of this episode.

17. Edna Staebler, "The Lord Will Take Care of Us," *Maclean's*, March 15, 1952. Reprinted by permission of the author.

18. Edwin L. Pitt, "The Hutterian Brethren in Alberta," 90.

19. Eaton and Weil, *Culture and Mental Disorders*, 142.

20. "Report to the Honourable the Legislative Assembly of Manitoba of the Select Committee . . ." (Winnipeg, 1947), 27.

21. A brief report of this claim appeared in the *Winnipeg Free Press*, April 29, 1965.

22. This case history was related to me by Mr. E. Howe, provincial agricultural representative at Altona. On a subsequent visit to the colony I did not meet the man, who was engaged in some field work, but I did discuss the case with the father.

23. Based on tape-recorded interview, Winnipeg, September 1957.

24. *Constitution of the Hutterian Brethren Church* (see Appendix). See also *Hansard* for April 1951; *Winnipeg Free Press*, April 4, 1951.

25. Peter Hofer is the holder of a State of South Dakota second (in 1907) and first (in 1915) grade teacher's certificate. The first-grade certificate records the following marks: Reading, 96; Writing, 91; Orthography, 98; Arithmetic, 92; Geography, 92; Grammar, 98; Physiology, 90; U.S. History, 90; Civics, 97; Didactics, 100; Current Events, 92; Physical Geography, 90; American Literature, 100; Drawing, 89; S.D. History, 98.

Chapter XII. Kindred Societies, Converts, and Neighbors, pages 171–184

1. V. F. Calverton, *Where Angels Dared to Tread* (New York, 1941).

2. See J. W. Eaton, *Exploring Tomorrow's Agriculture* (New York, 1943), 231–239; "Communists Turned Capitalists," *Time*, September 7, 1959; and Bertha M. H. Shambaugh, "Amana That Was and Amana That Is," in *The Palimpsest* (publ. by State Historical Society of Iowa, Iowa City), 44, 3 (1963).

3. See George B. Lockwood, *The New Harmony Movement* (New York, 1905).

4. Zieglschmid, *Das Klein-Geschichtsbuch*, 461.

5. *Ibid.*, 461–462.

6. Hans Joachim Schoeps, *Die letzten dreissig Jahre, Rückblick* (Stuttgart, 1956), 43.

7. Circular letter by Elder Elias Walter, March 20, 1931, reprinted in translation in the *Mennonite Encyclopedia*, I, 163.

8. Eberhard Arnold, *Ein anderer gedruckter Sendbrief* (Bruderhof Neuhof, Hesse-Nassau, 1932), 9.

9. See Michael Horsch, in *Mennonitisches Gemeindeblatt* (Karlsruhe, 1937), No. 12/13; and M. Horsch, *Die Auflösung des eingetragenen Vereins Neuwerk Bruderhof* (Ingolstadt, 1937).

10. Gracia D. Booth, *Saturday Night*, August 31, 1940.

11. "Die Bruderhöfe in Alto Paraguay," *Mitteilungen*, 4, 11/12 (Institut für Auslandsbeziehungen, Stuttgart, 1954); J. Kapitän, "In der Schule bei den Hutterischen Brüdern in Paraguay," *Die Sammlung*, 14, 7/8 (Göttingen, 1959). As a postscript it may be added that the Society of Brothers has since left Paraguay. Their community farms were sold to Mennonites in that country.

12. "English Accent of Hutterites Amazes Traders," *Winnipeg Free Press*, January 5, 1950.

13. One source for this section was the diary of Rev. Samuel Kleinsasser. *Vorsteher* Peter Hofer, the late Mr. Kleinsasser, and others were interviewed on this subject.

14. Cf. Margaret Böning, "Persönliche Erinnerungen an Käthe Kollwitz," *Der Pflug*, 2, 1 (1954).

15. Excerpt from the *Urteil* (sentence) passed by the assembled *Schmiedeleut'* Hutterian leaders with *Vorsteher* Peter Hofer presiding: ". . . wegen ihrer Abtrünnigkeit und Abfall von ihrer Gemeinde, und dadurch von allen andern hutterischen Gemeinden, auf dessen Grund sie getauft sind, sollen die schuldig befundenen Personen von nun an für Abgefallene gehalten werden; ja als Abtrünnige und Bundbrüchige, und sollen als solche gemieden, damit sie in sich gehn und für ihre Untreue Busse tun. In der Gemeinde der hutterischen Brüder können sie nicht wieder kommen als nur durch den Ausschluss nach getaner Busse und rechtschaffener Ergebung." (". . . because of their disloyalty and backsliding from their congregation, and thereby from all other Hutterian congregations, in whose faith they were baptized, those persons found guilty are henceforth to be considered apostates; yea, renegades and traitors, and as such shall be shunned, that they may repent and make atonement for their faithlessness. They shall not be taken again into the community of the Hutterian Brethren until they have done penance and shown wholehearted submission.")

16. "Electricity Helps in Community Farming," *Electrical Farming* (Winnipeg), June–July 1957. See also Associated Press story, "Sect on Farm in Ontario Practices Communal Living," *Fargo Forum*, November 28, 1963.

17. *The Hutterites and Saskatchewan: A Study of Inter-Group Relations*, Conducted by Saskatchewan Division, Canadian Mental Health Association (mimeographed, Regina, 1953), Table 2.

18. *Ibid.*, 38–43.

Conclusion, pages 185–190

1. P. McL., "The Hutterite View: 'One Manner of Law,'" *Winnipeg Free Press*, February 3, 1955.

2. Gerald Wright, "The Carillon News Visits a Hutterite Brethren Colony," *Carillon News*, Steinbach, Manitoba, July 17, 1959.

3. Bertha M. H. Shambaugh, "Amana That Was and Amana That Is," *The Palimpsest*, 44, 3 (1963), 116.

4. Douglas Sanders, "Alberta Has Been Shown Up Badly," *Edmonton Journal*, December 24, 1963.

5. "Terms Hutterites' Attitude 'Disappointing,'" *Winnipeg Free Press*, February 27, 1964. See "Hutterites to Take Children from Public School in S.D.," *Fargo Forum*, September 29, 1961, quoted on pp. 140–141.

6. Circular letter, James Valley Bruderhof, Manitoba, Canada, March 9, 1959, p. 2.

7. Lowry Nelson, *Rural Sociology* (New York, 1948), 202–203.

INDEX

71 72 73 74   12 11 10 9 8 7 6 5 4 3 2 1